CONG CATCHERS

A SOLDIER's MEMORIES OF VIETNAM

LEE HALVERSON

Published in the United States of America

ISBN 978-1-963379-41-9 (SC)
ISBN 978-1-963379-28-0 (Ebook)

Lee Halverson Books
112 Meadow Oaks Lane
Jackson, MS 39209
https://congcatchers.com

Order Information and Rights Permission:

Quantity sales. Special discounts might be available on quantity purchases by corporations, associations, and others. For details, contact the publisher at the address above.

Book rights Adaptation and other rights permissions
Leave message at: https://congcatchers.com

Dedication

This book is dedicated to my wife, Ginny. It was her prayers and our faith in Jesus Christ that kept me alive and sane in Viet Nam. It was her love and understanding that restored me when I came home.

Lee Halverson

Acknowledgements:

I'd like to thank my parents, Bendix and Margaret Halverson, for raising me in the Christian faith.

My daughters, Missy and Ginger, deserve to be recognized for understanding when I couldn't take them to a fourth of July fireworks display. They took it in stride when I dove into the bushes when I heard a sound similar to a rifle shot. They attended our MP dog handler reunion in St. Louis and visited with the guys in my unit. Afterwards, they told me, "Dad! All those things you told us are true!" And finally, they knew I needed to see the wall for its healing effects. Afterwards, they gave me a picture of a man standing at the wall touching the name of one of his lost friends. I love you.

A big thanks to Ed Nielson, who got me going on the book. The foundation that he wrote from my articles got me started and helped me to finish.

I appreciate Ginny Smith, editor of the Sioux Rapids portion of the Spencer Daily Reporter, who accepted my articles and reminded me when another one was due.

I can't forget Mrs. Fortune, my English teacher in high school who always assured me that someday I would appreciate prose and poetry. You were right, Mrs. Fortune!

And finally, thanks to Ginny. When we went to St. Louis for our reunion; the guys could have cared less if I were there…they wanted to see Ginny! She supported me and helped me through this entire undertaking. And boy, do I love you!

Contents

Foreword

I grew up on a farm in Northwest Iowa. My base of values came from a strict working class family and the Lutheran church where I was baptized and confirmed. Therefore, Christian values and the values of a good work ethic had been ingrained within me.

After graduation from high school, I attended Iowa State University. While at Iowa State, I met my wife, Ginny. She too had been raised on the farm and in a Christian family and had very similar values as mine. Early in our relationship we made a commitment that Jesus Christ would be the center of our marriage. Together we would pray and seek guidance from him.

When I completed my studies at Iowa State, I went about the process of finding a job. This was 1968 and the Viet Nam war was in full swing. I soon learned that an able bodied young man who was eligible for the draft would have trouble finding good employment. The reason being that once someone had gone to the work of training me, I could be drafted. Understanding this, I went to speak with the recruiters. At the time, there was a two year enlistment available. It seemed to be my only option, so I took it.

Ginny and I wrote letters to each other every day while I was in the service and saved not only those letters, but the letters I received from others. Consequently, there were a lot of letters. In the back of my mind, I had always wanted to write a book about my Viet Nam experience. The trouble was that to do that I had to read the letters. We were married for 22 days when I left for Viet Nam. The whole year I was gone was very emotional for both of us. One day in early 2000, we were sorting through some boxes that we had stored and came across the boxes of letters. We immediately took some out and began to read. Within a very few minutes, we were both in tears. It was amazing how much had been hidden down deep in our hearts.

Then in 2008, I began to write a column for the local newspaper and I found that if I used just one letter at a time and interspersed the articles with memories of my growing up on the farm, I could get through the letters. Every letter has brought back memories for both of us. Some of the memories make us laugh and some still make us cry. But the best part of it all is being able to share those memories with our family. Our daughters Missy and Ginger grew up hearing these stories. We took them to a reunion of the 981st MP Company several years ago. After wandering around for a while talking to my compatriots, Ginger came back to us and said, "Dad, all those stories you have been telling us are true!" Yes, to the best of my memory, they are true. I have taken the liberty of changing some of the names but the events are real.

Most of the books about Viet Nam deal with troop strength, weaponry, battles, body counts and so on. Not this one. For the most part I am an optimist and when I returned to the world, I decided it was important to focus on the good things that happened. The letters and our belief in Jesus Christ brought me through that year of separation and the transition I had to make when I returned home. I still have occasional nightmares though they have diminished over the years. But there is not a day that goes by that I don't thank God for bringing me home safe and mostly sound.

CHAPTER 1
ENTERING THE ARMY

In 1964, when I turned eighteen, I had to go to the Buena Vista County court house and register for the draft as was the obligation of every young American male. I never thought much more about it until years later when the war in Viet Nam came to a head. Many young American boys were being drafted to fight and there were few exclusions: Quakers, conscientious objectors, those who were physically or mentally handicapped and those of us who were given a deferment from the draft because we were in school. Many made a career of going to college in order to avoid the draft.

When I graduated from Iowa State University, I walked across the stage to accept my diploma, went back to my room at Alumni Hall and found my draft notice hanging on my door. That's how efficient the whole system was! Imagine the people responsible for drafting young men having done enough research to know the exact day Lee Halverson would graduate?

The letter said, "Congratulations! Your friends and relatives have selected you to represent them in the United States Military." I was told to report to Fort Des Moines for a physical. I reported for the physical and was told that I had a small rupture. It would prevent me from getting into the military, but it wasn't bad enough to be classified as 4-A the classification that said one was medically unfit for the military. I asked "What do I do? No one will hire me because I'm classified 1-A. You won't accept me because I have a small rupture, but you won't classify me as 4-A. I'm stuck between a rock and a hard spot!"

I had received eight job offers from companies who really wanted me. One of them was Hormel Foods in Austin, Minnesota. I wanted the

1

job and they wanted me. But not as long as I was classified as 1-A and might be drafted.

I decided that my problem was my hernia. It was either going to get worse and I would become 4-A or it would get better and I could pass my physical, do my duty and then get on with my life. So I bought a set of weights and began to lift weights in earnest. Either the weights would bust the hernia into one large enough to be excluded or they would build muscle and I would pass.

My next appointment for a physical came a few months later. Ginny and I drove from Sioux Rapids to Des Moines. We had decided to become engaged and would shop for wedding rings after my physical. She planned to watch Soap Operas until I returned. Ginny left and I entered the waiting room. I sat down amongst a group of nervous looking young men. The guy next to me had tattoos and long hair. He looked confident. "I've got 'em beat," he confided. "Ya rub soap in your armpits and it'll raise your blood pressure so high you'll fail." I nodded and got up to walk around. I didn't want to offend him, but I didn't want to sit next to him and continue his conversation. I walked around the room for a while and finally sat down by a rather large fellow. "I've got 'em beat," he exclaimed with a smile. He spread his legs and showed me a small vial resting between them. "It's a urine sample from a friend of mine. He's got sugar diabetes. I'll pour it into my pee cup and I'll be out of here quicker than you can blink your eyes." I nodded to him and got up to walk around the room again. This time I found a bank of empty chairs and sat down there.

A tall, young man entered the room. He moved with the grace of a dancer. There was no question that this young man was a good athlete. He stood in the shadows of the door and looked the room over. He looked at the guy with the tattoos and the fat guy with the urine sample and then at me. Then he walked over to my area and sat nervously beside me. He was on my left and I looked at him out of the corner of my eye. I noticed that the entire right side of his face was covered with a bright red birth mark. I immediately felt sympathy for him and I extended my hand and said "My name's Lee." He hungrily grabbed my hand and said "Smith. William Smith, but everyone calls me Smitty."

2

We talked for a while and I soon found out that Smitty was a farm boy just like me. He had just graduated from high school and had received his draft notice, since he was not going on to college. So there we were…an eighteen year old and a twenty-two year old being drafted together.

At that time, an army sergeant entered the room. "All right, everyone follow me for your physical."

We entered the area and were told to strip. There were stalls for each of us to hang our clothing and leave our personal belongings. Then we were ushered to another room where we were told to line up, lean over and spread our cheeks. A few of the guys leaned over and grabbed the cheeks of their mouths, pulling them apart. "No, you idiots! Your butt cheeks!" The rest of us laughed as the guys in question made the proper changes as the doctors made their observations.

"All right. All of you grab a little cup and pee in it." I noticed the fat guy was already foiled in his attempt to deceive them. They had us walk into the area naked. There just wasn't any way for him to carry his little vial.

Then we went through the normal physical routine of taking our blood pressure, breathing while the doctor listened with that cold stethoscope, looking into our mouths and being tested for a hernia. "Cough," the doctor would say as he felt the muscles of the abdomen for weakness. The calm was shattered when the guy with the tattoos shouted "What? What do you mean…Perfect! My blood pressure is high…not perfect!" The doctor smiled at him and said, "Tried the old soap trick, huh? Sorry, son…it doesn't work."

"Do any of you prefer boys to girls?" Most of us started laughing, but one fellow who obviously bordered on being mentally challenged said "I like boys!" The laughing got even louder as two doctors whisked the young man into a private room. Shortly thereafter, the young man was released. The military did not accept gays nor anyone who was in question of being gay in those days. And the military did not call them gays…they called them queers.

Smitty went through a routine that would become very familiar to me over the next few years. He twitched his shoulder and tipped his head at the same time. "Looks like we got rid of Sheela!" Everyone in the room

3

roared with laughter and I knew that Smitty was a guy that had a natural ability to impact people.

This time I passed the physical with flying colors. Apparently, the weight lifting had strengthened my muscles. I wasn't crazy about going into the army, but at least I would no longer be in limbo. I'd do my two years of service, get it over with and come back home.

"How were the soap operas?" I asked Ginny. She didn't look happy as she explained that NASA was sending up another rocket today and every network had covered it. No soaps! I knew that this was a good time to keep my mouth shut, so I said nothing as we drove to Zale's in down town Des Moines. Ginny looked at every ring in the store. I quickly browsed the ring section, pointed and said "That's it!" I had selected a matching set of wedding bands that were gold with the Greek key symbol of love etched into them.

"Oh, those are nice," she said, "but we have to look at more."

"Are you kidding? These are perfect. Let's buy them and go bowling!"

We shopped for the rest of the day and eventually came back to Zale's and purchased our wedding bands with the Greek symbol of love.

On January 7, 1969 my Mom and Dad drove Ginny and I to the Des Moines airport in their white Rambler with the pretty blue seats. Ironically, Ginny and I had met exactly two years earlier on this date. Everyone was in good spirits for this event. After all, Basic Training is something every young man must take upon entering the military. We all perceived it to be more like going to Boy Scout Camp or something similar. "Surely they won't send a college graduate to Viet Nam," Mom said. "Once they see your abilities in Basic Training, they will want you to be in a more important, useful position."

"I remember when I took Basic Training," Dad said. "Those drill sergeants will scare you to death, but you'll come through it just fine."

Ginny was all teary eyed at the prospect of being apart, but she bravely took it all in stride. I shook hands with Dad and he told me to stand tall. I hugged Mom and she promised to write letters. "We'll see you soon!"

And with that, Ginny walked beside me through the airport and right up to the steps that led to the airplane. As we walked, this song played over the sound system:

All my bags are packed, I'm ready to go
I'm standing here outside your door
I hate to wake you up to say goodbye
But the dawn is breakin'; it's early morn
The taxi's waiting, he's blowin' his horn
Already I'm so lonesome I could die

So kiss me and smile for me
Tell me that you'll wait for me
Hold me like you'll never let me go
Oh baby, don't let me go.
I'm a leavin' on a jet plane
I don't know when I'll be back again
Oh babe, I hate to go.

We kissed, held hands and then I walked up the stairs to begin another chapter in our lives.

CHAPTER 2
BASIC TRAINING

I landed in Dallas and found Smitty waiting at my gate like a little boy lost at the state fair. We joined a number of recruits at the USO where we would wait for a flight to Fort Polk, Louisiana. Funny, when you're away from home you identify with anyone from your neck of the woods. We immediately noticed Mike, another GI who had gone through his physical with Smitty and I. We came together as if we had grown up with one another, kind of like when you go to Disney World and see someone from a neighboring town that you've never even spoken to, but you recognize him and converse as if you've known each other forever.

Mel, a perfect stranger, joined us as well. He was a chain smoker and I gave him the nickname "Smokey the Bear." He called me "Short Stuff", but that nickname never stuck because Smitty quickly said, "No. He's my Dad while I'm away from home!" From that point on; I was known as "Dad" to everyone I would encounter. At 22, I was the "old man" in the group. John was 18 and fresh off the farm. He became "Farmer John." Dave was from a gang called the Outlaws, in Waterloo. He was in trouble with the law and a judge had given him a choice of going to jail or signing up for the Army. Dave made it clear to us that he was one tough dude and wouldn't put up with any guff from anybody. I nicknamed him, "Percy!" Everyone laughed and that was the end of his playing the tough guy. Everywhere he went he was greeted with "How ya doin' Percy!"

Somehow, we knew the importance of nicknames. We were of all faiths, backgrounds, communities and histories with the law. We didn't want to use proper names because we were leery of each other and didn't want to get too close to someone we didn't trust. Later, in Viet Nam, we used nicknames because we didn't want to get too close to a buddy knowing that he might get "blown away."

6

We flew from Dallas to Fort Polk, Louisiana, and were assigned to a holding company, a holding company being nothing more than a large warehouse with a glorified secretary noting who had arrived. This secretary was a man who looked like a bulldog and in my estimation was meaner to boot! He barked orders at us and apparently knew which company each of us was assigned to. He sorted us into little groups and each group would eventually be taken to its respective company. Smitty and I reclined on our duffle bags and rested. We were already getting used to one of the most popular rules in the Army: Hurry up and wait!

At two a.m. in the morning we were awakened by our bulldog secretary. "All you rubberheads in Company B, 5th battalion, get ready to load up."

We grabbed our duffle bags and were herded into a waiting deuce and a half truck. There were benches on either side of a deuce and a half that comfortably seated 12 men. However, the seats were folded up to the side and no one would be sitting down for this ride. The drill sergeants accompanying us barked and pushed until they had loaded 50 of us onto the truck. We were packed in like sardines with no room to breathe let alone move into a comfortable position.

The drill sergeants continued to call us vile names and they seemed to be especially partial to "rubberhead." They didn't talk; they yelled at the top of their voices, and made it evident that they were there to instill the fear of the Lord in each and every one of us.

The driver took special care to swerve the truck from side to side, resulting in all of us falling against one another to maintain our balance. The truck had a tarp over the top and I'm sure they had plumbed the exhaust to exit beneath the tarp. The exhaust fumes were suffocating us and we were all fighting each other to maintain our balance as the truck continued to swerve from side to side and the drill sergeant continued to yell at us through the window from the cab.

Finally, the truck stopped and the end gate dropped. Our drill sergeant yelled at us to disembark and line up. None of us knew how to make a formation so we meandered around trying to do the right thing, while the drill sergeants yelled at us, called us names, and told us we were doing it all wrong. Some of the recruits began to cry.

"Oh, poor baby want to go home to Mommy?" the sergeant jeered. "Look at me when I'm talking to you rubberhead, and address me by my proper title!"

"Yes, sir," the recruit would say.

"Don't you cuss at me! I'm not a sir!"

The recruit began to cry even more.

"I'm a drill sergeant and you will address me as drill sergeant! Don't you ever cuss at me again. Got it?"

"Yes, sir," came the reply, and the whole episode began all over again.

About the time recruits got the hang of saying, "Yes, drill sergeant," an officer would confront the new recruit.

And this time the poor, dumb slob would respond by saying, "Yes, drill sergeant!"

And of course the officer would reply, "Don't you cuss at me. You will call me SIR!"

And this little game continued to repeat itself as the officers and drill sergeants circled like sharks looking for the weakest among us so they could attack again. None of us knew military insignias, and were completely confused, and scared to death. We didn't know what to say to whom. And that was the design of Basic Training in those days. The objective was to completely humiliate each recruit and reduce them to a quivering mass of Jell-O in order to begin proper training.

Finally, the drill sergeants called our names in alphabetical order and assigned us to a bed. They were bunk beds lined up about four feet apart. Our barracks building had two stories with 50 recruits on each floor. Each of us had a footlocker at the end of the bunk bed and a wall locker beside the bed. We threw our belongings into the wall lockers and climbed into bed as drill sergeants screamed names at us and ordered, "Lights out!" I laid there awake and pondered what was in store for us. I'd never been so scared, disoriented, and petrified in my life.

We were awakened at four a.m. by our drill sergeant yelling and hammering his baton on the ends of the beds. "Get up, you bunch of rubberheads! Do your three S's (shit, shower, and shave) and get ready for breakfast!" We stood three deep in the shower while he continued to scream obscenities at us and demand that we hurry up. "Formation outside the barracks in 10 minutes!" he yelled. We all scurried as fast as we could and went outside for formation.

"Dress it up," he demanded.

That meant that we in the front row all had to extend our right hands to the shoulder of the person on our right. As soon as we were an arm's length apart, the rows behind us had to line up directly behind the person in the front row. Our company lined up with twelve men in front all an arm's length apart. Three more lines of men stood directly behind the man in front of them. It was a beautiful thing!

"Ten hut!" he yelled meaning that we all had to stand at attention.

Then our drill sergeant went from man to man inspecting our dress, shoes, and shave. He carried a razor with him for the poor unfortunate soul who didn't get the job done right.

"Did you forget to put a blade in your shaver, you rubberhead?"

Then he would take his BIC and dry shave the poor slob right on the spot. The recruit would stand there crying with blood dripping down his face from the dry shave. All of us took notice and vowed that we would be sure to shave ourselves well in the future, I sometimes shaved as many times as three times a day.

"What did you do to your shoes, shine them with a Hershey bar? Drop down and push away that Louisiana soil! Give me 50!" the drill instructor barked to another recruit.

The recruit had to drop and do 50 pushups for not shining his shoes. Once again, we all vowed silently that we would have our shoes shined in the future too! We all remained at attention for what seemed like hours while Company A went through the food line at the mess hall. We were in Company B and would be next.

"Fall out and get in the food line!" he barked.

We all scrambled to get in one of two lines. We were told that we couldn't eat unless we knew our serial number and yelled it to the drill sergeant who stood at the head of the line. Half the guys didn't know their serial number and had to go back to the barracks and, upon returning, would be back at the end of the line. My serial number was RA (Regular Army) 68070861 and I yelled that number at the top of my lungs.

"You've got five minutes to eat. If you're not done, we'll throw you out!"

I grabbed a tray and got my helping of chipped beef on toast (SOS) and sat to eat. Outside I could hear the continuous yelling of NG (National Guard serial numbers), ER (Enlisted Reserves), and more RA serial numbers. NGs and ERs were often sent to the back of the line because the cadre (non-commissioned officers) didn't show respect for them. That's because many young men joined the National Guard or the Enlisted reserves to avoid being sent to Viet Nam. They had to attend basic training as a part of their military obligation, but when basic ended, they would be going back home. The cadre at basic training were hard core army and looked upon these men as cowards. Only RA's were smiled upon because we weren't trying to dodge service in Vietnam, they felt there was no distinction between RAs who had been drafted and RAs who had volunteered. We were considered to be exemplary soldiers who had joined to do our duty.

Those of us who had been at the head of the line had to wait outside until the remainder of our company finished eating.

"Smoke 'em if you've got 'em," our sergeant would yell.

Being first in line became a must for those of us who smoked, since this was a rare opportunity. During other activities that we did together, being at the front of the line often offered other chances for a cigarette while the rest finished.

"And make sure you field dress those butts!" he would yell.

That meant that we had to tear the paper from our cigarette butts and sprinkle the remaining tobacco on the ground. Filters had to go in a pocket to be disposed of later.

After eating breakfast that first day we paid a visit to the barber. There were some recruits who still had 50s-style pompadours and there were a number of "Hippy types" who had ponytails. The barbers watched for the two types of recruits like vultures waiting for a cow to die!

"How would you like yours cut?" they would ask nicely.

Then, regardless of the recruit's reply, they would shave a strip of hair right down the middle of his skull, spin him around to look in the mirror, and wait for the recruit's reaction. Some of the recruits would cry with their signature hairdo gone, and the barbers would laugh with glee each time that happened. Every one of us left the barber shop with what the Army called the "whitewall." That's a butch hair cut with the sides trimmed so short our heads looked like a whitewall tire!

Next the drill sergeants took us to the clothing warehouse and issued our GI clothing. First we got a duffel bag. It was olive drab in color, about four feet tall, two feet wide, and had a strap with a clip on it. As we were issued our clothes, we would fold them up and pack them into this bag. Once the bag was full, the upper flaps folded over onto a ring. The clip could be attached to this ring and also formed a shoulder strap so we could carry our bag. For two years everything I owned went into that bag. I think of the suitcases full of clothing and personal items we take on a weekend trip now and remember that literally everything I owned for my tenure in the Army fit into one bag!

The supply people really knew their business. "Forty-six long!" the clerk said when he looked at me. And that was exactly the size of my suit coat! "Eleven and a half, D!" he shouted. And that was the exact size of the shoes I wore. And so it went. Before long my bag was stuffed with shirts, underwear, socks, pants, shoes, and a Class A uniform. Everything, except for the Class A uniform, was olive drab in color. I grew to hate that color and I still do!

We marched back to our barracks and were told to unpack everything and place our clothing in either the footlocker or the wall cabinet. Everyone completed that task and then our next lesson came.

The wall cabinet was similar to the lockers we had in high school. There was a small shelf at the top. Instead of hooks like our high school lockers had, there was a pipe to accept the hangars for our class A uniforms and any other clothing we wished to hang. The foot locker was about the size of my mother's cedar chest. It had a tray on top that sat on railings on either side of the locker. This tray would hold our socks and underwear. Beneath the tray we could place our folded pants and shirts. Both lockers had hasps so we could use a padlock to secure our belongings.

"Don't you rubberheads know how to fold clothes?" our drill sergeant yelled.

I looked and saw piles of clothing in each footlocker. Some had made an attempt at neatness, while others had just dumped their clothing and slammed the lid!

Now we would learn the Army way of folding clothes, the Army way of making our bed, and the Army way of waxing the floors. Beds had to have hospital folds and the blanket had to be so tight the drill sergeant could bounce a quarter on it. Socks had to be rolled into a small ball with the upper folded over the entire sock. We simply rolled the toe of the sock towards the top of the sock and when two inches was left, folded the upper over the rolled sock. Socks were then arranged in rows in the top tray of our footlockers and it was surprising how neat this row of socks looked. Underwear, both shorts and T-shirts, had to be folded into four-by-four squares. Those were also lined up in order in our footlockers. Class As, field jackets, and pants could be hung in the wall locker with exactly one inch of space between each item. Our class A hat sat on the top shelf of the wall locker along with our field hat. Boots and personal belongings were at the bottom of the footlocker. I have to admit; everything was pleasing to the eye when it was done. And we never had to search for anything….we knew exactly where every item was!

Next we had to learn how to spit-shine our boots. We all put a little water in the lids of our shoe wax cans and, after spreading polish on our boots and brushing them, we would take cotton balls soaked in water and finish the boots off so they had a mirror like shine. The officer's boots really did look like mirrors because they had shined them so many times. And all they needed was a hanky and a little spit to bring back the "spit shine."

Drill Sergeant O'Dell smiled as he presented a gallon can of paste floor wax to us. "You will make this floor so shiny that I will be able to shave by using it as a mirror," he said. The floor already looked shiny to me so I thought waxing it would be an exercise in futility, just another aggravation in Army life. My jaw dropped as O'Dell grabbed the end of a bunk bed and dragged it to one end of the barracks and back to the other, gouging huge scratches into the floor.

"You will make those lines disappear and make this floor into a mirror," he said. We worked well into the night applying wax and rubbing it into the shine with our socks.

"No letter writing! You will need your sleep because we have an IG inspection tomorrow," O'Dell declared. "Lights out and everybody better be in bed when I check later." O'Dell grinned at us with his yellowish teeth. He was six feet three and weighed a hundred and fifty at best. I knew other men of his size and stature in the past and the old saying about him standing sideways, sticking out his tongue and looking like a zipper came to mind. That would have been true of O'Dell too except for the fact that he had a huge Adam's apple and an even larger nose. I decided that he looked and sounded like "Foghorn Leghorn" in the Disney cartoons.

After O'Dell made his nightly inspection, we disobeyed his orders and went back to waxing the floor for the Inspector General's visit. We didn't want to be gigged (A GIG was a penalty for not doing something correctly. Companies were compared by the number of GIGs they had.) for the floor because that would mean KP duty. Everyone dreaded Kitchen Patrol because of the potato peeling and the washing of pots and pans.

The Inspector General arrived the next day and we all stood at attention at the foot of our beds waiting for him to admire the wonderful work we had done on the floor. To our surprise he put on a pair of white gloves and ran his finger over the window sills. The finger tip of his glove turned brown immediately. As if driven by some evil force, he went to Perry's footlocker, which looked like a rag bag. "Everyone in front leaning rest!" he ordered. Front-leaning rest is the Army term for the top position of a pushup. We all took the position of front-leaning rest while the general informed us that we were in the Army now.

"One person screwing up can screw up the entire company," he said. "You let one guy make a mistake and you could all die! So you had better learn to watch the other guy and compensate for him. If one guy screws up, you all suffer!"

My arms began to shake after being in the front leaning rest for what seemed like an eternity. Others experienced the same thing. *That damned Perry*, I thought. *If it wasn't for him I wouldn't be going through this.*

Others were thinking the same thing. When that inspection was over, Perry paid!

13

Perry became the first victim of a GI Party. He got hauled out of his bunk late one night as "friends" threw a blanket over him so he couldn't see, and a number of GIs commenced to beating and kicking him. Perry lay on the floor weeping after it was all over, but he had gotten the message loud and clear. I helped him up and got him back into bed.

He looked at me with mournful eyes and said, "I want to go home. I miss my Mama and Papa." I didn't reply because we both knew he was here to stay and there would be no going home.

"Dad," he asked. "Can you help me fold my clothes?"

Perry had grown up in Tennessee and his Army boots were the first pair of shoes he'd ever worn in his life. Owning more than one pair of pants and shirts seemed like a luxury to him. He had never folded a shirt or even seen a hanger in his life. Teaching him to fold clothes became agony because he just couldn't seem to get the hang of it. I spent a number of days with Perry, and he finally learned to fold his clothes and arrange them in his footlocker.

The Army method had worked. Perry was no longer afraid of the drill sergeant. He was afraid of his own peers! He never got gigged again. The GI Party was an effective way of taking care of problem soldiers and was administered by peers, rather than by officers or cadre.

There were a number of GIs who had never taken showers before. They had no understanding about personal hygiene. They got to smelling to high heaven after a day of drills and marching. They would be hauled out of bed in the dark of night, a blanket thrown over their heads, and would then be escorted to the shower where other GIs would scrub them down with long handled course brushes called GI brushes. The course bristles would scratch the skin and draw blood. But when the GI Party was over, they would get the message and shower regularly from that point on.

We were not allowed to write letters back home. "You're going to war and the only thing you can depend on in war is your fellow GIs. So get the idea of depending on your parents or your girlfriend out of your heads right now!"

When we were busy with training, getting ready for an inspection by an Inspector General, or doing all the other things required of us, there just wasn't any time to write. I had promised Ginny that I would write every day and I was going to stick to my promise. I wondered, *Where could I go to write a letter and not be caught by the drill sergeant?*

There was a simple answer to that question: the latrine! So I wrote letters sitting on the toilet! Since we had stalls with doors on them, I had privacy and good lighting. Whenever the drill sergeant entered the latrine, all I had to do was make some convincing grunting noises and continue with my writing. It worked like a charm.

Eventually, I got a flashlight at the PX and wrote my letters in the dark of night with a blanket over my head to conceal the flashlight. Soon, others purchased flash lights and were doing the same thing. I had Ginny mail me stationery and stamped envelopes because the Army wouldn't allow us to buy stationery, envelopes, or postage. I had to run to a mailbox near the compound to mail my letters because if the mailroom was used, the cadre would find out. They would return the letter to the offender the next morning at formation, have the offender assume the front leaning rest position, and give us a sermon about going to war in Vietnam.

They stressed that we wouldn't be able to rely on mommy, daddy, or girl friends while on the battle field. "Look at this rubberhead in front leaning rest! He's letting you down. You won't be able to depend on him in the heat of battle."

All this talk of war in Vietnam was taking its toll on everyone. Many of us didn't believe in the war in Vietnam, but had been drafted and had no choice in the matter. A number of GIs frightened of going to Vietnam walked into the headquarters building holding hands and kissed in front of the captain. They were immediately discharged from the Army. Basic Training was teaching us the Army way. We were learning to deliver our own justice, work together, and forget about our ties back home.

One night I was under my blanket writing a letter to Ginny when my blanket was pulled from my head. *Oh boy,* I thought. *I've been caught and tomorrow I'll be on K.P, or I'll be the victim of a GI Party.* I turned expecting to see drill sergeant O'Dell ready to lower the boom and there to my surprise was Perry, tears rolling down his face. "Dad," he asked. "Can you write a letter home to my wife for me? I never learned to read or write."

Perry dictated his letter and I wrote. I felt out of place hearing such personal information let alone writing it. But I wrote the letter and mailed it along with my letter to Ginny. Perry looked at me with his puppy-dog eyes and didn't even have to say thank you. His eyes said it all.

Ginny sent me a letter every day. Mail was less expensive in those days. Regular letters had a six-cent stamp with FDR's face on it. Air mail had five rows of stars and cost 10 cents. Each was addressed to Lee Halverson, RA68070861, Company B, 5th Battalion, 2nd BCT Brigade, Fort Polk, Louisiana 71459.

There will never be a happier face than a GI whose name has just been called because he had a letter. And there will never be a sadder face than a GI at the end of mail call who didn't get a letter.

Ginny was still at Iowa State University working on her degree in English and Speech. She lived in Maple Hall and got plenty of support from her roommate and other friends there. Once in a while she would send a picture of herself and her friends. My favorite picture is of her and four other girls all saluting us. They were saluting with the wrong hands, but that didn't matter. They were all cute and the other GIs in my platoon were envious of the pretty girls I knew, and wanted to come home with me when we had leave so they could meet them. Rumor had it that the Army put saltpeter in our food to hold down the sexual urges of the men, but you certainly couldn't tell it by their reactions when they saw Ginny and her friends!

We spent most of our early time in Basic Training working out and going to classes. Of course, the Army wanted us to be in top physical shape and that required lots of calisthenics and pushups. We would begin our day by "Policing the Area." That meant that we had to stand at one end of the calisthenics field and dress ourselves an arm's length apart. Then we would bend over and walk side by side to the other end of the field picking up trash and cigarette butts as we went. The drill sergeant would be saying, "Get it all. I don't want to see anything but assholes and elbows!" I was certain that all the smoking officers went to the field so they could throw their butts down for us along with any candy or gum wrappers. The non-smoking officers probably raided the ash trays in the office so they could make their contributions too!

Next we were led in calisthenics by someone who always resembled Atlas himself. We spent at least an hour every morning and another in the afternoon doing jumping jacks, sit ups, leg lifts, push-ups, crab walks and toe touch windmills.

We soon got used to the regimen that the Army wanted us to follow: Lights out at nine p.m., up at four a.m., shower and shave, form up for inspection, run a mile, and then have breakfast.. We usually had one class in the morning. That would be followed by more calisthenics, lunch, and another class or two in the afternoon.

We marched in formation to each class and were ordered prior to entering class that there would be no coughing, sneezing, or sleeping during class. Amazingly, nobody coughed or sneezed, and we sure didn't sleep!

Our first class was the Military Code of Conduct:

Article I: I am an American fighting in the forces which guard my country and our way of life. I am prepared to give my life in their defense.

Article 2: I will never surrender of my own free will. If in command, I will never surrender the members of my command while they still have the means to resist.

Article 3: If I am captured I will continue to resist by all means available. I will make every effort to escape and to aid others to escape. I will accept neither parole nor special favors from the enemy.

Article 4: If I become a prisoner of war I will keep faith with my fellow prisoners. I will give no information or take part in any action which might be harmful to my comrades. If I am senior, I will take command. If not, I will obey the lawful orders of those appointed over me and will back them up in every way.

Article 5: When questioned should I become a prisoner of war, I am required to give name, rank, service number, and date of birth. I will evade answering further questions to the utmost of my ability. I will make no oral or written statements disloyal to my country and its allies or harmful to their cause.

Article 6: I will never forget that I am an American fighting for freedom, responsible for my actions and dedicated to the principles which made my country free. I will trust in my God and in the United States of America.

We all received cards with the Code of Conduct printed on them and were told to memorize the above six articles. When we lined up for breakfast the next morning, a drill sergeant asked us to recite one of the articles. Anyone who couldn't recite the article requested went to the back of the line. We soon learned that, if we didn't have the articles committed to memory, we didn't eat.

Next we had an introduction to the Uniform Code of Military Justice, UCMJ for short. They told us that in the event of minor infraction, our commander could issue an Article 15. An Article 15 is like being sent to the principal's office for throwing spit balls in class. Be that as it may, a solder can request a court martial if he feels his commander's punishment is out of line.

But the UCMJ was meant for serious infractions and they spent a lot of time addressing certain articles. Violating any of those articles could result in a court martial, which could result in serious penalties such as being sent to the stockade, the Army 's term for jail or even death. Following are the articles from the UCMJ that they stressed:

Article 86: AWOL. We could not be absent without leave.

Article 85: Desertion. Deserting our post and leaving our fellow soldiers in jeopardy was really stressed. They mentioned that deserters in the past have faced a firing squad.

Article 89: Disrespect to an officer. We were taught to respect rank regardless of the person.

Article 91: Insubordination. We could not actively disobey an order given by an officer.

Article 92: Failure to obey an order. While insubordination is a definite action, failure to obey is a non-violent action that could be just as bad in the eyes of the military.

Going to classes meant marching. Usually, the platoon leader got picked on the basis of prior service. Anyone with prior service knew how to call cadence and give orders: column left, march in step, double time, and so on. Some platoons didn't have anyone with prior service and resorted to a GI who had taken ROTC in college.

I had the good fortune of having a good voice, and also picked up on commands quickly. Our platoon leader had been picked because of his prior service, but he had a voice that didn't carry and didn't know the commands for marching. Drill Sergeant O'Dell called me to the front during one of our marches and said, "You're our new platoon leader! Start calling cadence."

Bucky, our previous platoon leader, had to fall into ranks and I began calling cadence. "Your left, your left, your left, right, left...your left, right, left. Look to the left and what do you see? Company C in misery! Am I right or wrong"

The platoon would then respond with, "You're right!"

"Tell me if I'm wrong!"

The platoon would respond with, "You're right!"

These cadence calls were designed so that when I said, "left" each individuals left foot would hit the ground. And when I'd say, "right" the soldiers' right foot would hit the ground. A good cadence caller would have everyone in the platoon stepping in unison to the point that one's chest could touch the back of the soldier in front of him as they marched and no one would trip. It really was a beautiful thing to see when a platoon could march in synchronization.

My favorite marching cadence was, "Bring 'er on down." I'd say:

Your left, your left, your left, right, left.
Your left, right, left.
Cadence count, one, two.
Cadence count, three, four.
Bring 'er on down.

Then everyone in the platoon would shout:

One, two, three, four.
One, two, THREE, FOUR!

My platoon soon became the company commander's pride and joy. We could outmarch and outshine every other platoon in the company, and when the entire company had to attend a class Company B was always out front. It felt good calling cadence for them and having officers on the side lines pointing at us with smiles on their faces. It was one of the few things I enjoyed about Basic Training.

The "perks" I got as platoon leader surprised me. Sergeant O'Dell told me that I would get my own room. No longer did I have to sleep in the rows of bunk beds with the other G.I.'s. I would have the privacy of my own room—a single bed, a desk, and a lamp. Of course, the desk and lamp were there for me to do the paperwork required of the platoon leader.

This paperwork would require me to be up after lights out took place. While the others had to go to sleep, I would still be up. What it really meant to me was that I could now write letters without having to hide under my blanket with a flashlight. What O'Dell didn't know wouldn't hurt him!

The platoon leader would never be assigned to KP or to guard duty. *Wonderful!* I thought. *No more fire guard duty!*

We were assigned "fire guard" for an hour each night. Our barracks were wooden, clapboard buildings and would burn in a minute if a fire were to start. Before I was platoon guide, someone woke me at two in the morning and told me it was my turn to be the fire guard. I had to walk our floor from one end to the other for an hour and watch for a fire. If there had been one, I was to wake everyone and get them out of the building immediately. At three I would wake up the next fire guard and he would take over. And so it went every night. Every one of us had to take turns standing fire guard from dusk to dawn.

Four a.m. arrived quickly for those of us who had lost an hour of sleep during the night because of fire guard duty. But as soon as four a.m. arrived we would race to the head to shower and shave prior to the morning's formation. There the officers and cadre would inspect us for dress and shaves. Then we would go on a mile run prior to breakfast. I was never a good runner and the mile run was a killer for me. I started out running with Benny, a kid from Pennsylvania. Benny was at least fifty pounds overweight and ran the kind of pace I could match. Smitty ran like a deer and had the track medals from high school to prove it. He would quickly disappear into the horizon as Benny and I slogged along together. But in time, Benny lost his fifty pounds and I improved in my ability to run. I pushed myself to keep up with Smitty and towards the end of Basic; I could keep up with him…. never catch him, but at least he didn't disappear into the horizon anymore. I would arrive huffing and puffing at the end of the mile and Smitty would be ready to run another one!

Our drill sergeant demanded that everyone finish before we could eat. We did a lot of physical activity at Boot Camp and our only food was the three squares we got daily, no lunches or snacks. So we were mighty hungry for each meal and it was agonizing waiting for our over-weight troops to finish so we could eat.

"Why should we have to suffer because he's out of shape?" we would ask.

"You're going to have to depend on each other in war," our drill sergeant would reply. "So you'd better get used to helping each other out. We work as a unit and that means everybody! So if you want to eat, you'd better help him out."

Benny was one of the culprits who was always lagging behind. So I would carry Benny's M14, Smitty would take his backpack, and together we would each grab one of Benny's arms to help him run. It was hard work carrying two M14s and half a guy, but we soon had Benny finishing with the rest of us and got to eat sooner. We quickly learned to help each other whenever needed because all of us suffered if we didn't.

The day came when we would have our final physical training test. Top qualifiers in each category would get weekend passes; Smitty was a shoo-in for the mile run. Although he was a natural all around athlete, I could beat him on the parallel bars and the obstacle course. But that mile run was a killer for me. I remembered running wind sprints in high school football practice. I'd always come in last and Coach Sandine nicknamed me one of the "Gold Dust Twins."

Smitty took off for the mile run just as he always did, seemingly exerting no effort at all. He ran like a deer! Imagine if you will: He was running in sand while wearing combat boots and Army fatigues, yet turned in a mile in just under five minutes! I went through the parallel bars two rungs at a time since it was my best event, and did a chin up at the end just for good measure. We both participated in the rest of the exercises, but didn't keep track because we knew Smitty had won the mile and I had won the parallel bars and that was enough to clinch a pass. The company commander wanted us to set a new record, which we did, and honored the passes even though our company was restricted to the area.

I thought to myself, *What the heck good is a weekend pass? Ginny is back in Iowa. I don't carouse or frequent bars. So what will I do?*

I should have known that Smitty would take care of everything. "Hey Dad! We're going to New Orleans for the weekend!"

It turned out that one of Smitty's acquaintances was a guy named White. His father was a famous person and had a penthouse on the top floor of a swanky building in downtown New Orleans and all of us who had passes were invited to a party there!

We arrived at the building and found that the top four floors were accessible only by a key card. Those floors were occupied by some really rich people and they didn't want any riffraff bothering them. White entered his key card and before long the elevator doors opened to the most impressive living quarters I had ever seen in my life. The penthouse was the entire top floor of the building. Fine furniture, art work, beautiful pictures, paintings, mirrors, and other fine furnishing were everywhere. A chef on duty there would make anything our hearts desired. The bar had hard liquor, beer, wine, and pop. Best of all, there was a recreation room complete with pin ball machines, a pool table, air hockey, ping pong, and a large television. It was a dream come true! I beat everyone at ping pong, and then retired to the pin ball machines and had the chef make me a hamburger and French fries.

I didn't drink alcohol in those days, so I stuck to Pepsi. Smitty, on the other hand, spent the entire weekend sampling every bottle on the shelf. When it came time to leave and go back to the compound, I put an arm around Smitty and helped him to the elevator. He was a little wobbly, but he was having a good time. The elevator didn't go straight to the bottom like I had anticipated, but stopped at the next floor down. A large-breasted woman with a ballroom gown and a fancy hairdo with diamonds in it stepped into the elevator with us. I remember the look of disgust on her face as she sidled to the back of the elevator to be as far away from us ruffians as she could get.

Just when we reached the bottom and the doors were opening, Smitty passed gas, so much gas that it would have made a Belgian draft horse proud. It truly was a magnificent performance. Smitty immediately turned to the lady behind us and said, "Lady, you ought to be ashamed of yourself!"

She was still in the back of the elevator with a look of shock on her face when the doors closed.

When we got back, we had to go through the gas chamber to qualify with our gas masks. We were taught the procedure step by step. First we had to loosen the elastic straps on our mask. There were six straps and each had a little buckle that allowed the strap to be loosened if pulled one way and yet held the strap firmly in place if pulled from the other direction. Then we were to arrange the elastic straps on the back of our heads and pull the mask down over our faces. When the mask was in place, there were tabs on each elastic strap that could be pulled tight to hold the mask tightly around our faces.

Next we performed the pressure check. We held our hands over the exhaust valve and blew. That would make sure that the intake valves were closing properly. If the mask was in proper working order, a sound like a Bronx cheer would erupt. If we didn't get the Bronx cheer, we knew that the intake valve was faulty. The other check involved covering the intake valves and breathing in. That was to make sure the exhaust valve was working properly. A good check meant that the mask would be sucked into our faces because we would create a vacuum with our suction. We were told that the exhaust valve was faulty and needed to be repaired if we got air with this check.

Once we had properly donned our masks and done our checks, we were to stand in line for the gas chamber. We were told that the chamber was being filled with CS riot gas. As the name implies, it is used for riots to disperse people. Its effects are choking, stinging eyes, burning skin, labored breathing, and perhaps vomiting in the most drastic cases. We were told that the effects were temporary and that our breathing and our sight would return to normal in no time at all.

We were to enter the chamber with our gas masks on. One of the drill sergeants would pull our mask away from our face, at which time we were to take a deep breath. When we began coughing and choking, the sergeant would allow the gas mask to snap back into the place and we could leave the chamber.

I had learned early on to never be first in line for anything in the Army, so I feigned difficulty with my straps and waited for others to get in line. I watched as they were ushered into the chamber. After a few minutes, men would leave the chamber coughing and leaning over in pain, trying to get their breath back. Lots of them were rubbing their skin because of the stinging sensation. This didn't look good at all.

My turn finally came and I entered the chamber. It was cloudy in there because of the gas and I could barely make out the drill instructors. One came up to me and pulled my gas mask away from my face. I waited. He waited. Nothing!

Finally he said, "Take a deep breath."

I took a deep breath. I waited. He waited. Nothing!

"Go get in line again," he said in desperation.

I came into the chamber a second time and he was waiting for me. He pulled my mask away from my face and said "Take a deep breath."

I did. I waited. He waited. Nothing.

Finally he took my gas mask completely off and stood there. I don't know what the deal was, but the gas simply had no effect on me.

The drill instructor shook his head and smiled. "Halverson, I can't figure it out. For some reason you seem to be immune to the stuff."

I told him, "If you had cleaned as many chicken houses as I have, you'd be immune to it, too!"

We were confined to our company area the entire time we were in Basic Training. Too many men were going AWOL because they were afraid of going to Vietnam. So we had guards around our company area and weren't allowed to leave for any reason, except on weekends when we could go to a bank of phones just outside the perimeter and make a phone call home to loved ones. There were six phones in the phone bank with lines of 20 soldiers waiting at each phone. It was difficult to have a private conversation with so many people behind and beside me. Usually, I'd be trying to say, "I love you" to Ginny, while the guy behind me was saying, "For gosh sakes, hurry up will ya!"

The only exception to that rule was that someone from a platoon could go to the PX (grocery store) and buy necessities for everyone in the platoon. I frequently got that job. I had to meet with everyone in the platoon to create a list, collect money, buy the products, and then give everyone their change back when the job had been completed. And that's the reason I frequently got the job: I could make change. It amazed me how many guys there were in my platoon who couldn't count and, therefore, couldn't make change. If I had learned how to count in Sioux Rapids Consolidated School, why couldn't someone from New York or Brooklyn? It seemed to me that the schools there would be superior to a school out in the middle of farm country, but apparently not.

Our days were pretty uneventful. We were stuck in our company area doing the same things, day in and day out. Mornings began with calisthenics and a mile run. Then we went for breakfast. That usually consisted of oatmeal, and eggs and bacon or chipped beef on toast.

After each meal, we had to walk the horizontal bars just outside of the mess hall. The horizontal bars were like a 30-foot long ladder supported about 10 feet from the ground. We had to jump up and grab a rung, then walk hand-over-hand the length of the ladder. I got so I could go three rungs at a time and swing through it like a monkey. I always felt sorry for the overweight guys because they usually ran out of strength after 10 feet and would plummet to the ground, at which time they would receive lots of verbal abuse from the cadre.

We marched, usually double-time, to our classes in the mornings and afternoons.

The obstacle course was always a part of our day. We began by running on logs. Pity the poor guy who lost his balance and fell into the mud between the logs. At the end of the logs were more horizontal ladders and then a six-by-six, again about 30 feet long that we had to hang from and go hand over hand along its length. Again, pity the poor guy who lost his grip and fell into the mud below. Next came a wall about 12 feet tall with ropes on one side. We had to grab the rope, climb to the top of the wall, swing over, and drop to the other side. Smitty could hit the wall in stride and step up to the top, grab hold, and swing over without ever touching the rope! I was never a good runner, so I used the rope.

The low crawl came next. Barbed wire was strung about two feet off the ground and over an area about fifty yards long. We had to crawl under that wire. I excelled on this part of the obstacle course because I wasn't a good runner but I was a great crawler! Then we had to crawl through a culvert that was three feet in diameter. At the end of the culvert was a rope bridge across a river. This bridge consisted of a single rope for our feet and another rope about seven feet higher for our hands. The trick was to walk on the lower rope and use the top rope for balance, rather than to use the top rope to support one's weight. When we got to the other side of the river, we were done and could rest until the other guys finished. The guys who were out of shape usually took quite a while because they would fall into the mud or get hung up in the barbed wire.

Mom used to say that, "Sometimes solitude is the best companion," and I found that I enjoyed going to a place of solitude after completing the obstacle course, rather than congregating with the rest of the guys who had finished. The cadre liked to have everyone in one place so they could keep an eye on us. One day, I had found a nice grassy knoll about 20 yards from the group. As I lay there enjoying the sunshine and my thoughts, a lieutenant came up to me and said, "Who in the world put you in this position?"

"My draft board," I replied.

We usually had two classes every day while we were in Basic Training. One class usually dealt with combat in some way, shape, or form. We might learn about such things as weapons, camouflaging ourselves, self-defense, gas masks, and chemical warfare. The other class always dealt with our mind set. We learned that God was on our side. We learned that fighting for our freedom was supremely important. We learned that communism was out there somewhere, trying to take over the world. If we didn't stop them in Vietnam, they would eventually end up in the United States and take away all our freedoms. If we didn't do something, Vietnam would fall, followed by Cambodia, then Laos, and eventually that domino effect would end up in Sioux Rapids, Iowa.

Our class one day dealt with our forefathers fighting in the Revolutionary War. We were told that five signers of the Declaration of Independence were captured and tortured before they died, Twelve had their homes ransacked and burned, and nine of the signers died from wounds. Carl Braxton, a wealthy planter and trader, saw his ships captured by the British Navy. He sold his home and properties to pay his debts and died in rags. Thomas McKean was so hounded by the British that he was forced to move his family constantly. He served in Congress without pay and his family was kept in hiding. His possessions were taken from him and poverty was his reward.

Twenty-four of the signers were lawyers and jurists, 11 were merchants, and nine were farmers. They all signed the Declaration of Independence knowing full well that the penalty would be death if they were captured. Of course, the message to us was that our predecessors were willing to die for freedom and so should we. Indeed, it is honorable that these men should make such a commitment but I wondered, *What happened that made them do it?*

So I went to the library and did some research. The 13 colonies were subject to Great Britain, so Parliament passed laws that affected the colonies. None of the members of Parliament came from the colonies. That's why the phrase "Taxation without Representation" came into being. In essence the members of Parliament had no idea what life in the colonies was like and were passing laws to fatten their purses. They were not representing the people. They were passing laws to satisfy their own greedy desires.

Parliament passed the Quebec Act, giving the land between the Ohio River and the Mississippi River to the Canadians. Quebec would sell furs to England and pay the hefty tariff that England demanded, thereby bringing income to Great Britain. The colonists were selling furs to France and Spain, which kept more money in their pockets. The Quebec Act took away the livelihoods of many colonists and gave it to Canadians.

Tea was popular in the colonies. Parliament placed a tax on tea, partly to increase income to the government and partly to save the British East

India Company from bankruptcy. Soon, Parliament placed a tax on other necessities: glass, lead, paper, sugar, molasses, and even a stamp act that placed a tax on wills, diplomas, and marriage certificates. The colonists felt that they were being taxed to death and began to revolt. The Boston Tea Party was a harbinger of things to come.

Thomas Paine wrote a book called *Common Sense*. The book became so popular that the printing presses couldn't produce enough copies to satisfy the market. The main theme of his book was that government can be diverted into corrupt purposes by the representatives within. The simpler the government, the easier it is for people to discover corruption and make the necessary adjustments needed. This book fueled the colonists. Parliament was so complex that the colonists, even those who wanted to remain faithful to the crown, didn't know who to point their fingers at. But a simple government would make it possible to identify a corrupt representative and vote him out!

The end result was that the colonists won their independence and formed their own government. Great Britain was 250 million pounds in debt and had to raise taxes on its own populace to pay for it. France, who supported the colonists in the Revolutionary War, was 187 million pounds in debt. Only half the national revenue in France went to serve the debt from the war. That eventually led to the French Revolution when its government tried to raise taxes even further to pay its war debt.

I looked around at all the hundreds of men that were in basic training with me. Our taxes were paying for all this training. And this was just one battalion! How many more battalions might there be? I thought of the tremendous expenditures that paid for not only the Army, but the Air Force, the Navy, the Marines and so on. And that's just the training. Imagine the cost of moving all of us into a war zone after the training is done. And imagine the cost of fighting the war in terms of equipment, weaponry, food, transportation, clothing, medical supplies. Would our taxes be raised as a result? Would average citizens question their leaders about placing our nation in debt? And who would they point their fingers at? Was our government too big for its britches too? It seemed like half our congress was in favor of the war in Viet Nam while the other half was against it. It seemed idiotic to me that we should be sending young men into battle and put their lives on the line when our own leaders couldn't agree whether or not it was the right thing to do.

Be that as it may, I realized that I was now in the middle of it along with a bunch of other guys from all over the country from all different walks of life. We would have to overlook our differences and learn to work together towards a common goal.

Going to college and meeting folks from other places was a real learning experience for me. Until then I never realized that there are people in the world that weren't like the people I'd grown up with in Sioux Rapids, Iowa. Our little town was a homogeneous group of farmers or people who depended on farmers for their livelihoods. Most of us went to church regularly. We knew that work had to be done whether the weather was inclement or not. We knew we needed a high school diploma and it was even better to go on to college. We were patriotic. Memorial Day and the Fourth of July were strictly observed. Labor Day was a day off for city people—we had livestock to care for and hay to bale. Dad worked and Mom kept house. In school, boys took shop and girls took Home Economics. One day we would marry and complete the cycle.

It surprised me when I went to Iowa State University and found atheists who not only didn't go to church but didn't believe in God! A large number of ISU students didn't come from a farming background or community. They thought eggs and milk grew in the grocery store. They would skip class if the weather got too cold. They burned the American Flag and demonstrated against our government's involvement in Vietnam. Labor Day was an important holiday to them. Some of their parents were CEOs of large companies and others had parents who were union members. Some had stay-at-home fathers. Boys were attending interior decorating classes and girls were in my welding class! Be that as it may, we were still a pretty homogeneous group, because for the most part we all came from families that had a mom and dad and a belief that a college education was important.

As I looked over the other men in my unit, I realized what a melting pot the Army was. We had very little in common with one another, except that we had been drafted and wore the same uniform.

Chain was an African-American from the streets of Atlanta. He had been a leader of a gang there and had received his nickname by beating another gang leader almost to death with a length of chain. His mother was on Welfare and he had no idea who his father was.

Arturo Willimino Pollicelli was a member of the Sicilian Army from Boston. He carried six knives on his person at all times, even in the shower. His father was a second generation cop from Boston. After the Army Art would become a cop and carry on the tradition of his father and grandfather.

Clyde was an honest to goodness hillbilly from Kentucky. His father raised pigs, a milk cow, corn, and hunted for meat. His family depended on deer, rabbits, squirrels, and fish for their very lives. Often, Clyde had been given a rifle and one bullet and was expected to return with something for the table when he came back. He was a crack shot at the rifle range. His Army boots were the first pair of shoes he had ever worn.

Speed was from Alabama. He got his nickname from running moonshine. He had been successful in outrunning the "Revenuers" many a time, but finally got caught in a road block. He said he could outrun their cars, but he couldn't outrun their radios. Once he'd been caught he was given the choice of jail or the Army.

There were young men whose fathers were lawyers, doctors, union members of all kinds, farmers, grocers, printers, and so on, all mixed with young men who had no families to speak of and had grown up on the streets making up their own rules along the way.

As you can imagine, conflict was a regular part of our day. Mixing young men with such diverse backgrounds made for an explosive situation when somebody's toes got stepped on. Fistfights were common place, something completely foreign to me. I was able to survive using my two magic weapons: Treating people like I'd want to be treated myself and telling rotten jokes!

Ginny made cards for me. That seems to be a lost art in today's world since we have computers and Hallmark. But she would cut pictures out of magazines and paste them onto construction paper to deliver a message. One card showed a fireman on the front. It said, "Sorry I haven't written lately, but I've been busy putting out a fire in the bathroom." When I opened the card, the inside showed an outhouse that

30

had been partially burned. The caption read, "Fortunately, it didn't reach the house." Her letters and cards always gave me strength as I knew I had something better to look forward to. I shared her cards with the other guys and soon she had a reputation for being just the kind of girl each of them had dreamed of for themselves. Whenever I got a card in the mail, there would be a waiting line of guys saying, "Hey, Dad, can I see what she made for you this time?" Ginny and I had become a symbol for many of the younger guys in the platoon. They all wanted a girl just like Ginny and our relationship had cemented my nick name of Dad.

Monte was 17 years old. He had lied about his age to get into the Army. He wasn't physically developed yet and this made the physical fitness training difficult for him. He just couldn't get the hang of doing anything right, largely because he didn't listen. When he made a mistake, the entire platoon would have to do pushups.

"All right, Monte screwed up again!" the sergeant would yell. "When one guy screws up, the whole platoon suffers. So get down and push that Louisiana soil away." We all groaned, fell to the ground and began doing push-ups.

Soon, everyone was mad at Monte. He came to my room one night in tears, fearing he'd be next for a GI party. As platoon leader I could counsel individuals from the platoon and having my own room made it private. I listened to Monte as he cried and lamented the fact that he just couldn't hack it. But that was all I could do, listen and console him. We were all in the Army now and there would be no excuses or exceptions to the rule that we were in it together and responsible to the entire unit. He'd have to shape up and we both knew it. I showed him the medallion that Ginny had given me. "Are you a Christian?" I asked.

"No. I've never been to church," he replied.

"Well, I'm a Christian," I said. "Part of my faith is written on this medallion…All things are possible through Christ who strengthens me. Jesus Christ said that if you pray to him he will answer. You don't have to go to church to be a Christian. All you have to do is believe in him and pray to him and he will answer your prayer. How do you think I got a girl like Ginny?"

"That's how you got a girl like her? That's why you get letters every day? I haven't gotten a letter since I got here!"

I told him that right now is the time to change all of that. "Would you like to pray with me?"

"I don't know how to pray," he said with a dismayed look on his face.

"Prayer is just another word for talking," I said. "Just talk to Jesus like you're talking to me. Tell you what…I'll start and then you take up where I leave off…how's that?"

We both bowed our heads and closed our eyes. "Jesus, I have a friend here that's going through some tough times. We've both been thrown into the Army and it's a little difficult adjusting to the people and the new way of life we have to live now. I ask that you help us to adjust to this new way of life. I ask that you will help me to be a good platoon leader. And now Monte would like to talk with you."

"Jesus, I don't know you but if you would help me to listen and quit screwing up so I don't get a G.I. party; I sure would appreciate it."

I said "Amen."

Monte had a different look in his eyes as he left my room and we never had to do push-ups because of Monte ever again. The Holy Spirit had entered and changed Monte.

It had been three months since I had seen Ginny and I couldn't wait for graduation from Basic Training. Historically, they had given at least a three-day pass to graduates prior to being sent to Advanced Individual Training. How wonderful it would be to have three days with her once again! I went to the captain and inquired about the three-day pass and wanted to get his recommendation on accommodations. He looked at me with a blank expression and then turned and looked out the window. There was only one window in the white, cramped office and he stared through it as if he wished he could be on the other side of it. After quite some time he finally turned to me and said, "I'm sorry Halverson. The entire company is on quarantine. Because of the Vietnam War we've had too many men go AWOL after Basic Training. We just can't take a chance on losing good men after we've invested so much in their training. You won't be getting a pass. The best I can do for you is to allow your girl friend to sit in the front row of the stands during graduation ceremonies. You can spend some time with her after the graduation ceremony, but after that you're quarantined to your company area. I'm sorry."

I saluted and left the office. I thought on the way back to the barracks about how I could write a letter to Gin and explain that it wouldn't be worth her time to come down for graduation. We had been planning her trip and this would be a real letdown. I sat down on my bunk and began to compose my letter when Smitty came running up. "Dad! You'd better come quick! I think Billy just tried to kill himself."

I dropped my pen and paper and followed Smitty down to Billy's bunk. Billy was sitting on the footlocker with a faraway look in his eyes. Others tried to talk to him but he was entirely unresponsive. I had worked as an orderly in the hospital at Iowa State University and recognized the symptoms of a drug overdose immediately. I slapped Billy in the face. He looked at me and said nothing. I slapped him again, only harder.

"What the Hell are you doing, Halverson?" one of the guys asked.

I didn't pay any attention to him because I was focused on Billy. I knew that I had to get some information from him immediately before he passed out. I slapped him again and he seemed to come around.

"What did you take?" I asked him.

His eyes located mine and he said, "I don't know."

I slapped him again to force him to stay alert. "Where's the bottle?" I asked.

He looked at me and said, "I threw it into the trash in the latrine." Smitty! Go to the head and find that bottle—*right now!*"

I got Billy onto his feet and forced him to walk while Smitty ran to the latrine.

"Here it is, Dad," Smitty yelled, as he ran in and handed me a bottle.

I stuffed it into my pocket and guided Billy toward the headquarters building. The captain was gone for the day and Drill Sergeant Odell was in charge.

"I've got to get this man to the Dispensary immediately," I told him. "He's had a drug overdose."

"Permission denied," Sergeant Odell replied. "If you're in combat you won't have a Dispensary handy and you'll have to take care of each other. Better get used it."

I walked Billy outside and headed for the Dispensary. We got about half a block when Billy passed out. I threw him over my shoulder and carried him the rest of the way. When we got to the dispensary, I asked for a doctor.

I gave the doctor the bottle and said, "This is what he took."

The doctor and a few nurses disappeared with Billy on a gurney.

An hour or so later the doctor came back. "He's going to be OK. It's a good thing you brought the bottle along. Without that we wouldn't have known exactly what to do and I think your friend would have been a goner. We'll have to keep him a few days for observation, but he's going to be fine. It's a shame how many of these cases we get when orders to Vietnam come out."

I went back to the barracks alone, happy that Billy would be all right.

Sergeant Odell was waiting for me. "Halverson!" I've put you up for an Article 15 for insubordination!"

I couldn't believe what I'd just heard, I'd just saved a guy's life and I was going to be punished for it. I looked at Odell and replied "I'll take a court martial."

I knew that accepting an Article 15 meant that I'd be admitting guilt. A court martial meant a jury in front of my superiors. I was willing to gamble on that one.

I never heard another word about the incident.

Drill Sergeant O'Dell was madder than hops that I had refused the Article 15 and chose a court martial instead. I knew that a court martial would never fly and so did he. Be that as it may, he was still my drill instructor and I was still his private. I knew there would be hell to pay one way or another.

The next morning I called my platoon together for formation and stood at the head of the ranks waiting for Sergeant O'Dell. He stood in front of the platoon and looking directly at me and said, "I've tried to instill in your rubberhead minds that sticking together for the good of your unit is the only way you'll stay alive in Vietnam. What do you think will happen if you have a leader like Halverson babysitting some namby-pamby momma's boy while the rest of you get shot all to Hell by Charlie while he's gone?"

And with that, he pulled my stripes from my arm and gave them to Jackson. Jackson was a bully and loved to push the smaller guys around. He had been a thorn in my side because of this and we had come close to blows a number of times. Jackson was just the kind of guy O'Dell wanted: he would take and give orders and enjoy every minute of it. Jackson looked at me with a sneer on his face as he took command of the platoon and I fell into its ranks.

"Halverson! You're on KP tonight," O'Dell said, grinning.

I did a number of nights in a row on KP and, just when I thought he might let up on me, he ordered me to the Supply Office. "We've got a new shipment in that needs to be stocked," he said. "A bright college boy like you should know just where everything goes!"

Working the Supply Room was supposed to be punishment. But the supply sergeant had heard about my taking a young man who had overdosed on drugs to the hospital despite O'Dell's orders. "Heard you turned down on Article 15 and asked for a court martial," Sergeant Prell said, winking at me.

"This here's demanding work," he continued. "Might make a fellow tired and, if that fellow needs to catch up on his sleep, there's a cot in the back room. I don't want anyone messing up my supply room because he's too tired to think straight."

He smiled and told me to unpack gas masks and store them on the shelves. The gas masks came in burlap bags about 10 feet long. They reminded me of the gunnysacks that feed came in when I was in back on the farm, only these were three times longer.

"What shall I do with them?" I asked sergeant Prell.

"Oh, just fold them and pile them on the upper shelf. They might come in handy someday."

"Don't forget the cot," he said as he left.

He knew that I had been working nights on KP but was still required to go to drills during the day. Apparently, I wasn't the only one that had a difference of opinion with O'Dell. I did go back to the back room to catch up on my sleep and wondered if sergeant Prell really would be okay with it. He was. It wasn't long before O'Dell came and inquired about how long Halverson would be tied up in the Supply Room.

Prell told him, 'Oh, we've got a lot of work to do here and it might take another week or two before I can let him go."

Smitty caught me at the end of the day. "Hey Dad," he said as he gave that familiar shrug of his shoulder. "We're gonna have a blanket party for O'Dell!"

"Are you nuts?" I asked.

We had given blanket parties (or GI parties) to those in the unit who smelled because they didn't take a shower or because they didn't keep their lockers in order. It was a disciplinary method used by peers to send a message to someone who was out of line. We'd throw a blanket over them in the dark of night so they couldn't see who was involved and punch them and kick them so they got the message to straighten up. But an NCO?

"We can't throw a blanket party for an NCO," I said.

Smitty shrugged his shoulder again and said, "Hey, Dad. You're the best platoon guide in the whole battalion and everybody knows it. You saved that kid who overdosed and everybody knows that. O'Dell shouldn't have demoted you and everybody knows that, too. He was wrong and deserves a blanket party, and everybody wants in on it. Hey, didn't he say he wanted everybody to stick together for the good of the unit? Well, we're just going to do what he wants us to do." Smitty had an amazing way of using logic.

There was no arguing. Smitty had arranged it and had quite a following of others who wanted in on the party. I told Smitty about the burlap bags that the masks had come in.

"Perfect!" he said. "We'll throw the bag over his head, tie him up in the bag just like a pig, and let him have it."

Sergeant O'Dell played pool with the boys every Wednesday night and usually left pretty well lubricated. We waited in some bushes for him to leave. He was walking down the path all alone when Smitty jumped from the bushes and pulled the bag over his head. A dozen others jumped out to help pull the bag over his entire body and finished by tying it shut. Then they commenced to punch and kick, while O'Dell kicked and screamed from inside the bag.

The next morning at formation, O'Dell was standing beside Jackson sporting two black eyes and more bruises than I could count. There were a dozen of us who had to quash the urge to laugh out loud. We simply looked straight ahead at attention. I did manage a smile.

After formation, Jackson came up to me and said, "I'll get you for this."

Smitty looked at him and gave that familiar shrug of his shoulder. "Better watch it, Jackson, or you'll be next."

Again the company commander put out the word for me to come to his office. An invitation from the commander usually meant that someone had done something wrong, but for the life of me I couldn't think of anything I'd done. When the commander calls…

"You've got the highest test scores I've ever seen come through my office," he said. "That's pretty surprising for someone that hasn't been to college."

"But I *have* been to college," I told him. "I graduated from Iowa State University."

"That's not possible. Your serial number shows that you haven't been to college. They have specific numbers for college graduates."

I showed him my billfold card, which I.S.U. gave us at graduation and through his questioning told him that I had studied FORTRAN at Iowa State University."

FORTRAN was one of the first programs for computer language and ISU had one of the first computers. It was an awful system requiring one to fill out piles of index cards in order for the computer to do its job. But it was part of the computer evolution and that had everyone's attention.

"I'd like to put you in for computer school," he said. "We need sharp young men like you in the Army." He looked at my file and said, "Someone at the reception station made a big mistake. He assigned you a number showing you're a high school graduate and nothing more. That's too bad because with these test scores you should be sent to computer training or a similar type of school. But that's not going to happen because of your serial number. That's too bad, too, because that's how the Army makes a decision on your next duty station."

"Can't my number be changed?" I asked.

"Nope, once you're assigned a number, it's written in granite. Of course, you could go to Officer Candidate School upon graduation from Basic Training. You've shown definite leadership skills as a platoon guide and with these tests scores you'd be a shoo-in."

"What's involved with that?" I asked.

"Well, you would have to sign up for three more years to go to OCS. Uncle Sam would have to invest a lot of time and money to train you as an officer, and then he'd expect a return on his investment."

I left his office with lots of thoughts racing my mind. College graduates usually get sent to a school that keeps them out of combat. Or they get sent to Germany or some other safe place of duty. And here I am facing duty in Vietnam because some idiot didn't get my serial number right! OCS would be a good choice for more reasonable duty, but three more years? I couldn't stand the Army the way it was and I sure didn't want an additional three years of it. Besides that, how could I lead a group of guys into something I didn't believe in myself?

I went back to my office in the barracks and pondered my situation. I've always believed that God has a plan for me and this must be part of his plan. After a while, I made the decision that I would do whatever happened for the next two years, but I sure wasn't going to sign up for more time in the Army. I had spent a month in the Army and hated it. Why would I want to spend any more time in it than I absolutely had to?

I led the "show platoon" for our company. I called the best cadence, we had scored high on our tests as a platoon, and we had the highest scores in overall training to date. I could develop my own cadences as platoon leader. So I decided to rebel against the Army in my own way and wrote a cadence that quickly became my platoon's favorite and also spread to other platoons throughout the battalion. It's sung to the tune of *Baby, Oh Baby Mine.*

Five more weeks of rocks and grass,
Honey, Honey.
Five more weeks of rocks and grass,
Babe, Babe.
Five more weeks of rocks and grass,
Then Fort Polk can kiss my ass!
Honey, oh baby, mine.

I had made up my mind long ago that I wanted a Christian girl as my wife. It made sense to me that since I was a Christian, married life would be much less problematic if my spouse was too.

I tell my daughters that Ginny is the first girl I ever dated. They laugh at me because they know I dated a number of girls. But Ginny was the first girl I ever took to church who grabbed my hand when we said the Lord's Prayer. I was a bit surprised when she did it during that first service we ever attended together, but I thought, *What a neat thing to do! Holding hands during the Lord's Prayer!* It just made sense to me that this would be a symbol of both our love and our faith.

When I got drafted, I was concerned about marrying her because I thought, *What if I'm sent to Vietnam and get killed? I don't want Ginny to be a widow. She should wait for my return and if I didn't return, she should be able to find another without the baggage of having been already married.* But she had no doubt about my returning safely. She said, "Before you graduated from college, or considered going into the army, I woke one night and sat up in bed. There was a voice telling me that you would go to Viet Nam and you would be safe. It was God." She never questioned my return for a minute and that was one of the first indicators to me that I would be marrying someone with a rock-hard faith.

When we graduated from college, she gave me a small package. Inside was a necklace with this inscription: "Philippians 4:13 - All things are possible through Christ who strengthens me."

I wore that necklace all through Basic, Advanced Individual Training, and most of Vietnam. I lost it in Pleiku during a football game. We stopped the game and everyone got on their hands and knees to locate the necklace, but to no avail. I hated the thought of telling Gin what had happened. Eventually I had to tell her, and I was afraid she'd either start crying or have a temper tantrum. But she didn't bat an eye at my revelation. She simply said, "Someone needs it more than you do. God let it fall to whoever that is and I'm sure they'll find the strength to go on because of it."

We shared scriptures in our letters to each other. Of course, I Corinthians, chapter 13, was included in those letters: "Love is very patient and kind, never jealous or envious, never boastful or proud, never haughty or selfish or rude. Love does not demand its own way. It is not irrational or touchy. It does not hold grudges and will hardly even notice when others do it wrong. It is never glad about injustice, but rejoices whenever truth wins out. If you love someone you will be loyal to him/her no matter what the cost. You will always believe in him/her and always expect the best from them and always stand your ground in defending them. All the special gifts and powers from God will someday come to an end, but love goes on forever. There are three things that remain: faith, hope, and love, and the greatest of these is love."

Her faith sustained me while I was in the Army. One of those times came when we had just finished at the firing range. We kept a strict inventory of ammunition and spent rounds were counted as part of that inventory. Our drill sergeant announced that the inventory showed that some live rounds had been stolen by someone during our qualification and that whoever that was would be up for a court martial.

That night Mike came into my office. Mike was in the Army because he had been given a choice: go to jail or join the Army. He was street tough from the Bronx and didn't take any crap from anyone.

He said, "I stole the rounds and if they want to put me in the slammer, they can. That's where I was going if I didn't come here anyway."

We talked for a while. He wanted to go AWOL because he didn't want to go to jail. I suggested that he go to the commander's office and own up to what he'd done.

Mike got belligerent and said, "What's the big deal? It's just a few rounds."

I said, "Those rounds are Uncle Sam's, just like you and me. You stole something that isn't yours and it's a court martial offense."

We seemed to be at a standoff when he noticed my necklace. "What's that?" he asked.

I told him that Ginny had given it to me and we believed in what it said: All things are possible through Christ who strengthens me.

He softened and said, "My folks never went to church, but I always envied the kids who did."

I asked him if he would like to pray and surprisingly, he said, "Yes."

He knelt and I said the words. "God, Mike's just a kid who was playing around. He never thought he was stealing anything. He was just pulling a prank. Please let the commander have understanding and accept that Mike didn't mean anything by what he's done. Amen."

Mike looked at me with tears in his eyes. Something had happened to him because he was no longer that street tough I had known. I believe the Holy Spirit had descended upon him.

"What's next?" he asked.

Together we went to the commander's office. Mike owned up to what he had done, and said he was wrong to have done it and if he had to go to jail he would go.

The captain got a wide grin on his face and stood up extending his hand. The captain and Mike shook hands as the captain said, "It takes a good man to admit when he's wrong. I wish we had more men like you. Now go back your barracks and get a good night's sleep. We've got a big day ahead of us tomorrow."

I grabbed the medallion as I left his office and looked upwards to sky and said, "Thank you, God."

Mike was a changed man from that day on.

We got orders to go on bivouac. The Boy Scouts call that "Camping Out." But they didn't have to carry everything for their camp out and they didn't have to march twenty miles to do it! It was February, we were in Louisiana, not Iowa, but it was still cold. The trees had frost on them and the temperature was in the 30s. We had to carry a full backpack and our M14 rifles. Our backpacks had a change of clothing, C-Rations, an entrenching tool, a pup tent, a sleeping bag, magazines loaded with blanks (we weren't allowed to carry live ammunition, but we had to get used to carrying the weight), dummy grenades, and personal items.

We all wore heavy clothing because of the weather: winter jackets, an olive drab skull cap for underneath our helmet liners, and olive drab cloth glove inserts inside our black leather gloves. I also wore two pairs of socks. Most of the guys wore only one pair but I had learned to wear two pairs when I did chores on the farm during those Iowa winters. They kept my feet warm and dry and on a march like this one; they would prevent blisters from forming.

We marched 18 miles and set up camp. The first thing I did was find the highest spot in the area. It's a good thing to be on high ground in case it rains. I set up my tent using the entrenching tool (a foldable spade) as a hammer to drive in the tent pegs. Since it was spring weather, the clay soil was pliable and the pegs drove in quite easily. Once the tent was up,

I dug a trench around it. The trench was about four inches deep and six inches wide. The trench provided a channel for water in case it rained.

Longleaf pine trees are prevalent in Louisiana. Their needles are about 6-10 inches long and every tree sheds an abundance of needles. I gathered armfuls of the needles to make a mat in my tent. A bed of needles about two inches thick made a pretty good mattress beneath a sleeping bag and sure beat sleeping on the rough ground. I always carried a length of cotton clothesline with me. I'd string it between a couple of tree branches and hang my socks, underwear, and gear on it. That way everything stayed dry and organized.

We had the camp all set up by suppertime. C-Rations offered beef, pork, and spaghetti, as I remember. The beef and pork weren't bad if they could be heated to melt the fat. Otherwise the congealed fat was nauseating to eat. I always tried to make sure I got spaghetti. We opened the cans with P-38s, foldable can openers. Most of us had a P-38 on our necklace, along with our dog tags. We were issued two dog tags and wore both on our necklace. If we were killed in action; one tag would be attached to our big toe to identify our body and the other would go to our next of kin. Each ration had cans containing four crackers, peanut butter, and jelly. It took a long time to open all the cans. Dessert consisted of peaches, pears, or applesauce. I hate pears. The apple sauce wasn't too bad. But I really wanted the peaches. And finally, the C-ration had a small Hershey bar, a gourmet dessert for a gourmet meal, and we all loved it.

Each kit also had a small packet of toilet paper. The packet had six toilet paper sheets that were about four inches square. That's not much to work with, so you can imagine how accurate our wiping had to be.

Lastly came a small pack of cigarettes: Lucky Strikes, Chesterfields, Pall Malls, Salems, Newports, or Camels. The blacks seemed to love Salems and Newports. There were always dedicated Camel and Lucky Strike smokers. So I could easily get spaghetti and peaches if they weren't in my C-Rations by just trading smokes for whatever I needed.

We had mail call that night and I got a big box from Ginny. Inside were Valentine cookies with little messages like: I Love you, You're cute, Be Mine, and so on. I gave everyone a cookie. The cookies were a nice treat after the C-rations. Everyone wanted to come home on leave with me to meet Ginny. That made me proud.

I did a little research on the history of C-Rations and share it with you here.

They began as "Iron Rations" in 1907. They were developed in anticipation of WWI and were designed to keep the "iron willed" soldiers alive in case they were so far ahead of the front line that a Mess Hall wouldn't be available. Iron Rations were three cakes of beef bouillon cooked into thoroughly-ground wheat flours, three bars of chocolate, a salt packet, and a pepper packet. As you might expect, the chocolate was very popular, but the beef/wheat mixture tasted like silage! It wasn't very popular at all.

As WWI continued, soldiers on the front complained and the Army decided to improve the rations and, in 1917, the "Reserve Ration" came into being. The Reserve Ration included twelve ounces of bacon, one pound of corned beef, two cans of hardtack (biscuit), instant coffee packets, sugar packets, salt packets, pepper packets, four ounces of tobacco, and cigarette papers. The Reserve Ration served the Army until 1937. The only change came in 1925 when the bacon and corned beef were discontinued and replaced with pork and beans. In 1938 the Reserve Ration got replaced by the "Field Ration-Type C."

As I write this I am thinking about when the United States really entered WWII. The Japanese bombed Pearl Harbor in December 1941. Yet preparations for feeding ground troops began in 1938. Draw your own conclusions.

The C-Ration became known as a "wet' ration." That meant that the food was cooked in its own juices and canned. The "M Unit" was the meat unit and offered one of the following: Chicken in broth, chicken loaf, chicken and noodles, ham and eggs, fried ham, beans with meatballs, beans and weenies, ham and lima beans, beef and potatoes, turkey in broth, pork steak, spaghetti, meatloaf, meatballs in tomato sauce, beef steak, or pork steak.

The "B Unit" was the bread unit and offered the following: Four crackers and a tin of peanut butter, cheese spread or jelly, cocoa powder, and one of the following: pound cake, fruit cake, date pudding, or a pecan nut roll.

The dry goods in the C-Ration included instant coffee, plastic spoons (Soldiers were very possessive of their spoons, wearing them either in the elastic band on their helmets or in the pen slot of their breast pockets), P-38 can openers, toilet paper, matches, a packet of Chiclets gum, creamer, sugar, salt, pepper, and cigarettes. Soldiers often traded for their favorite cigarettes: Marlboro, Lucky Strikes, Camels, Chesterfields, Larks, L & Ms, Salems, and Newports.

Fruit came along later: peaches, pears, apple sauce, apricots, and fruit cocktail.

Everything was packed in cans painted olive drab, which was high in lead. So if the cigarettes didn't kill you the lead paint would!

The C-Ration was used throughout WWII, Korea, and the beginning of the Vietnam War. They proved to be a problem in Vietnam for a number of reasons that hinged largely on the fact that there were no "fronts" like there had been in earlier wars. Soldiers in Vietnam had to hump the boonies in search of the enemy. The cans rattled while being carried and that sound gave away soldiers' positions to the enemy. For that reason soldiers got extra socks and packed the C-Ration cans in the socks so they wouldn't rattle. Because the C-Rations were a "wet pack," they were heavy to carry. The North Vietnamese carried dry rice and added water when they did their cooking. Consequently, they had less weight to carry and more energy than US soldiers who got tired from carrying extra weight. U. S. soldiers learned this lesson and carried rice and dried fruit while on patrol.

In 1966 the Army resorted to lightweight dehydrated foods that were light to carry and made no noise in transit. The new rations were called LURPs, for Long Range Patrol dehydrated food packets.

On the first night of bivouac the heavens broke loose with a thunderstorm. I lay comfortably in my sleeping bag on the bed of pine needles. Whenever the lightning made that possible, I could see the rainwater flow in the channels I'd dug around my tent. I thought to myself how I pitied the guys who hadn't dug their channels, when someone dived into my tent and crawled in beside me.

You guessed it: Smitty! At least Smitty had brought his own blanket along. Thankfully, he had done that and hadn't crawled in beside me under my blanket. His pup tent had flooded because he hadn't dug any channels around it. He lay down beside me, covered himself with this blanket, and looked out at the pouring rain. "Hey Dad! It's raining like a cow pissing on a flat rock out there! Look at those poor boobs that didn't set up camp right. They'll be soaked to the bone before this is over. They sure don't know how to handle the rough life like us farm boys, do they? Just look at the water running through those channels!" Smitty watched the rain water flowing through the channels around the tent with a satisfied look on his face, just as though he had dug them himself.

Smitty had been born with a giant birth mark on the right side of his face. He was a very handsome young man looking at him from his left side. But if observed from his right side, I first found it hard not to focus on the bright red color stretching from his eyebrow to his chin. But after a while, it was just a part of Smitty. He wouldn't have been the same person without it.

"Hey Dad?" Smitty asked. "Do you think my birth mark is ugly?"

Where in the world that question had come from I had no idea. But obviously it was on Smitty's mind.

No," I said. "To be honest with you, I don't even notice it anymore. I judge people by their personalities and not their looks. If we judged people by their appearance, those that have a large nose or a big wart on their chin or crossed eyes or a funny laugh would never have a friend. We all have deformities in one way or another, whether it's physical or emotional. So when it gets right down to it, it's just like the old saying says 'Don't judge a book by its cover.'"

"That is the way I feel," Smitty replied. "Mom and Dad wanted to take me to a doctor who said he could take the birth mark off. But I told them that if people didn't like me with my birth mark, they probably wouldn't like me without it either. So I never went."

We both laid there in silence, satisfied with our conversation. It seemed to have solidified our friendship even more.

"Hey, Dad! I'd give anything to be back on the farm in Panora right now," he said. "We'd just be finishing milking those good ole Guernsey cows. There's no milk better than the milk from a Guernsey. Then we'd go to the house and Mom would have bacon and eggs and toast and jelly. And afterwards, we'd have coffee and talk and laugh. Boy, I sure do miss home." Smitty's birth mark took on a deeper reddish hue as the emotion of the moment surged through his body.

I thought about my favorite times at home. Sunday was my favorite day because we only had to do livestock chores. Dad observed the Sabbath and, consequently, there was no field work on Sunday. We would quickly do the livestock chores in the morning, giving the animals a double dose of feed so we wouldn't have to feed them in the afternoon as we usually did. Then we went to Sunday school and church. Afterward, Mom made her usual Sunday dinner: fried chicken, mashed potatoes and gravy, creamed peas, and Jell-O or salad. Dad would read the *Des Moines Register* and I would read the funnies.

Finally, Mom would summon us to the table at which time we would say grace together. Faith and I fought over the legs and thighs, but I usually got away with the gizzard without any fuss. We discussed the latest gossip gathered from others after church and nodded our heads in understanding or agreement. We brought up funny incidents from the past and laughed in unison at whatever it was.

When dinner was over, Dad would conclude with a resounding BUUUUUUUUURP and Mom would shout, "Bendix!"

Lying there in that tent with the rain coming down, Smitty and I were both in our own little worlds, remembering what was really important in life: Family and the good times we had shared with them.

The next morning found soldiers squeezing the water from their blankets and clothes. Smitty and I built a camp fire and soon, everyone was warming their hands and jabbering about the rainfall from the previous night. Among them were our drill sergeants, most of whom had not dug channels around their tents and had been soaked to the bone as well. They didn't say much but did announce that bivouac would be cut short and we should "Pack Up" for the march back to the compound.

One day I got a letter from Bill Patten, my old college roommate. Bill grew up on a farm near Aurelia, Iowa, not far from my home so we had many things in common. We spent many a night in our dorm room talking about baling hay, pitching manure, gathering eggs, and so on. Bill had been raised in a Christian home just like me and, consequently, we shared many of the same values.

So it was without reservation that I asked Bill to "baby sit" Ginny while I was in the Army. She still had a semester of college to finish at Iowa State University. I knew that she needed to get out and be with other people, rather than sit in her room and mourn my absence. One tends to become depressed sitting alone all the time. So Bill took her to dances, movies, church, etc. It was nice to have a friend that I could trust.

There were plenty of "friends" who felt Ginny would feel deprived of attention while I was gone and they'd be plenty happy to fulfill her needs. Ginny was a beauty and there were plenty of guys who wanted to provide companionship for her. One of them was Leonard, the picture of a sweet, innocent young man who also lived in Alumni Hall. He asked Ginny to go to a dance with him. When the lights got low and the music played, Leonard became an octopus and his hands went everywhere. Ginny slapped him and left the dance!

Bill was a perfect gentleman and, like a good friend, his intentions and his actions were honorable. He provided a sounding board for Ginny and they had many a conversation about things that were important and timely: Would I go to Vietnam? Should we get married before I went? Would I be safe and sound? Should Ginny get a job if I went to Vietnam? Could she go to Germany with me if I got stationed there?

There were so many decisions to be made; but we were hanging in limbo. Isn't that the way it is with anything in life? Uncertainty makes life difficult. Take health for instance. Knowing that something is wrong but not knowing what the problem is can make life difficult. It's almost a relief when the doctor identifies what is wrong so you can make a decision about how to deal with the malady.

I remember a comment by my mentor, Ellis Brooks about his tractor. "The tractor runs just fine but makes a funny sound," Ellis said. "I wish the darn thing would break so I would know what to fix!"

And so it was for that period in our lives. We were uncertain where we would go or what we would be doing. That uncertainty caused mental anguish because we didn't even know what we were dealing with, let alone how to deal with it. Bill said that Ginny would break down in tears during their conversations and he would get teary-eyed himself. I'm just glad he was there for her.

When we got married, Bill was my best man. Since then, Bill has married and raised a family, and so have we. When Ginny and I lived in Chicago, we met Bill and Rosie in Galena, Illinois, about half way between where we lived and Marshalltown where Bill lives. We met there frequently to renew our friendship. Rosie and Ginny shopped while Bill and I wandered and talked, and kayaked on the little river nearby. The topics of our conversations have changed since those early days, but they are still meaningful and sometimes teary eyed.

Wayne Munkle worked in the dining hall with us and was her faithful counsellor throughout these first days of my service. He was a Viet Nam vet from the mid-sixties and was the one who kept drilling into her the importance of letters, cards and boxes of goodies from home. Wayne was the inspiration for the home-made cards and booklets that helped sustain me through my time away from home. He knew from experience what I would need. I thank God for Wayne and his great advice. Wayne and Ginny would sit in the dining hall for hours after work just talking. She learned so much from that man.

> There is nothing in all the world so precious as a friend who is wise and true.
>
> —*Herodotus*

We had done "compass courses" during the day a number of times. We'd be broken into small groups, given a map and a compass and an M14 rifle loaded with blanks and told to find our way back to base camp. The map had the coordinates of the location where the deuce and a half had dropped us, and the coordinates of base. It was a piece of cake!

Next we got a real test: a night course. We would have a map, a compass, and a flashlight. We were given red armbands to wear and told that this test was the real thing. Ex-Vietnam vets were randomly located in the course. They'd be wearing blue armbands to identify that they were the enemy. They would torture us as enemy combatants if they caught us. So not only did we have to find our way back to camp, but we had to avoid being captured by the enemy. Stories filtered through the troops about what these ex-vets would do to us: We could be hung by our thumbs. They could pull out our finger nails. They could beat us as long as they didn't break any bones. It was like sitting around a campfire telling ghost stories when we were kids. The stories got scarier each time they were told. By the time we had heard these stories, we were all petrified of getting off the truck.

48

"Now don't shoot at anybody within twenty feet of you," the sergeant told us. "Those blanks shoot a cardboard wad and it would put an eye out let alone hurt!"

That comment made Smitty's eyes light up like a neon sign.

The deuce and a half drove for half an hour or so into the countryside before it stopped by a small embankment. The sergeant dropped the end gate and told us to climb up the embankment and begin our way home. I remember a rather pudgy guy trying to climb his way up the hill with all his gear when I saw Smitty level his M14 and fire it at the pudgy guy's behind.

"OW!" And just like that he was over the hill!

"Hey, Dad! Did you see him jump?" Smitty said with a laugh.

We lost the rest of our squad in the dark of night, so Smitty and I took off together. I could read the map and the compass and knew what direction to go. We could have taken a course through the woods, but the map indicated a road not too far away that would make for easier traveling. So we headed for the road.

Just as we came into a clearing in the woods, I noticed four guys with blue armbands hiding in the bush near the road. I froze. "What are we going to do?" I asked. "They'll see us for sure. We'd better backtrack and come back to the road about a 100 yards farther down."

"Wait right here, Dad." Smitty said as he peeled off his red armband.

He walked right up to the foursome. As mentioned earlier, the right side of Smitty's face had a birthmark. That usually shocked people and Smitty knew how to use it to his advantage. Once people were looking at his birth mark, he would repeatedly twitch his right shoulder and tip his head towards his shoulder. At that point, people would be looking first at his birth mark and then at his shoulder, and by then he had them right where he wanted them.

"Hey, guys! You seen that dumb-ass sergeant in charge? He dropped us off in the boonies back there and forgot to give us our blue armbands! What a dummy!"

They laughed at his remark and agreed that the sergeant was an idiot. Since they were posted near the road, they all agreed that he would be returning after posting the other blue soldiers, and agreed to stop him and send him over to us.

"Are you kidding? That drunken bum would get lost trying to find us and then we'd have to organize a search party to find him!" Smitty said.

They all roared with laughter and Smitty knew he had them in his hip pocket.

"Tell you what, just give us two armbands so we can identify ourselves and when the sarge comes, get replacements from him."

They all agreed and wished Smitty good luck in capturing some of the newbies.

Smitty walked back to me and we both put on blue armbands. We got on the road a hundred yards down from our present location and walked into base camp like we owned the place!

Smitty was magic!

When it came time for us to qualify on the rifle range, the drill sergeant looked at us and said, "The top five qualifiers on the rifle range will be first in line for a leave!"

I noticed that he didn't say we would absolutely *get* a leave; he said we'd be first in line for a leave. However, his comment had given all of us the incentive we needed to fire well on the range. Believe me, if a leave was possible, I wanted to be the first name called out!

Our first qualification was with the M14. I had no experience with a weapon that powerful. I had grown up with a BB gun and advanced to a single-shot .22. But I had learned with a single-shot to make every bullet count because I wouldn't get a second chance. That meant that I had to hit my targets in the head rather than wounding them. I had shot a number of squirrels that way. A shot to the head meant that they would die instantly and I wouldn't have to chase them.

The Army taught us to recite the word "BRASS" in order to shoot well. B stands for Breathe; before firing; we should take a deep breath and hold it. R stands for Relax; you'll never hit your target if you're tense. A stands for aim; sight in on the target. The first S stands for slack; every trigger has some slack in it; if you don't pull the slack out of the trigger, you'll shoot low because when you pull the trigger from its natural position you will hit the slack spot and pull the barrel down. The last S stands for squeeze; squeeze the trigger and fire the shot. Do not yank the trigger…slowly squeeze it. I had learned to do every one of

50

these steps with my single-shot .22 out of necessity and never knew there was an acronym describing those steps.

The M14 was a wonderful weapon. The shells were as big as my little finger. I thought to myself, "If a .22 can shoot a bullet a mile with the tiny little bit of powder in its case, how far can this thing shoot?" It had a gas line that connected the front of the barrel to the bolt. Thus, just before the bullet left the barrel the gas would follow the line, drive back the bolt, eject a shell, and chamber another one! That was quite a change from using a bolt action .22! It had a peep sight rather than a notched rear sight. I found that I could allow for distance by adjusting the level of the front sight within the peep sight. The M14 had very little kick and that surprised me. I learned later that the M14 had an ingenious internal spring that served as a shock absorber. This spring absorbed so much of the recoil that the gun had little more kick than a .22 rifle and certainly nothing like a 12-gauge shotgun.

Our targets were plastic silhouettes of a man and were hydraulically driven. They would pop up anywhere from 50 yards to 500 yards away. There was no pattern to where or when they popped up, so I had to keep my eyes peeled on the entire range in order to know where to shoot. Many of the guys focused their attention on one area of the range and didn't even see some of the targets that popped up. When we had been at this range before, the targets would remain up until we hit them. But for qualifying the targets were timed. They would pop up only a few seconds and then fall back down whether we hit them or not. Timing the targets had quite an effect on one's score because there was a tendency to fire quickly since the targets would only be up for a few seconds. It was a challenge to remember to follow the steps of BRASS rather than to yank the trigger and shoot quickly.

I lay in a prone position with my rifle resting on a sandbag and waited. My target popped up and I followed the steps: breathe, relax, aim, slack, and squeeze. Going through those steps seemed like an eternity and I was so afraid the target would fall back down before I shot it. Down it went!

I remember thinking, *Did I hit it or did I run out of time and it fell down on its own?*

Nonetheless, I followed the steps with each and every shot. I hoped I had hit the targets successfully so I'd earn a leave. That was the underlying motivation for all the qualifications I went through, that I would earn a leave and be able to see my beloved Ginny for just a few days.

When qualification ended, I learned that I had fired third highest in the company! I'd done my part. Now it was the Army's part to come through with a leave!

Next we had to qualify at grenade throwing. We marched to the grenade grounds from a hill. It was early in the morning and the dew twinkled in the rising sunlight like little diamonds in the grass. I remember looking at all the longleaf pine trees on either side of the trail and wondering *Could this really be Louisiana?*

I thought Louisiana was all bayous and swamp grass surrounding "Sin City, The Big Easy" otherwise known as New Orleans. But Louisiana from what I had seen was a huge forest that grew in a red clay type of soil. That red clay, I found out later, was Yazoo Clay and had been deposited by the water that melted from the glaciers clear back in the Ice Age. There are places in the gulf states, especially Louisiana and Mississippi, where the clay is 80 feet deep! It was a wonderful soil for the raising of cotton and the southern portion of Louisiana is as flat as a table top.

The plantation owners who built the magnificent antebellum homes had their fields in Louisiana and their homes in Natchez, Mississippi. At one time, over 80 percent of the millionaires in America lived on the bluffs of Natchez. Back in those times people believed that germs were carried in the air. Living in a higher place meant thinner air and fewer germs, so antebellum homes dot the landscape on the bluffs of Natchez. The landowners rode their carriages from Natchez to the fields of Louisiana to check on their crops.

While that clay was good for growing cotton, it wasn't good for the training we were doing. When it rained, which was every other day, the clay turned into a sticky muck that clung to our shoes and covered our uniforms. Combat boots are heavy anyway, but add five pounds of red clay and they were like lifting an anvil with each step. Our olive drab uniforms would be red by the end of the day. Thank goodness for laundry service or we never would have been able to stand for inspection.

The grenade area consisted of two lines of what looked like foundations for really small apartments. The walls were about eight feet high. As I looked into the stalls, there was a back wall and a wall on either side but no front wall. The first series of stalls would be used for practice. Cadre assisted us one by one, showing us the proper way to throw a grenade. It's done very much like a quarterback throws a football. I was told to look at my target, pull the pin, extend my left hand toward the target, cock my throwing arm with the grenade, count to three, and then throw. Dummy grenades were used in that drill.

Upon the sergeant's approval we went to the next series of stalls where another non-com waited for us. There was a small truck parked about 30 yards from the throwing area and the object was to try to hit the truck. Most of the guys throwing grenades got within 10 or 20 feet of the truck, but no one had it hit so far.

Benny was our platoon screw-up. He was the fat guy with the pop-bottle glasses who Smitty and I had carried, along with his weapon and gear, when we first began training. Benny performed properly for his sergeant as far as form was concerned. However, when he threw the grenade, he hit the wall and the grenade bounced back into the throwing area.

When that happened we found out why there was a non-com in every stall. The sergeant quickly yelled "Hit the deck!" He grabbed the grenade and dropped it over the wall just before it went off. Benny was crying. We all gave a sign of relief and rose to our feet. The sergeant got lots of free beer at the club that night.

When my turn came, I vowed that I was going to hit the truck. I used the proper form and threw with all my might, which was considerably more than usual because the adrenaline was flowing after Benny's mistake. I hit it!

I turned around with pride and everyone cheered. Then it was Smitty's turn. He was the most natural athlete I've ever met in my life. Smitty threw his grenade and cleared the truck by at least 20 feet! The troops went wild! Smitty looked at me and winked. "How 'bout that, Dad?"

On our final day of qualifying with the M14, we got up at 5 a.m., showered and shaved. Qualifying days were always nice because the Mess Hall served excellent food so we would all be in a good emotional state. That day we got bacon, eggs, toast, orange juice, and coffee instead of the typical chipped beef on toast (and you know what we called that!).

We also got to ride to the rifle range in a deuce and a half rather than marching. Usually, we had to make a six-mile forced march to get to the rifle range. That meant we had to carry full gear: a backpack and an M14 rifle. We trained with M14s simply because they were heavier than an M-16 and therefore better for training purposes.

No one could fall out during a forced march. If someone became light-headed, we had to carry his backpack and rifle so he could regain his strength. In the event someone passed out, we had to carry him, too. Again, they wanted us in top form for our final day of qualifying.

We had qualified with the M-14 two times before, and this was our final chance to improve our marksmanship scores. We understood that we couldn't score lower than we had before, but we could improve and our cadre hoped that some of us would score higher because we had a chance of setting a new battalion record. Our previous qualifying trips were meant to make us comfortable with the process. For final qualification we should understand everything we were to do and not be nervous.

Each company had their drill sergeant accompany them to the firing line. Two drill sergeants were to the left of the officer's tower and two were to the right. Each drill sergeant had a paddle that was red on one side and green on the other. The officers in the tower would watch and manage the entire episode.

The normal procedure went something like this: One of the officers took command of the tower. After all of us were lying down with our rifles steadied over a sandbag and zeroed in on our first target, he went through the following command steps.

First he said, "Is there anyone down range? Is there anyone down range?"

That gave anyone who might have been setting targets who had not gotten out of the way the opportunity to announce his presence and be given time to get out of harm's way.

If no one yelled, the officer would say, "There is no one down range." Then he would look to his left and ask, "Ready on the left?" At this point our drill sergeants had the option of showing the green or red sides of their paddles. The red meant that they weren't ready and the green meant that they were.

Of course they showed the green side of their paddles and the officer would announce, "The left is ready." He would them look to his right and ask, "Ready on the right?"

Those drill sergeants would show the green side of their paddles and the officer would announce "The right is ready." His final statement came: "The firing line is all clear. Commence firing!"

And eighty to one hundred rifles blasting away would be the immediate response.

This final day of qualifying turned out a little differently. You see, we had an officer with a speech impediment in control of the tower that day. We had all piled out of the deuce and a half trucks and had laid down with our rifles on the sandbags, zeroed in our targets, and were ready to set a new qualifying record for our battalion. We were like thoroughbred race horses stamping at the starting gate and waiting for the race to begin.

The officer grabbed the microphone and in a loud voice asked, "Is thewr anyone down wange? Is thewr anyone down wange? Thewr is no one down wange. Weddy on the weft? The weft is weddy. Weddy on the wight? The wight is weddy. The fiwing wine is all queer. Commence fiwing!"

Not a single rifle cracked. All of us were laughing so hard we couldn't pull the trigger!

Eventually, another sergeant grabbed the microphone and in a majestic voice went through the rendition one more time.

When the final scores were tallied, I had still retained third place and a week end pass. Four more, including Smitty had earned a pass as well. I had no idea what we would do with them, but I was sure that Smitty would come up with an idea or two!

We were told that 90 percent of the GIs at Fort Polk, Louisiana were going to Vietnam. They were the draftees who were obligated for two years of service. The other 10 percent had signed up for more than the required two-year hitch. So if we wanted a chance at staying out of Vietnam, we could re-enlist for more time in the Army, attend a school, and possibly get stationed somewhere else. Those of us who had been drafted had to weigh the alternative: decide whether to go to Vietnam and serve two years, or sign up for more time.

It made me think of Larry Bleeker. Larry was an All-American boy who had grown up in Ames, Iowa. His father owned the Bleeker Furniture Store there, and Larry had grown up stocking the store and selling furniture to the public. The exposure to selling at a young age had formed him into a very personable young man.

I met Larry through a mutual friend, Phil Hurst. Phil and I were college roommates, which is another story in itself. I was a member of a Christian organization called the Navigators. Phil and Larry belonged to another group called Campus Crusade for Christ. Phil thought Larry and I should meet so he invited Larry to our apartment for a visit.

Larry immediately impressed me with his outgoing personality and enthusiasm, the kind of guy anyone would want for a friend. Any father would be pleased to find his daughter in love with Larry. He had the ability to speak at ease, make everyone laugh, and yet make a serious point without offending anyone.

Yellow Submarine Days, named after the popular Beatles song, were a part of campus life then. Hippie Types roamed the streets with signs advocating getting out of Vietnam. ROTC students had to stand at stiff attention while Hippies stuffed flowers down the barrels of their rifles. Pro-war professors had their classes picketed. There were demonstrations against military recruiters preventing them from even coming on campus to do their jobs.

Our entire society was torn over Vietnam. There were the "hawks" and the "chickens." The peace symbol made popular by those against the war was called a "Chicken Track" by those on the other side. Those who felt the war was wrong were called unpatriotic. Those who felt the war was correct called themselves patriots.

In was in the midst of this upheaval that Larry Bleeker decided to enlist in the Marines. He set an example for others—he did the right thing by being patriotic. Larry arrived in Quang Tri Province on October 8, 1967, as a Second Lieutenant Basic Infantry Officer. He died October 26, 1967.

Phil and I went to his funeral at the Baptist Church in Ames. I remember standing in front of his coffin. He was in a Marine uniform and his once energetic face was pasty-white and lifeless. I thought to myself, *How can such a bigger than life person be dead? Why should a person doing the right thing have to die? It doesn't make sense.*

It reminded me of one of the Bible passages that Larry had quoted at one of our meetings. They were the words of King David near the end of his life: "For we are here for but a moment, strangers in the land as our fathers were before us; our days on earth are like a shadow, gone so soon, without a trace."

There is a trace of Larry left. He's on Panel 28E, Line 072 on the Vietnam Wall in Washington D.C.

Pugil stick training was next on the list. We had to get up at three a.m. because it was a long march to the pugil stick practice field. We marched in the dark for two hours and arrived at the field just as the sun peeked over the horizon.

The sergeant in charge showed us the pugil sticks and explained how they were used to mimic fighting with a bayonet. The stick was about six feet long, two inches thick, and heavily padded on each end. It had been invented by Dr. Armond Seilder of the University of New Mexico and used for training during WWII. One end was marked as the butt of a rifle and the other end was marked as the bayonet.

Two experienced soldiers began an exhibition, showing us how to thrust and parry. The sergeant explained that anyone who had recently had a brain concussion would be excluded from this activity.

Great! I thought. *This is my way out!*

I raised my hand and told the sergeant that I had experienced three brain concussions in football.

"How long ago?" he asked.

"Oh, about four years ago," I said, "when I played high school football."

"Nice try," he said. "Didn't you hear that I said recently, you rubberhead? Do you think a Viet Cong is going to ask you if you've had a brain concussion before he rams his bayonet into your guts? You just volunteered to be first in line for pugil stick training!"

I stepped forward, remembering the advice that experienced GIs had told me: "Keep your mouth shut and *never* volunteer for anything."

As I put on a football helmet and accepted the pugil stick, the sergeant asked for a volunteer to fight with me. The biggest black man I had ever seen stepped forward with a huge grin on his face. He put on his helmet, grabbed a pugil stick, and before I knew it he had hit a home run by using his stick as a bat and my head as a baseball! I saw stars for a few hours while the others in my company took their turns.

When the pugil stick training had ended, we were given a demonstration in first aid. "You must be able to take care of your fellow soldiers if they are wounded by a bayonet," the sergeant told us. "Remember, your fellow soldiers are your new family. They depend on you and you depend on them. Forget Jody [the military name for your girlfriend back home] and your Mommy and Daddy. They won't be there in the battle field with you, so get used to your new family."

We were all issued a square package of gauze and an atropine syrette. We were told to fasten the syrette to our helmet with an elastic strap and wear it at all times.

"The bayonet will leave a bleeding wound that must be stopped," the sergeant said. "You must take the gauze and apply pressure to the wound to stop the bleeding."

We all paired up and took turns applying the gauze to an imaginary wound on our partner, as the sergeant and others roamed among the troops and gave advice. They stressed that we must apply a lot of pressure to stop the bleeding. "Bleeding is going to cause low blood pressure," we were told. "Atropine will counteract that."

Atropine is made from the deadly nightshade plant. We farm boys knew how deadly nightshade could be for our farm animals because it effects the nervous system. That's why the atropine works. The vagus nerve, which is actuated by a wound, normally slows down the heart rate.

Atropine blocks this action and thus stimulates the heart and increases blood flow.

"Atropine has an immediate effect and wears off quickly, so if you happen to screw up and stick yourself it won't harm you," the sergeant said.

He demonstrated on a dummy how the atropine syrette should be used. "Just take off the protective cap and slam the end of the syrette on the wounded person's thigh. The spring loaded mechanism inside will automatically eject the needle and administer the atropine. And, remember, if you accidentally inject yourself, it won't harm you."

When I saw the look in Smitty's eye, I knew that was all he needed to hear. We paired up again for atropine injection practice and I made sure not to be Smitty's partner.

"Don't take the protective cap off the syrette," the sergeant said. "This is a practice drill only. We will be watching to make sure your actions are acceptable."

We all rammed the syrette against our partner's thighs as though we were doing the real thing. An alarming "OW" rang out and all the officers congregated around Smitty's partner who writhed in pain. Smitty, with the most innocent look on his face, explained that his syrette's protective cover must have fallen off. The officer assured the wounded GI that the effects would be temporary and that that he would be fine.

As we lined up in formation to march back to the barracks, Smitty looked at me with that devilish grin and said, "Hey Dad! Did you hear that guy holler?"

Our society was split on our being in Vietnam. Since most of us had been drafted, many of us questioned the justification for being there. In those days we didn't have an all-volunteer Army whose members were homogeneous in their thinking. On the contrary, some of us had serious questions: Were we really fighting for our freedom? Did our way of life really depend on what happened in Vietnam? Did we really have to follow the orders of an officer just because he happened to be an ROTC graduate who had no more common sense than a box of rocks?

The Army had experienced men going AWOL, fleeing to Canada, and even deserting because of those reasons. They were pulling no punches in making it clear that we were now "government issue" and belonged to the Army in body, mind, and spirit.

Basic Training to me was a process dedicated to these goals: (1) Get us into good physical condition. Soldiers need to be in good shape to fight. (2) Eliminate individuality. Soldiers need to think about their entire fighting group and make decisions based on what is best for all concerned, rather than what is good for themselves. This includes family. Soldiers need to view their counterparts as their new family. (3) Discipline. Soldiers must respect rank and follow orders. "The Army does not pay you to think," was a popular comment from our superiors. (4) Learn to kill. That is the ultimate goal of the soldier. It requires knowledge of a variety of weapons, how to use them, and how to maintain them. It requires knowing when to hunker down in a defensive position and how to attack in an offensive condition. (5) Country First. Many of our school sessions were aimed at conditioning us to believe that country must always come first. We were told that personal feelings, family, personal desires, loved ones, and even our very lives must take a back seat to country.

Being a college graduate made it difficult for me to go through Basic Training. I had been taught to think, question, read, and consider alternatives. I had taken philosophy courses and read the writings of Plato, Descartes, Thoreau, Tolstoy, Voltaire, Dostoevsky, Machiavelli, and so on. I was constantly plagued with questions like, "What if the Puritans had put country first? They never would have landed on our shores and started this great country!"

I had also taken Logic. If A=B and B=C, then A must also equal C. Therefore the syllogism: "If Terry dies in a gunfight in a certain location and if Joe dies in a gunfight in that location, then I, too, will die if I stay in that location."

Yet I was told not to think. I must follow orders and act only in what my superiors decided was in the best interests of the entire unit, which meant I must stay in that location, too. But what if my superiors were wrong or acting in their own self interests rather than in what would be best for the whole unit? The conflict between what I was being told I must do and what made sense to me was constantly there, and only the threat of punishment and the desire to do my duty kept me and others like me in line.

One of our class sessions was led by our chaplain. He began the class by asking what was really important in our lives and, therefore, worth protecting.

"Family," one soldier said. "I would die to protect my family."

"That's true," replied the chaplain. "What else is worth fighting for?"

Another GI shouted, "Freedom! I'll fight for free speech and the freedom of religion."

"That's also true," replied the chaplain. "What else is worth fighting and dying for?"

Another answer came from the group. "God. Anybody that tries to stop me from worshiping God is in deep trouble!"

The chaplain smiled and a number of GIs in the group shouted, "Brownnoser!"

"Is there anything else we should add to the list?" the chaplain asked.

"Good jobs and a good way of life," someone from the back of the room yelled.

The chaplain asked for other suggestions but the room fell silent. The things that were important to us had all been said.

"All right," the chaplain said. "Let's try to put these things in order with the most important thing on top and the least important on the bottom. What do you think should be at the top of the list?"

Some voted for family, some voted for jobs, some voted for freedom, and some voted for God.

The chaplain then said, "What about country? Because without our country, the United States of America, none of the other things would be possible. Without our country we wouldn't have freedoms. With the freedom of religion, you wouldn't be able to worship your God. Without the USA and its capitalistic economy, you wouldn't have jobs and you wouldn't be able to support your family. So doesn't it make sense that the first thing you should be willing to fight and die for is country?"

I had grown up in the First Lutheran Church in Sioux Rapids and had been confirmed there. Bible study, commandments, creed, the Lord's Prayer, and so on had been drilled into us in confirmation class. I raised my hand and asked the chaplain if he had read the Bible.

"Of course I have," he replied.

I asked him if he had gone to seminary.

He looked at me with a questioning face and replied, "Of course I have. I had to go to seminary to become ordained."

"What is the first commandment?" I asked.

The chaplain turned beet-red in the face and had me removed from the room.

I believed in the first commandment: I am the Lord thy God. Thou shall have no other Gods before me. I had become the leader of our entire company. Originally I had been the platoon leader, a platoon consisted of 60 men. A company is four platoons. So when I led marches, counseling, holding court, etc., I did it for over 200 men. That had all come about because of the strong foundation I had in terms of religion, family, and principles. When I was a platoon leader, I counseled the men in my platoon. Many would come into the privacy of my office and break down in tears. They couldn't handle being away from home. More often than not, these fellows never got a letter from home.

Others came to me because they were in trouble. Some had stolen things from the Army. Quite a few of the men in my platoon were there because they had been given a choice: Two years in jail or two years in the Army. The main reason they were there was that they didn't have good principles.

My principles had come from my Christian faith, so it made sense to me to share that faith by holding devotions. I had Catholics, Baptists, Methodists, and lots of guys who had no faith at all. They simply knew that they needed something beyond what they presently had.

I soon found some complications: Baptists wanted to pray out loud; Lutherans didn't like to pray in public; others just didn't know how to pray. So I made some rules. I would read the scripture and then we would have silent prayer. Afterward, anyone that wanted to stay and have a conversation on the subject could do so.

One of my principles was this: Don't tell people what to do. Ask them and say please. My people appreciated that. I don't think anyone likes being ordered what to do, at least I don't. Apparently that's true of others, too, because guys would do anything for me and as a result our platoon was always at the top of the list for honors. The combination of all these things is what resulted in me leading the entire company. Others joined our devotions, came for counseling, and participated in activities because they were being asked and not ordered.

That got me in trouble with the company commander. He pulled me aside and told me that in the Army we don't ask people to do something; we order them to do it. He told me that I was too friendly with my people. "And we NEVER EVER say PLEASE!" He made it clear that if I didn't start ordering my people what to do and quit being friendly, he would fire me and find someone else.

I thought about his threat for a while and finally said, "These are my principles and I'm not going to change. We've been the honor platoon for weeks now and there's a reason for it. I guess you're just going to have to find someone else for the job."

I thought he would back down and he did. He said, "OK. You're still my man."

I got another care package from Ginny one day. A note was inside: "Know what a 500 pound canary sounds like? Here KITTY, KITTY, KITTY!" The package had caramel popcorn, Starlite Mints, and Black Jack and Clove chewing gum. She knew that I loved the flavor of those chewing gums. Mom used to buy Black Jack, Clove, and Teaberry gum from a mail order catalogue. It arrived in small boxes and I'd pick it up at the mailbox. The gum's shape wasn't in stick form as we now know it, but rather in small chunks about an inch square and half an inch thick.

I shared the gum with the guys in the platoon and they all got a kick out of the Black Jack because it made their mouths black. They enjoyed opening their mouths in front of the brothers in our unit and saying, "Now I'm just like you!"

We had been camping out on maneuver for the past week. Many had colds and sore throats, so the mints were appreciated for their soothing effect.

Back on post I sat on the step in front of the barracks and munched on the caramel corn, thinking about the Clay County Fair. In my mind's eye I could picture myself standing in front of the booth where caramel corn was being made. What a smell! And then I imagined the other welcoming smells in the air: the Tom Thumb donut stand, the Dixie Cream Donut stand, cotton candy, the foot long hotdogs, and all the stands that had onions cooking on their grills. Once I ordered a plate of cooked onions at one of the stands. (I really love onions!) The attendant looked at me as if I had lost my mind. "We don't sell them, buddy. We just cook them to bring in the customers!"

It had been a momentous week. I had received orders to go to Military Police School at Fort Gordon, Georgia, relieved that I wouldn't be going to infantry training. We were all afraid of being a "ground pounder" in Vietnam. Sadly, 90 percent of the company received orders to attend infantry training right where we were, in Fort Polk, Louisiana. It was known as "Tigerland" because of the close proximity of Louisiana State University, but none of us wanted to be a tiger.

Ginny had finished her schooling at Iowa State University. She had a teaching degree in English and Speech. She had been interviewing at a number of schools, one of which was in Humboldt where she had done her student teaching. The students and the staff there loved her and wanted her to remain full time. However, the school board balked at hiring her because she was married to a soldier. Their feeling was that she would only teach for a year or two until I got out of the service, at which time she would be leaving the school to be with me. So what had looked like a no-brainer resulted in her not being hired. She interviewed a number of other schools with the same result. They liked her and liked her ideas, but were afraid to hire her because she would probably leave as soon I got out of the Army.

"We'd love to hire you, but as soon as your husband comes home you'll be moving and we want someone who will stay for a number of years," they typically told her.

It didn't seem fair that I had been drafted and it didn't seem fair that she couldn't get a job because of me being in the military. What a dilemma. She had a teaching degree and students, teachers, and school boards liked her and her ideas about managing a class room, but no one would hire her because she was an "Army bride."

We couldn't help but feel cheated. I had been drafted and she couldn't get a job because of it.

My draft notice had begun with the line: "Your friends and relatives have selected you to represent them in the United States Military." Well, I didn't mind representing my friends and relatives in the Army—I considered that my duty—but I do wish my "friends and relatives" would have treated my future wife better.

Basic was finally over. Our company got placed on quarantine because most of the guys got orders to Vietnam and the Army didn't want anyone going AWOL. I had lots of time on my hands since I wouldn't ship out until the next day, so I relaxed in my bunk and wrote a letter to Ginny.

I reflected what I had learned in Basic Training and what I had learned surprised me. I would have thought it would be how to stay in good physical shape, knowledge of guns, hand-to-hand combat, living off the land, and so on. But what I really learned was quite different.

I had learned that all people have good qualities that need to be sought out and developed. People can overcome bad qualities if they receive commendation for their good qualities. I learned that people will do anything if you pitch right in with them. Leadership by example tends to make people strive for the best that's in them. When men are bossed around, they will do no more than the absolute minimum that's required.

I learned not to take my loved ones for granted. I missed Sunday dinner with the family. I missed having Ginny by my side, of having a hand clasp mine with nothing but a smile to go with it, an evening talking of love and the future, enjoying a movie or a canoe ride, and holding hands during the Lord's Prayer during Sunday worship.

I determined that when we were together eventually that I would take special means to thank her for making brownies. Until I had received them in the mail and shared my brownies with the guys, I had not realized that I had taken for granted something as simple as making a pan of brownies.

We were called out for a special formation. Sergeant O'Dell then presented the rank of E-2, a higher pay grade, to Jackson. My platoon booed both of them and made snide remarks that I should have gotten the promotion.

Lieutenant Daniels took the forefront and called eight men forward, surprising me when he called my name. Daniels called us "honor soldiers" of the company and presented each of us with a shiny new Zippo lighter. He looked at O'Dell and said, "And you're paying for them!" He then shook hands with all eight of us and said, "Job well done."

And that was the other lesson I learned. Bootlickers and those who kiss up to their superiors seem to get ahead in life. But do they? Well, if you measure success by financial gain, the answer is yes. Kissing up is an effective way to gain a promotion no matter what business one may be in. It is also an effective way to rise above one's capabilities.

Another measure of success is the recognition of one's peers. A man may be promoted by kissing up, but how effective will his leadership be if those below him have no respect for him?

Perhaps the best measure of success comes from within one's own soul. Success in my mind is remaining true to one's values, principles, and beliefs. Judas sold his beliefs for a sack of silver, and then went out and committed suicide. He had financial gain but that didn't make him successful. That's why I admire people like Jesus Christ, Joan of Arc, Harry Truman, Gandhi, Nelson Mandela, John Galt, and others. They all stuck to their principles and became successful as a result.

CHAPTER 3
ADVANCED INDIVIDUAL TRAINING

I waited in my barracks after graduation ceremonies from Basic. Some of the guys had family who came to attend the graduation. There had been a lot of pomp and circumstance for the graduation, and those who had family present received cheers and whistles. Most of us, however, received our diplomas in silence, since most of us were miles from home and it was too far for our families to come. Or as in my case, I had told my family not to come because of the limited time the Army would let us spend together. Families got to spend three hours in the parking lot, under guard, with their graduate. The rest of us were not allowed to leave the company area, even to make a phone call home. It seems contradictory to me that the soldiers who would be going to Vietnam to fight for America's freedom were not free to spend time with their families whether in person or by telephone. Oh, well, such were the times.

Smitty and I were up at three the next morning, ready to leave Fort Polk. I now knew how a convict must feel standing at the prison gate, ready to be set free after serving his term. We boarded the typical gray-colored bus that the Army used to transport soldiers. The bus took us to Alexandria, Louisiana, where we boarded a plane that took us to Shreveport. We boarded another plane that took us to Jackson, Mississippi. We boarded yet another plane that took us to Atlanta, Georgia. When we saw our next plane, I knew that we were close to our destination. We climbed into a C-130.

The C-130 is to the Army what a semi truck is to a farmer: It's built to carry cargo… lots of cargo. The wings are overhead and massive. Four huge engines with wide, flat-tipped blades adorn the wings, and it looks like it must have at least 18 wheels! The plane is easy to enter because its belly is barely a few feet off the ground.

Inside, the plane is very large and absolutely wide open. The open decking allows the plane to carry pallets of supplies, dollies loaded with bombs, Jeeps, and even tanks. The floor and sides of the plane have rigging hooks to secure whatever load it needs to carry. It is not glamorous. The inside is not finished for appearance, but looks like an unfinished basement where nothing is visible but studs and braces, the necessary structural pieces. Aluminum benches fold up on the sides. These were unfolded to give us a place to sit. No longer did we have the comfort of padded seats like we had on United Airlines.

The C-130 lumbered down the runway and miraculously lifted off the ground at what seemed like five miles per hour. The massive wingspan area gave the bird impressive lifting power.

We landed in Augusta, Georgia, where a bus picked us up and delivered us to Fort Gordon, home of the Military Police. Our first stop was the mess hall, since we hadn't eaten since five that morning. I waited at the front door for permission to enter.

One of the officers laughed and said, "You're not in Basic Training anymore, son. You're in leadership training with the Military Police. We're the best-dressed, most orderly and mannerly soldiers in Uncle Sam's Army. Just go in and enjoy yourself. No one is going to babysit you anymore."

We were allowed to sit with anyone we cared to be with and could carry on a conversation, none of which we could do in Basic. We could take our time and enjoy our meal, while we had been allowed five minutes to cram food down our gullets in Basic. A selection of different foods was available and we could take whatever portion we wished, rather than have a Mess Hall sergeant slop spoonfuls of his creations onto our tin plates. I took my tray of food and sat down.

"Hi, Lee," I heard as I sat down. I looked up and saw my cousin, Allen Halverson, grinning at me from across the table. I hadn't seen Al since the Halverson reunion a few years ago near Linn Grove and here we were, two Northwest Iowa boys sitting at the same table in Augusta, Georgia!

It's a small world, isn't it?

Because our unit had such a high number of college graduates, we had scored very high on the written tests we were given. In addition, we had scored well at the firing range, probably because so many of us had come from the Midwest and had hunted as boys. Our company commander announced that we were in a position to set a new combined scoring record and he really wanted the record. He said our last hurdle was the.45 pistol. He proclaimed that, if the company as a whole did well with the.45, we would indeed set a new company record. To sweeten the pot he told us that the top three qualifiers would get three-day passes!

I had never fired a .45 pistol in my life but I knew one thing: I was going to have that three-day pass. After all, I had qualified during Basic as an expert with the M-14, the M-16, the M-60, and the grenade launcher. I had never before fired any of those weapons either, so it made sense to me that I could qualify as an expert with the.45.

I hadn't seen Ginny since I had left her at the Des Moines airport three months earlier when I flew out for Basic Training. I sure did miss her! I called Ginny and told her to be on a plane the next weekend. "Make reservations at a motel in Augusta," I told her, "because I'm going to have a three-day pass and I'll meet you there."

Little did I know what a challenge the.45 pistol would be. The pistol is a heavy one and it took a strong arm to hold it in position. It also had a hard trigger pull. A normal person could pull on that trigger too fast, which pulled the barrel down and resulted in shooting the target in the foot instead of the heart.

Sergeants were thick because an inexperienced person could be deadly on the firing range. Very few people even hit the target, let alone the bullseye. I heard a scream followed by sergeants shouting for help. A qualifier had pulled the trigger so hard that he had shot *himself* in the foot!

I've often remembered that day because I prayed, "Dear God, help this bullet to hit the bulls-eye so I can get a three-day pass and be with Ginny."

It seemed incongruous to pray while shooting a weapon designed to kill someone. Be that as it may, I prayed for very single bullet I shot. Soon I had a group of sergeants behind me cheering because I had a good shot group, right in the bullseye. I ended up firing expert and had the highest qualifying score of the company.

Mom used to say that the fondest dreams of mice and men often go astray, and that's just what happened. President Dwight David Eisenhower died that week. We were told that all leaves were suspended and that the entire battalion would stand honor guard that weekend.

I went straight to the commander's office. "A deal's a deal," I announced. "I did what you asked and my fiancé is coming for the weekend. If I don't get my leave, I'll go AWOL!"

I could hardly believe I had said those words myself and neither could the commander. I had assisted him on a number of projects and he knew how dependable I was. But he also knew I meant business. "I'll have to call the base commander, Colonel Thompson, and see what I can do," he said.

I waited in his office while he made the call.

Meanwhile, Ginny was about to land in Augusta, along with Carol Steele, my cousin Al's fiancé. My brother-in-law, Gabe Blaskovitch, had volunteered to take them to the airport in Des Moines. They had arrived late and missed the flight that they were supposed to be on and were given standby tickets on the next flight. Thank goodness that flight had seats available for them.

However, their good luck changed when they got to O'Hare Airport in Chicago. "Those standby tickets are for morning flights, not afternoon flights," they were told.

The manager of American Airlines was about to get a lesson he'd never forget. You see, Ginny has the innate ability to argue or cry to her advantage, and she's darn good at knowing which to use and when. She knew she was in the big city and that crying would never work with these people, so she argued!

"I'm supposed to be in Augusta to meet my fiancé this afternoon...AND YOU'RE GOING TO TAKE ME!" she screamed.

Before long she had three managers around her, trying to get her to be quiet. "Ma'am, our seats are filled," one of them said. "All we have left are two seats in first class and your tickets aren't good for first class."

That's all he needed to say. You see, as soon as he said he had two seats, he was dead in the water! It wasn't long before Carol and Ginny were riding first class to Augusta.

They arrived in Augusta and took a taxi to the Dixie Motel where she had booked rooms. The Dixie Motel was on the wrong side of town, but it was the only place available because the Masters Golf Tournament was taking place that same weekend and most motels were sold out. It looked like a log cabin. I suppose she was praying for a room just like I was praying for my bullets! We remember our reunion each year when the Master's comes around.

They deposited their luggage and waited at the bus stop across the street for a ride to the base. The bus never came. After about an hour of waiting, two non-coms came along and offered them a ride to the service club where we were to meet.

Ginny hesitated to ride with strangers but Carol said, "I'm going."

Ginny told them where we were to meet and they said, "That's the wrong service club. You need to be going to the MP service club, not this one." But I had told her Service Club 6, so that was where they went.

They arrived at the service club where upon the two good Samaritans gave them a sermon about riding with strangers: "Don't ever do that again!" they said.

Inside, they met another wife waiting for her husband to get off work. As they chatted, the wife told them that they were at the wrong service club. "You want the MP Service Club," she said, "and this isn't it."

Her husband arrived and agreed that they were in the wrong place. As a precaution, he took Ginny through the whole service club opening doors and checking in every room to see if Allen and I were there. But of course we weren't. After some discussion, they decided that he would take Ginny to the MP's club and Carol would wait just in case. Arriving at the MP Service Club and finding no evidence of me, Ginny resorted to her other God-given strength: she began to cry.

Immediately the husband who had driven her to the club decided to call the commander of my company. "I've got Halverson's fiancé here at the club and she's crying her eyes out." It just goes to prove that there are good people everywhere and she had just met four of them.

I heard the telephone conversation because I was standing right next to my commander. He looked at me, shrugged his shoulders and gave me my three-day pass. So, Al and I hopped into a cab and met the girls at the MP service club. Ginny, of course, wanted to know why I had told them to meet at the wrong service club.

And I resorted to one of my strengths: I blamed in on Al!

It was wonderful to have Ginny beside me. I hadn't seen her since we said goodbye at the airport when I flew off to Basic three months before. We had so much to catch up on, friends and family back home, my experiences in the Army, her studies at Iowa State, and our upcoming wedding. We arrived at our motel which looked like an arrangement of little log cabins. Opening the door of our little cabin, we observed our room. It was a Spartan little place with no fringes but it was ours for the week end! I immediately noticed that we had twin beds! We had agreed that we would remain virgin until our wedding night, but I sure wanted to hold her in my arms as we slept! So we scooted the two beds together and made one bed out of the two of them.

I had one big advantage in being so far away from home: It was impossible for me to be involved in all the decisions to be made about our wedding. Gin talked about the church, the color of the flowers, the cake, the color of the bridesmaids' dresses, the color of the tuxes the men would wear, and so on.

I said, "You take care of it all. I'll just show up and say, 'I do.'"

We had both heard about the Augusta Masters Golf Tournament, how beautiful the course was, and how beautiful Augusta was. The entire city was all dressed up with flowers, the streets were clean, and the citizenry were all dressed up and on their best behavior to welcome the crowds coming to enjoy the tournament.

We began our day by going to a restaurant for breakfast, the first meal I had eaten in months that wasn't served in a mess hall. It felt good to order whatever I wanted. By the same token, it was nice to have my own toilet and bed at the Dixie Motel, instead of the rows of bunk beds and community toilets that we had in the barracks.

Gin and I decided that a bus ride would be just the ticket to see the sights of Augusta. So we left the cafe and went to the bus stop right outside the door. We walked up the steps of the bus and quickly found seats. The bus didn't move. Suddenly, the driver said "Hey!" He pointed the coin drop and said, "You gotta pay!" Neither of us had ever ridden on a city bus and that was quite evident to everyone. We deposited our quarters and sat back to enjoy the sights. As the bus progressed and made more stops, the bus began to fill—with black people! Ginny and I were the only white people on the bus. Most of the other passengers carried a sack lunch with them and we could see that they were all working class people, maids, waitresses, city employees, parking lot attendants, and so on.

I was just a farm boy from Iowa in the big city for the first time and must have appeared pretty naive when I exclaimed, "Wow!" Look how tall that building is! I wonder what it is."

A nice man turned around and smiled, 'That's the court house," he said.

"Look at that statue," I said.

Another man turned and explained what the statue was.

Before long, we had people gathered around us pointing out historical spots, elegant buildings, shopping malls, places to eat, statues, and other points of interest. We were all having such a good time together.

One person would stand and say, "This is my stop. Just wanted to shake your hand and tell you how nice it was to meet you."

And another person would take his or her place pointing out the sights of the city. Soon the bus driver joined in the activity and said, "Joe! Tell them about the old theatre!" And the driver would laugh and smile as Joe told us about the old theater, nodding his head each time Joe mentioned something the driver felt was important.

Everyone wanted to know more about us: What was it like in Iowa? When were we getting married? Would I have to go to Vietnam? Iowa...that's where they raise all the potatoes, isn't it? Are there any Indians in Iowa?

I told a few jokes and everyone laughed. It seemed like the more I told, the more they laughed. We were really having a good time.

Suddenly, I noticed that our happy little crowd had diminished and soon Ginny and I were the only people left on the bus. The driver stopped the bus and turned around with a huge smile on his face. "Folks, I've really enjoyed having you on my bus. But this is where you got on. If you want to go around again, I'd love to have you. I just thought I'd let you know."

Sheesh, a hayseed in the city!

I got promoted to assistant squad leader in my MP training and once again had my own office. While the rest of the guys roomed in a large barracks with bunk beds, a foot locker at the end of the bed, and a wall locker between the beds, I had a room with a single bed and a desk, along with my foot locker and wall locker.

Our schedule began at 3:30 a.m. every morning and ended at 10 p.m. The hours and the training wore on everyone. Tempers were short. We had very little time to write letters or make phone calls home. Men who had wives found it difficult to maintain the communication required to sustain their relationships. The same could be said of the men who had sweethearts. Consequently, marriages broke apart and unmarried men received "Dear John" letters.

Many of these guys would come to the privacy of my room to talk. I didn't mind being a sounding board and letting them unload their concerns.

One such fellow looked at me and asked, "You're always happy and never let the Army get you down. You and Ginny have something special. You never seem to worry about whether she's faithful to you and you certainly have never gotten a Dear John letter like I did. How come you're so lucky?"

To be honest with you I had never considered that Ginny would be unfaithful to me—it just never crossed my mind—and that is because Ginny and I based our relationship first of all on our belief in God and Jesus Christ. Our families had brought us up as Christians and we attended church regularly. We believed that a man and a woman should cleave together as one. We had many discussions during our courtship and had decided that trust was the ultimate factor in a successful relationship. Trust requires a lot of hope and faith, and a relationship cannot be strong without it.

As I discussed that belief with John (yes, John was his real name and he had gotten a Dear John letter), he asked me "When did you know she was the right one for you?"

I took a moment to reflect and then realized when it was.

Before I met Gin, I had dated another girl who was quite popular and very attractive. I worked three jobs in college: janitor at Alumni Hall, food service at Oak Elm Dining Hall, and ward at the hospital. Money was tight for me. Nonetheless, I wanted to surprise her with a dozen roses. She looked at them, commented how nice they were, and then threw them down on her desk like an empty Big Mac wrapper. Things went downhill from there and I soon broke off our engagement. As a result, I wasn't interested in going through that again so I had a three date rule: Three dates and drop 'em!

Ginny was the only blind date I ever had. My roommate and hers were dating and they thought we would be perfect together. When those elevator doors opened and I saw Ginny's radiant smile, she hit me like a ton of bricks. She made me break my three date rule!

Ginny and I did a lot of study dates. I'd walk to her dorm and together we would walk to the library or Alumni Hall to study for the night. Then I'd walk her back to her dorm. One spring day, walking to her dorm, I noticed a patch of wild flowers by the sidewalk so I stopped and picked a handful for her. I remember wondering whether or not she would think of me as a cheapskate, and almost threw them away before I got there. But I had gone through the effort of picking them, so when she came to the door I presented them to her.

She broke out in a smile, gave me a kiss, and then immediately went to get a vase for them. We didn't leave for study until she had placed them on her desk and told everyone on the floor about her flowers. Likewise, she had to tell everyone studying at the hall what I had done. She made me feel like a king.

And that's when I knew she was the one.

John's Dear John letter would be one of many I saw before my tour ended.

Tattoos were considered manly things in those days. Marines usually had Semper Fi tattooed on their arms; Navy guys had an anchor; Army guys had a parachute if they were airborne, a rifle if they were infantry, or crossed pistols if they were military policemen. Whatever the tattoo, the man wearing it was considered manly and someone you didn't mess with.

We were in the Enlisted Men's Club when The Big Wop said, "Let's get a tattoo!"

Arturo Willimino Pollicelli was six feet six inches tall, weighed about 250 pounds, and had a 36-inch waist. He was very proud of his Italian-Sicilian heritage. He truly was a Big Wop. Art was a member of the Sicilian Army in his home town of the Bronx. Members had to vow to wear six knives on their person at all times, even in the shower! Not only did Art wear them, he knew how to use them. All I knew was this was a guy I wanted as a friend, not a foe. I always felt safe in the presence of the Big Wop.

Down the street we sauntered, looking for a tattoo parlor. Art was the first through the door of this dark, dirty, foreboding little business. The tattoo artist sat on a chair in the corner. My eyes had to adjust to the dark before I could see him. He was just as dirty as his building and had tattoos of dragons, snakes, a medusa, and fingers of fire covering his arms, legs, neck, and forehead. He had a cigarette dangling from his lips and sat there, silently glowering at us.

Art announced that he wanted an American Eagle on his chest. The artist pointed at a chair without speaking and Art obediently sat down. Art removed his shirt revealing a gigantic chest and awaited the artist with a brave smile on his face.

The artist grabbed his tattoo machine, which looked like it had gone a thousand miles without an oil change, and started to tattoo the outline of an eagle on Art's chest. He used no pattern—it was all freehand. I admired the man's work. He was forming a perfect eagle and I remember thinking that this man had a gift. He truly was an artist.

Art told us that we should look at the pictures of other clients that were hanging on the wall and pick the tattoos we liked. I looked at the crossed pistols and thought I should have them since I was a military policeman. And then I saw it, the perfect tattoo: a pair of lips! I would have a nice, big, red pair of lips tattooed on my right buttock. Then, when a drill sergeant made one of his stupid remarks, I would simply lower my drawers and show him my tattoo. I could convey my message without uttering a word!

While I dreamed about all the practical applications this tattoo would have, I heard a loud shriek, followed by whimpering. I turned and saw The Big Wop crying. The tattoo artist had completed the outline of the eagle on Art's chest and had poured Listerine on the pattern. The Listerine foamed and bubbled on the fresh wound the tattoo machine had made. Obviously that must have been painful because the big, strong Art that we knew had been reduced to a crying baby!

The tattoo artist said, "You'd better hang in there, buddy—I've got three more colors to go."

By that time I had seen enough to know that I wasn't going to go through with it. Everyone else decided the same thing, so we sat while the artist finished his job on Art.

Sometimes I have to deal with some really stupid people who make me wish I had gone through with it and gotten that lip tattoo. Like the saying goes, a picture is worth a thousand words.

We soon learned that an MP must set an example for the rest of the Army in terms of dress, grooming, military courtesy, and decorum. The whitewall was a must for every MP. The barbers loved to shave the sides of our heads to make the whitewall, and especially savored a troop who used to have long hair and wanted it back again. They took special care in shaving the scalp of such a person.

The shine on our boots came next on the list. We spent hours shining our boots so they took on the look of a mirror. We all became expert at putting water in the lids of our shoe wax cans, dipping a cotton ball into the wax and then the water, and rubbing away on our boots until the mirror finish appeared.

We learned that our chances of going to Vietnam were about 50-50. We could get an "early out" if we went to Vietnam, but we would have to serve our full enlistment if we stayed state-side or went to Germany. I didn't know which way to go. I had been drafted and wanted to be out of the Army as soon as possible. Maybe I should go to Vietnam, but if I did that I stood the chance of being killed and leaving Ginny a widow. On the other hand, I could go to Germany and be safe. The trade off for going to Germany was that it would be much longer before Ginny and I could be together.

I pondered my situation as we took off our pistol belts, pouches, canteens, first aid kits, and helmets to enter class. Everyone shucked their equipment quickly and sprinted for the air-conditioned class room.

I took a little more time to arrange my equipment and as I stood there alone. I noticed some movement in the trees near our formation area. It looked like an Army helmet, only it was moving. I soon recognized it as a turtle and found out later that it was a very rare turtle, native only to the woods of Georgia. They call it a "cumayumpin" turtle. Well, it came out of the woods, saw my helmet, cumayumpin, and raped my helmet!

Classes lasted four hours. The sergeant called class to order and as usual announced, "There will be no coughing, sneezing, or sleeping during class."

It's amazing, I thought, thinking of all the coughing that occurs during a preacher's sermon. *All he'd have to do is announce from the pulpit that there would be no coughing or sneezing during his sermon and that would be that!*

Nobody coughed or sneezed, but sleeping was the difficult part of that order. The classes were boring and long and I could sleep at the drop of a hat anyway. I always made sure I had a buddy beside me who would poke me if I fell asleep, and I'd do the same for him. Those who fell asleep got chastised on the spot and were given some sort of nasty detail, like KP.

There was only one exception to this sleep rule: Smitty always seemed to get away with it. Maybe they knew it was better if Smitty slept.

One day we were called into formation to go to the dispensary. That wasn't unusual as the Army often gave us "short arm inspections" to ensure that we didn't have any sexually transmitted diseases. After the inspection we'd get another sermon on how to prevent disease.

But this time was different. We had our regular short arm inspections, the doctors listened to our hearts, had us breath in and out, and then we had to bend over and spread our cheeks. It always amazed me that after this much time and this many inspections, some of the guys would still bend over and grab the cheeks on either side of their mouths and pull them apart!

We then fell into another line where doctors had a syringe with an amazing number of tubes connected to it. We were advised to hold very still when the doctor gave us a shot because the serum would be injected under tremendous air pressure. Imagine that! There was no needle at all! Whatever they were injecting into us would enter our skin entirely just by air pressure.

They told us that, if we moved, the air stream would make a cut that might require stitches. "So hold very still and don't jump away," they said.

None of us knew what the injections were for and that was also typical of the Army, too. We had no "need to know." All we knew is that there were eight hoses attached to each of the syringe-injectors. We figured something serious was coming down if we had to have that many shots.

It didn't take long for word to filter down to us. Our entire company would be sent to Vietnam and the serums were to prevent various tropical diseases.

Quite a few soldiers had returned from Vietnam to finish out their military obligations, and I had spoken with as many of them as I could. Randy was one of those vets with whom I became friendly and I took what he said to heart. He made it clear that there were roughly three types of duty for a military policeman. One type of duty was quite dangerous according to him.

"Military policemen always have to be the first into and last out of a combat zone," Randy claimed. "MP's direct traffic and secure an area ahead of the other elements of the Army, and keep the rear safe after their departure. This is dangerous work," he told me, "and lots of MP's get killed or injured.

"Other MP's are the cops in a compound," he continued. "It's pretty safe work because it's in a secure area, but it's discouraging work because you have to arrest soldiers who are drunk and most of them have a really good reason to be drinking. They're just trying to forget the awful things they've experienced out in the field. They can be pretty mean and don't even think twice about busting an MP in the chops for ruining their fun, if you want to call it that. There's nothing they'd love better than to be arrested and put in the brig. Then they wouldn't have to go back into the field!"

"Now if I had a choice," Randy said, "I'd want to go to 'Nam as a dog handler. The Gooks fight at night. You may not see them in the dark but your dog will be able to smell them. Heck, I'd rather have a mean dog with a good nose than an M-16! Besides that, everybody is scared of a dog. The officers aren't going to hassle you because they don't want to be anywhere near an attack dog. You can forget about spit-polishing your boots and shining your belt buckle! Dog handlers always have a compound of their own because the officers don't want a loose dog attacking them or their people. Yes sir, if I had to go to 'Nam again, I'd want to be a dog handler," Randy concluded.

Smitty and I signed up for MP attack dog training that day.

Our next class was hand-to-hand combat, a derivation of judo. We were told that judo is the art of using someone else's weight against him. Since we were practicing with each other, we first had to learn how to fall. It surprised me to learn that combatants are usually hurt when they are thrown or fall to the ground. They taught us to always look at the ground and prepare to hit it by "loading" our arms and our legs. That meant that we should prepare to slap the ground with our hands and kick the ground with our legs. Both actions acted as shock absorbers and cushioned our falls.

We then took turns rolling each other from our hips, and the person we were throwing would slap and kick upon falling. It worked! It fact, a fall that might normally knock the wind from me did absolutely nothing; I could get back on my feet as though nothing had happened.

Once we learned how to fall, the next lesson was the most simple of all judo moves: countering someone who attacked you. The normal reaction is to fight back against the aggressor. But judo taught us to grab the person's shirt, put our arm around their waist while pulling on their shirt, and use their inertia to pull them over our hip. Once their weight was on our hip, we would shift our hips upward while continuing to pull on their shirt and throw them over our hips with the hand we had around their body. This hip throw worked slick as a whistle and I stood proudly with my aggressor on the ground.

The next judo lesson was the arm throw. This move was effective if the aggressor came at us with a fist or a knife. Other than running, the natural tendency again is to stand and fight. But with judo we were taught to grab the arm of the person, spin around while pulling on their arm, and use their inertia and weight to get them onto their backs. The completion of this move was to once again raise our hips while pulling down on the arm and throw the person to the ground.

That resulted in the aggressor being thrown to the ground from a considerably higher elevation and landing on his back. Those who hadn't learned how to fall properly paid a high price. Without a slap and a kick the entire force of the fall would be absorbed by their bodies when they landed flat on their backs. They usually had the wind knocked out of them and would consequently lie in pain for quite some time before recovering.

When it came my turn to be flipped, I had to remember to keep my eyes open during the throw so I could focus on the ground, and coordinate my hand and foot in order to slap and kick just before I hit. It worked like a charm!

Handling an aggressor who kicked was my favorite exercise. The objective was to grab the person's foot, move backwards to utilize the inertia of the attacker, twist the foot while the opponent is in mid air, and let him land flat on his face! Since the attacker was in a position in which his legs could be used, the only defense he had to cushion his fall was to slap the ground with both hands. Some fellows got some pretty nasty bruises and cuts during that exercise.

An extension of that maneuver is to step over the fellow's leg while he's in midair. That allowed me to lay on the attacker's foot with my leg in his knee joint. I could control the attacker by the amount of weight I placed on his foot since it caused a lot of pain. In fact, I could dislocate the knee joint by placing maximum weight upon him.

Judo utilizes a psychological tool as well. We were told to stand sideways with equal weight on each foot, hold the hands forward and up and yell HIIIIIIIEEEEEEEEEAAAAAA as loud as we could. This would scare the bejeezus out of our attacker and, possibly, they would turn around and run.

Art was a street fighter from Boston and couldn't wait to use his new skills as soon as he could. That weekend he went to the local bar, picked out the biggest man in the place, and took the stance he had been taught.

Standing sideways with equal weight on both feet with his hands forward and up, he yelled HIIIIIIIIIEEEEEEEEEEAAAAAAAAAAAA at the top of his lungs.

The barfly looked at him with a quizzical look and punched Art right in the nose! And that was the end of that.

Eventually we were given something fun to do in the Army: We began classes in Jeep driving. Military Police are used as chauffeurs for officers and use jeeps to lead and follow convoys. It was easy to see who had grown up on the farm and who had been raised in the city. Farm boys took to the Jeep likes ducks to water. City kids had an awful time.

After classes on the overhead projector to show us such things as the gear shift, ignition switch, clutch, and brakes, we went to the parking lot. One by one, we were told to start the Jeep, drive it forward 20 feet, stop, and then back up to the original starting spot and park. A sergeant rode along in the passenger seat to turn the Jeep off just in case the driver lost control. Farm kids finished this exercise in a few seconds. City kids had by and large learned to drive on automatic transmissions if they had learned to drive at all and, consequently, the Jeep with its manual transmission proved a real challenge. Many couldn't comprehend the idea that the clutch had to be fully depressed in order to shift the Jeep into gear. Gears would grind and the engine would race as the driver's face would redden in frustration as the sergeant would shake his finger and yell at the recruit.

"Grind me off a pound or two," we farm boys would yell in laughter.

A Jeep was great fun to drive. The steering was quick, the engine was responsive, and the open air cockpit made me feel like I was one with nature. Driving it was easy after all the different pickups Dad had owned over the years. Dad was frugal, having learned to hold on to his money by B.A. Halverson, his father. Dad never owned a new pick up until his later years when he had retired. Until then, he bought the cheapest junkers money could buy, as long as they ran. Once he ran an ad in the newspaper requesting the best pickup money could buy for $200. Someone responded the very day the paper came out and Dad bought a 1949 Chevy pickup for $200!

The previous owner's horse had taken a big chomp out of the driver's seat but we easily filled it in with an old towel. The master cylinder leaked so we had to pump the brakes a few times in order to stop. The taillights had long since disappeared. In those days tail lights weren't protected like they are now. They were mounted separately on the backside of the pickup's body and therefore were susceptible to damage. It had no turn signals. But then, without tail lights, that didn't matter. The tires were nearly bald but still held air. The windshield wipers didn't work.

It had a windshield that opened at the bottom with a little crank on the dashboard and that was our air conditioning. It had a four-speed transmission that included a "super-low" gear. It would pop out of second gear unless we held on to the shifter to keep it in place. The gear shift had a little lever that had to be pulled up in order to put the transmission into reverse. One fender held on precariously to the frame by two rivets. It never did fall off, though we worried that it would every time we drove it.

I remember our last ride in that pick up. We had just picked up a load of coal at the elevator. We had loaded at least a ton of coal on the little half-ton pickup and the weight bottomed out the springs. We felt every bump in the road as Dad slowly drove down the street.

We went south on Highway 71 and just before we got to the gravel road to our farm, Dad yelled, "Oh Shucks!"

I looked behind and there was a highway patrolman with his lights flashing. Dad rolled down the window and made a left hand turn signal with his arm and turned onto a gravel road. The patrolman also made the turn and pulled us over with his lights blinking.

I can still see him smiling as he looked at Dad and said, "Got quite a load there!"

"Yes," Dad said. "It's only a few miles to home and I thought it would be OK."

The officer remarked that there were no tail lights or brake lights. Dad was speechless as we all looked at the wires hanging from the side of the box where the lights should have been.

"Let's see how your brakes are Mr. Halverson. Would you get in and depress the brake pedal?"

Of course the brake went clear to the floor.

"There's not much tread left on your tires, Mr. Halverson."

Dad was silent but I recognized a look on his face. He was deep in thought.

"There aren't any windshield wipers, Mr. Halverson."

About this time I saw a light come on in Dad's face. "Look officer. If you write a ticket for everything that's wrong with this pick up, there won't be enough room on the page. What if I agree to dump this coal and immediately take the pickup down to Vince Haldine's junk yard and junk it!"

The officer began to laugh and said, "That sounds like a pretty good deal to me."

He followed us home and had coffee with Mom and Dad while I unloaded the coal. Then he followed us to Vince's junk yard and gave us a ride home after turning the vehicle over to Vince. Dad and the officer parted friends. Dad was good that way.

Advanced Individual Training with the MP's was quite a bit different than boot camp. We usually got the weekend off to carouse, sightsee, visit friends, or just plain lay around.

My bunk mate was Kim Himrod from Gainesville, Florida. He had played football at the university there and had been drafted by one of the new American Football League teams. However, he had received his draft notice upon graduation and his football career had been put on hold. He was a quarterback and wanted to stay in shape by throwing, so I volunteered to catch for him. My gosh, could he throw. Every pass was straight as a string with no arc whatsoever. And when I caught them, it was like catching a shot put going 80 miles per hour. But I caught them and when I did he threw them even harder.

Finally, he said, "Dad, I wish you had been on our team. You catch better than any end I had in college." That made me proud.

At any rate, we built a good friendship and it happened that a number of Kim's friends were coming up to visit that week end. Kim was way out of my league; he came from a rich family and I was a plain old farm boy. But he really appreciated my catching his passes and said, "Come on and join us. I'll have my girlfriend bring along a date for you." I told him that wouldn't be necessary and he said, "Oh, right. Ginny. Well, just come along and enjoy yourself."

Kim and I were dressed in our Class A uniforms. All his male friends were decked out in suits and ties. All his female friends were dressed in ballroom gowns with lots of cleavage showing and hair dos that must have cost a fortune and might have been insured. It was to be my first exposure to a real southern Belle!

I could tell that none of them had ever milked a cow or pitched manure. They were from a different culture than me, but they also showed that southern hospitality that I'd heard so much about and they went out of their way to make me feel welcome. Kim told them what a good receiver I was and all the guys became fast friends with me right away. They all wanted to know where I had played football and their faces dropped when I told them that I had just played catch back on the farm. All the girls glittered with that "Isn't that Sweet" smile as they held their long-stemmed glasses of wine.

The night went on and the girls were enjoying their share of wine while the boys opened the next keg of beer. There was some dancing going on. I just stood on the sidelines and watched the merriment. Kim's girl friend was a real beauty and gyrated to the fast music with wild abandon, and I mean *abandon*, since she had drained that long-stemmed glass of hers a number of times. She had a very low cut dress on and I noticed that one of her breasts popped out during one of her more violent moves.

Kim noticed it too and, being the gentleman and quick thinker he was, he raced over to the window and said, "Hey everybody! Come over here and get a load of this!"

He smiled as she tucked herself back into the dress while everyone else went to the window and looked out at whatever Kim had told them to see. His chest seemed to swell as he pondered the fact that he had successfully distracted everyone and saved her the embarrassment of being noticed.

Suddenly, Kim realized that everyone was giggling and looking at him. Walking over to the window, he looked out. And there to his surprise were two dogs, and I guess you know what they were doing!

In late April of 1969, we stood in formation and received our orders. Our Advanced Individual Training had ended and we were now to be sent to our duty sites. That was one of the few times that our formation was silent.

When it was over, 90 percent of us were going to Vietnam. The other 10 percent had signed up for three or more years in the Army. That was typical of the time. Many young men signed up for three or more years with the promise that they would avoid duty in Vietnam. Many joined the National Guard or Enlisted Reserves for the same reason. Everyone who had been drafted for two years was destined for Vietnam.

The sudden reality of going into combat was sinking into everyone's minds. Some knew that they'd be heading up a convoy. MPs must survey new areas, determine the best routes to take, and then serve as convoy escorts. Visions of snipers and road side bombs were dancing through their heads. Some hoped they'd get duty as a driver for a general, relatively safe duty because a general usually stayed behind the lines. Chances of becoming a driver were very slim because those who had a father or a relative in Washington got those assignments because of their relatives' influence. Some hoped for duty as an MP within a compound, also relatively safe duty.

Smitty and I both received orders to become guard dog handlers. Others coveted that assignment because they knew that a dog handler didn't have to worry about being ambushed by the enemy since a dog would detect an enemy a long ways away. Dog handlers guarded ammunition dumps, food yards, and helicopter pads. Since all of those sites were within a compound, they would be relatively safe.

Formation ended and we fell out of our ranks. Most of us went back to the barracks, lay down in our beds, and contemplated what was to come. Some cried. Others became rebellious, yelling, "FTA (F**k the

Army).” The majority just lay in their bunks with a blank stare on their faces.

I remember staring at the ceiling and thinking that I no longer had control of my own destiny. From the minute I had been drafted, my future was in the hands of someone I didn't even know and would never meet. Somewhere in the vast fields of the Army was a person who determined where I would go and what I would do. What did he look like? Where was he? How did he determine where I would go? Did he throw a dart? Did he shut his eyes and place his finger on a list? It was a hopeless feeling to no longer be able to make a decision regarding where I wanted to go or what I wanted to do. I remember thinking, *They want me to fight for freedom and I don't have any!*

The guys who cried were the most severely affected. One broke into the armory and tried to get a .45 pistol to shoot himself. Two others held hands, walked into the headquarters, and kissed. They were immediately discharged because gays weren't allowed in the military in those days. Others cried uncontrollably, were taken to the dispensary, and given sedatives. The rebellious ones went to the PX, bought beer, and drank themselves into oblivion. They were rowdy when they came back to the barracks, tipping over bunks, and urinating on anything that had “Army” written on it.

We were restricted to our company area and were told that there were armed guards posted to make sure no one went AWOL. I wanted to call Ginny but the phone banks were outside the company and we were not to leave under any circumstances.

“Hey, Dad!” Smitty announced. “Let's go call Ginny and Nan!”

“We can't,” I replied. “The phone banks are outside the company area. They've got guards posted to keep us confined.”

“Hah!” Smitty grinned. “That lazy bunch of bums are all on the sidewalks where it's easy to look good for the brass. But they aren't watching the ditch out back. The ditch ends right beside headquarters and they sure won't be guarding that! I did a test run last night and made it out and back slicker than snot on an icy door knob! Let's go!”

Smitty took off on a dead run and I blindly followed along. We entered the drainage ditch and hunched low as we ran along to its end. Smitty sprinted up the hill at the end of the ditch with me right behind him. Smitty bounded onto the sidewalk and slammed right into some poor soul that was just walking along minding his own business, knocking him flat on his behind. I arrived at the sidewalk and saw Smitty standing over a man sitting on the sidewalk. I looked at his uniform and noticed something that scared me half to death. The man was a Colonel! And the base commander was Colonel Thompson!

Smitty helped the Colonel to his feet and the Colonel dusted himself off. I expected the man to begin screaming at us, but as usual, Smitty got in the first word before the man could speak.

"Are you Colonel Thompson?" Smitty asked.

"Oh, brilliant, Smitty!" I thought to myself.

The man nodded to Smitty's statement and Smitty said, "I don't know how you keep your sanity. You've got hundreds of trainees ready to go to Viet Nam and all they want to do is get away! And you've got to keep track of all of them! I don't know how you do it!"

Colonel Thompson visibly melted before my eyes and began listing all the problems he had running the base while Smitty nodded his head in complete agreement with everything he said. The Colonel wanted to know where we were from and not only got that we were from Iowa but also a description of how good it was to milk Guernsey cows! He seemed rapt with attention as Smitty told him about that good ole' black soil back in Iowa.

Finally, Colonel Thompson apologized for having to end this delightful discussion because he had an important meeting to attend. He saluted Smitty with a big smile and said how wonderful it was to have two good, wholesome boys from Iowa as military policemen. Smitty gave him his typical farmer wave and we double timed our way out of there to the phone bank. I got to talk to Ginny and Smitty talked with his girlfriend, Nan.

We entered the ditch once more, hunched over as we ran back to our barracks without a hitch. "See Dad! Piece of cake!"

Finally it was May 8, 1969 and in two days Ginny and I would be married. I had nothing to do but get a good night's sleep so I would be ready for our trip the next day.

I had reserved a taxi to pick Smitty and I up the next morning and take us to Atlanta to catch our 3 p.m. flight to Des Moines, Iowa. The taxi would arrive at 10 a.m. for the trip to Atlanta, which would take about two and a half hours. That gave us plenty of extra time in case the taxi had a problem or we got disoriented at the airport I had concluded.

"Hey, Dad! Get up!" Smitty yelled as he shook me out of my sleep. "I've got us a ride to Atlanta with Sergeant O'bradovich! We can leave right now!"

I looked at my watch and it was 8 a.m. "Smitty. I've got a taxi coming at 10 for us. We can't just go and leave the poor guy hanging!"

Smitty twitched his shoulder and tipped his head in that familiar movement I had come to know so well. "Dad, there's a whole company leaving today. There'll be plenty of guys looking for a taxi. He won't have any problem getting another customer. Besides, O'bradovich has a new Plymouth Roadrunner! He'll have us there in no time and maybe we can catch an earlier flight."

That "earlier flight" comment got my attention. "OK," I said, "Let's go!"

O'bradovich was parked behind our barracks in his lime colored Roadrunner. As soon as we came out the door with our duffel bags over our shoulders, he raced the powerful engine and grinned at us like a Cheshire cat. This was going to be fun!

As soon as I had set down in my seat, O'bradovich hit the gas. I pulled the door shut as the tires squealed and the dual exhausts echoed the engine's power up and down the street. "300 horses under that hood," O'bradovich exclaimed. "Detroit don't make 'em any bigger!" We were doing over a hundred once we hit the main road and the two and a half hour trip was completed in two hours. Wow! We were in Atlanta way ahead of schedule.

We checked for earlier, military stand-by flights when we got to the airport. There happened to be one leaving at 11 in the morning and it had two seats left! The ticket agent balked at giving us the seats because the plane was already loaded and they were closing the doors.

"Hey," Smitty yelled as he did his shoulder and head thing. The agent was torn between his twitch and the birth mark on his face. "We're military policemen going back home to that good old black soil in Iowa.

89

I'm tired of looking at this yellow stuff you call soil here in Georgia. And besides, he's getting married tomorrow!"

The agent began to laugh and replied, "We wouldn't want to delay that, now would we!"

Somehow, Smitty seemed to know just the right thing to say to whoever stood in his way. The agent called the captain off the plane and informed him that he would have to wait for two more customers.

We entered the plane and I found a seat near the front. Smitty ambled to the back of the plane where the other vacant seat was located.

As we rolled down the runway on takeoff, I heard from the back of the plane, "Hey Dad!"

Turning around I said, "Yah Smitty, what is it?"

He yelled so I could hear him. "Hey, we'll be milking cows tonight, Dad!"

The people sitting around me smiled.

We became airborne and once again I heard," Hey Dad!"

"Yah, Smitty, what is it?"

"By gosh, we'll be looking at good old black soil tonight; none of that slippery yellow clay!"

The people around me began to laugh and shake their heads in wonderment. Smitty entertained the entire planeload all the way to Chicago with his farm related comments.

As we began our descent into O'Hare, thunderstorms were in the area. The air became turbulent, the plane bucked and rolled, and everyone had the look of fear on their faces. There was a loud BANG and the captain immediately announced over the intercom that we were experiencing bad weather but everything would be OK.

"Bullshit!" yelled Smitty. "There's smoke coming out of that engine!"

Two stewardesses raced to Smitty and told him to be quiet. The co-captain came racing back to control him as well, but the damage was done. Everyone on the plane screamed bloody murder about being on fire. The captain came back on the intercom and announced that he had requested an emergency landing and that we should remain calm. Smitty had one stewardess in his lap, another at his side and a co-pilot staring him down to keep him quiet.

We landed in Chicago four hours earlier than our previously scheduled flight. Smitty went to check on an earlier flight to Des Moines, while I called Ginny.

Before I knew it, Smitty grabbed the phone from my hand and told Ginny to head to Des Moines right away. He grabbed my hand and said, "Come on Dad! We're headed to Iowa!"

We jumped a gate and ran down the loading ramp where the captain stood, looking from the plane's door with a puzzled look on his face. I learned later that, despite the ticket agent's objections, Smitty had jumped the gate, ran down to the plane whose door had already been locked, and knocked on the door.

The captain had shut the engines down, opened the door, and Smitty said, "Wait right here. We'll be right back!"

Once again, there were two seats left, one in the front and one in the back. I took the front one and Smitty went to the back. I looked around and saw men in tuxedos and women in evening gowns with lots of diamonds adorning their necks, fingers, and hair dos.

As soon as the plane began down the runway I heard, "Hey Dad!"

I thought to myself, *Just act like you don't hear him.*

However, Smitty just yelled louder.

A lady behind me tapped me on the shoulder and in a stuffy voice said, "I think your friend wants you."

I turned and said, "Yah Smitty, what now?"

"By golly, we'll be milking cows tonight, Dad."

No one laughed as they did on the last plane. These people looked at me as though I had walked on the plane with cow manure on my shoes.

The man beside me introduced himself and in the course of conversation I asked him, "Who are these people?"

He replied that it was the Iowa State Alumni Association's top 100 givers. They had attended a large fundraising event in Chicago.

I thought, *Oh, brother! People like this and Smitty's talking about milking cows.*

The man inquired about Smitty and wondered if he was from Panora.

Surprised, I said, "Yes, he is."

The man asked if I would introduce him to Smitty when we landed.

I was astounded and asked him why.

"Well" he said, "Smitty has a full ride scholarship to Iowa State to play in the sport of his choice. We'd sure like him to come to ISU when he gets out of the Army."

Smitty had the best guardian angel I've ever heard of. It seemed as though he led a charmed life. When we landed, I introduced them and left them to their conversation because I was only interested in one thing: seeing Ginny.

I had twenty two days to get married and go on a honeymoon. Then I would fly to Okinawa for dog training school.

Because we had gotten an earlier flight, we got to Des Moines sooner than Ginny. My sister Faith and her future husband, Gabriel Blaskovich, were driving Ginny to Des Moines and would then take us all home to northwest Iowa. It seems Gabe was washing his car so it would be nice and shiny to bring me home and since that was in the days before cell phones, no one could reach him to give him the change of plans. So, I sat down in one of the chairs and picked up someone's used Des Moines Register and commenced to read. Suddenly, my newspaper exploded! And the explosion had happened because Ginny had arrived and flew into my lap unannounced. I hadn't even seen her coming, but I was sure glad to see her!

Since our graduation from AIT had taken place on Thursday, and we spent the day Friday traveling it was evening before we made it to Des Moines. Our wedding rehearsal was scheduled for Saturday morning and the wedding would be that afternoon. We were squeezing the rehearsal and wedding together so we could spend as much time together as possible.

That morning the skies were sunny, then it began to rain, then it sleeted, and finally we had snow showers. The weather exhibited the same peaks and valleys that my emotions were experiencing. As I strode up to the church for rehearsal, I looked at the announcement sign in the front of the church. There in big, bold letters was "Congratulations Bendix and Virginia"! My mother had decided that all her children would go by their middle names. My whole name is Bendix Lee Halverson. My first name was in honor of my father, Bendix. I went by Lee and didn't really care for the name Bendix.

At the rehearsal, I made it clear to Reverend Campney that the sign **would** be changed for the wedding.

Only the critical people were there for the rehearsal: Ginny and I, her father and mother, Ginny's sister Jayne who was the bridesmaid along with my sister Karen, Smitty and Bill Patten, my best man. Reverend Campney gave us an overview of how the wedding would go and then said, "We'll dispatch with most of the ceremony here at rehearsal and just go through the vows. Everything went slick as a whistle until it came to the reverend's question, "Who gives this woman to be married to this man?" Her father Emery said, "Her father and I!" Everyone had a good laugh and the rehearsal was over. Ginny and her family went directly home to prepare for the wedding that afternoon.

Smitty and I had went to my home and had lunch with my family, then headed for the church. We got to the church with some time to burn, so we decided to drive to the Cook house (home of my future in-laws) and see how everything was going. We drove north out of Gilmore City, where the church was located, and found that the bridge was out near Bradgate. We took an alternate route on a gravel road and got lost. Finally, we realized that we had run out of time so we turned around and headed back to the church.

When we finally got there, the parking lot and the church were full. I quickly checked the welcome sign in front of the church and it said, "Congratulations Lee and Ginny." Thank goodness!

I met Ginny's grandfather outside the church in my jeans and shirt, and he said, "Hey! Aren't you getting married today?"

I looked around and said "Maybe I should get dressed!"

And I thought, *Jeez, here I am, late for my own wedding.*

Bill Patten, my best man, had been waiting for us and exclaimed, "Where have you been? Ginny is worried sick!"

The preacher gave a great sigh of relief and passed along the word that the wedding would take place after all.

Smitty and I sneaked in a side door to go into our room to change. When I took off my jeans, I was wearing my army issue boxers that had been designed by a parachute maker. Patten had a great laugh about my shorts.

The time came for us to move to the front of the church and I couldn't believe how many people were in attendance: my relatives, Ginny's relatives, and a host of our friends from college! I couldn't believe they had all found time in their schedules to be there.

Ginny appeared on the arm of her father. She looked gorgeous and I wondered to myself how a girl this pretty could be marrying a hayseed like me.

We were all afraid that, when the preacher said, "Who gives this woman to be married to this man?" my soon-to-be father-in-law Emery would say, "Her father and I," rather than "Her mother and I," just like he had done at rehearsal. But he did his part just fine and the only screw-up was mine when I said, "With this wing I thee wed!"

Ginny changed from her wedding dress as I waited. Eventually, she appeared in a yellow dress trimmed in white. It perfectly accented her flowing dark hair. She saw me and gave that smile that I had fallen in love with the first night I saw her when the elevator doors had opened and I thought, "She should be in Hollywood!" We had cake and mixed with our friends and family. At least I thought they were my friends, until we left the church and I looked at my car!

I had forgotten that I had built quite a reputation for decorating wedding couples' cars at previous weddings. They had all come for payback and, boy, did I get it. We tried to get in the car but couldn't because the inside door handles were tied together with fishing line. The entire inside of the car looked like a giant spider had spun its web in there. I found a small crack in the window and borrowed a knife to cut some of the fishing line so we could get the doors open.

Once we were in, the smell was insufferable! Limburger cheese had been spread everywhere, and Vicks VapoRub covered the steering wheel and all the door handles.

I started the engine and heard a loud bang, accompanied by smoke and sparks. The car bomb with its distinct sulfur odor added to the Limburger smell. I put the car in gear and, when I stepped on the accelerator, the engine raced but the car didn't go anywhere. My "friends" had put the differential up on blocks so the wheels were slightly off the ground. The crowd laughed in unison, and then a group lifted the car from the blocks so we could be on our way.

I looked through the shoe polish on the windshield and over the corn flakes and honey on the hood. When I tried to go forward again, we heard an awful racket. A rope with bowling pins and paint cans had been hidden beneath the car and trailed along about 30 feet behind us.

I hit the brakes and the horn blew! The horn sounded every time I hit the brakes for the next few days. The car stunk like Limburger cheese for weeks. One day while checking the oil I noticed a jar of it hidden on the manifold behind the carburetor.

We drove back to her parent's home to open presents. Emery looked at my car and said, "You'd better take my car. You can't go down the road in that!"

Our honeymoon was a short one because Ginny had one more class to finish at ISU. She had rented an apartment at the Motel 69 in Ames, Iowa. We spent two blissful weeks together doing the things that newlyweds do, going to her classes together, eating her wonderful cooking together and going on walks. It all ended too quickly.

Ginny, Mom and Dad, my brother Boyd, Emery and Cleo, and Ginny's sister Jayne escorted me to the Des Moines airport the morning of my departure for Viet Nam to say goodbye. I remember that everyone was very quiet. We were all on the verge of tears and knew that if we said anything at all the dam would break loose. So we all put on our bravest smiles and tried to act as though my going was a normal, everyday occurrence.

Smitty and his family arrived at about the same time and they were all bawling like babies. That gave my family a reprieve because they finally had a reason to focus on something other than my departure. Mom and Cleo gave support to Smitty's mother, while Emery and Dad talked with Smitty's father.

Smitty's mother and dad came over to me. "He calls you Dad," they said. "He's just a boy. Take care of him for us, will you?' I nodded in the affirmative.

I remember standing tall in front of Dad and shaking his hand to say goodbye. Men don't cry. I hugged Mom goodbye and found it difficult to hold back my tears while she sobbed that her son was leaving. I had the same problem when saying goodbye to my siblings and in-laws. Then came Ginny. There's nothing quite as painful as two young lovers being pulled apart by the events of the world.

She held my arm as she walked beside me to the airplane. And then over the sound system came an all too familiar song:

There's so many times I've let you down
So many times I've played around
I tell you now, they don't mean a thing.
Every place I go, I think of you
Every song I sing I sing for you
When I come back, I'll wear your wedding ring

So kiss me and smile for me
Tell me that you'll wait for me
Hold me like you'll never let me go
I'm leavin' on a jet plane
I don't know when I'll be back again
Oh babe, I hate to go.

It was indeed time to go. We were headed for Viet Nam and a year that would leave us no longer the boys we were but men who had done and seen far too much.

CHAPTER 4
OKINAWA

Smitty called me "Dad," but it wasn't just a nickname either. Smitty treated me like I really was his Dad. He was like a little boy with his father. Wherever I went, Smitty was at my side and he would absolutely fall apart if we were separated.

We arrived at a huge terminal at Oakland Air Force Base and there were hundreds of soldiers lying on their duffel bags waiting for the announcement that they would be next to fly to Nam. The sound system announced that the 981st MPs should line up for boarding. That was us! We lined up and a sergeant began counting us to fill the first plane. He ended his count with me. Smitty was next and that meant that we would be split up and Smitty would be on the next plane. Smitty's face was horror struck! He tried to change places with other soldiers so he could fly with me, but the sergeant stopped him.

"Dad, what am I going to do?" Smitty asked.

I assured him that he would be fine and that I would be waiting for him in Okinawa.

The sergeant led our group out of the terminal to another building where we would board our plane. Armed guards were posted at every door of each building. Many soldiers tried to go AWOL because they didn't want to go to Vietnam—the armed guards were there to make sure that no one ran away. No one entered or left a building unless they were led by the sergeant. Anyone leaving a building without an escort had to deal with the armed guards.

The new building we were led to had a soldier manning a machine making new dog tags for any soldier who had lost his. Dog tags were used to identify the body of soldiers killed in war. Each soldier is issued two tags, one to be attached to the body's big toe and the other to be sent to the next of kin. We thought it would be fun to send dog tags to our wives.

We asked the guy, offered to pay the guy, pleaded with the guy; but to no avail.

"Army regs," he told us. "Dog tags are only for soldiers."

"Hey Dad! What's going on?"

I turned around and there was Smitty. How he had gotten by the armed guards I had no idea. I explained that we were trying to get this guy to make dog tags for Ginny.

Without any hesitation, Smitty went over to the guy and said, "Hey, how long has it been since you had a coffee break?"

Mr. Dog Tags said, "Man, they never give me a break. I've been here for eight hours."

Smitty gave the guy a buck and said, "Take a break. I'll run this for you."

Mr. Dog Tags was ever so thankful and took off. Smitty made dog tags for everyone.

"Group 1, 981st MPs, ready to board" came an announcement over the loud speakers.

I realized that Smitty was in trouble. He'd be the only one left after we boarded and he'd be sent to the stockade for sure.

Smitty calmly grabbed a broom, threw it over his shoulder, and walked directly up to one of the armed guards and announced, "Well, guess I've got this place all cleaned up. Gotta go over there and take care of that building now."

And with the broom over his shoulder Smitty walked off like he owned the place.

After the plane took off, I leaned back in my seat and took stock of my situation: I'm going to war in Vietnam and I'm doing my duty for my country, even though I don't believe in the war and could not for the life of me see how whatever happened there would have any effect on life in America. But I had been raised by a WWII veteran and had grown up in the company of other such veterans. Like a lot of young men my age, I had been taught to be a patriot and do my duty for my country. So that was that.

I now understood how it felt to leave family and loved ones behind. I think that's the biggest sacrifice one can make. Folks talk a lot about the supreme sacrifice: giving your life for your country. In most cases, dying is an instantaneous thing and one wouldn't even be aware when it happens, but leaving loved ones is a very conscious thing to do and the feeling doesn't go away.

The Army took us to Okinawa for dog training school. Only there weren't any dogs there yet, since they hadn't been flown in from Vietnam. Still, we had to hurry up and wait. It reminded me of the trip I had just taken. We had to be at Oakland Air Force Base to leave for Okinawa on a designated date. But first we spent two days hurrying and waiting while they checked our medical records, financial records, orders, and gave us medical check-ups. The latter were primarily short-arm inspections since we had all been on leave—the Army wanted to make sure we had no sexually transmitted diseases.

Next, we went to the overseas replacement building where we hurried up and waited some more. That was the Army's answer to the endless question of how to keep busy all the time and accomplish absolutely nothing.

Finally, we were transported to Travis Air Force Base where we boarded a huge plane and flew to Hawaii. On that flight I met my "Lil' Brother," Dale Bladorn. Dale was from Janesville, Wisconsin, and shared the same values that I had. We played cards (slapjack) during the flight and others came to play, resulting in more new friends, all of whom I gave nicknames. For example, "Skip" was a big, blue-eyed Mormon from Utah and "Kawk" was an all-state football player from Ohio.

We stopped in Hawaii to refuel and had a few hours to kill, so Dale and I went to a restaurant where we enjoyed some fresh pineapple. Most of the other guys went to a bar for liquid reinforcements.

We boarded our next flight and left for Wake Island to again refuel. When I got off the plane there, the air was so hot and humid I could barely breathe. It didn't bother me at all that we didn't spend much time there.

The flight from Wake to Okinawa was long, so we mostly slept because there was nothing to see but clouds and ocean.

The plane finally began to descend and we all watched out the windows to see where we were landing. And there was Okinawa, a large, rocky island surrounded by turquoise water. It seemed to rise straight up out of the water with rocky bluffs all the way around it. Most of the cliffs were at least 200 feet high, except one area that had a beach along the ocean.

I remember thinking, *That must be where our soldiers landed in WWII, one small beach surrounded by cliffs. They must have been sitting ducks for the Japanese soldiers, who were probably up on the cliffs.* Then I looked closer at the cliffs. Tiny little caves dotted them from top to bottom. There were so many caves that the cliff looked like a giant honeycomb. Imagine landing on that beach with all those caves filled with Japanese soldiers shooting at you?

We landed and were immediately picked up in a deuce and a half truck and taken to our compound. We arrived early in the morning and our cadre immediately gave us work to do. They had us clean about 20 dog crates and 20 dog chains. We also had a pile of concrete blocks that we had to stack neatly. We all dove into our work and were done around 11 o'clock.

The cadre was shocked. "That job usually takes all day," one of them remarked, "but this class was hand-picked. All we wanted were farm boys and I can see why. You farm boys know how to work!"

Most of the dogs we'd be getting were already battle tested. Their present handlers were going back home to The World, and the dogs they had been handling would be coming to Okinawa to receive new handlers. Other dogs, donated to the Army by civilians, would be arriving from the States. These dogs were "green" and would require a lot of attention in their training. There were a few dogs in the kennel area, mostly washouts from previous training cycles. They'd get a new handler and another chance to become acceptable guard dogs. In the event they couldn't be properly trained, they would be put to sleep.

One of the sergeants told me, "That's the reason we checked personnel files to select farm boys. We figured our chances of getting these washouts trained would be better with you since you guys have worked with animals before. The city boys just can't get the job done and we'd end up putting down a lot of good dogs."

Since we had finished our work, they gave us the rest of the day off. We played football for the rest of the morning. Then we piled into the deuce and a half for the ride to our Mess Hall, about two miles away. Okinawa is a poor country, so Okinawans ran the Mess Hall because they worked cheap. The meal was wonderful. We had our choice of meats, vegetables, salads, potatoes, milk, Kool-Aid, iced tea, coffee, bread, and desert. They waited on us hand and foot. And the best part of it: no KP!

We also had a hooch servant we called "Charlie." He cleaned the barracks, made the beds, shined our shoes, and took care of the yard. He did all of this for tips. We were happy and so was he; we were good tippers.

That afternoon it began to rain and soon got more intense. Then it got so heavy that I couldn't see the dog kennels just a few yards away from our back door. It was somewhere between heavy rain and a river just falling on us. We all stood in the doorway awestruck.

"Monsoon," said Charlie. "Not bad here, bad in Vietnam."

That wasn't very encouraging.

While we were in Basic and Advanced Individual Training, the drill instructors did their best to take away our individuality and force us to become a unit. That's why everyone got haircuts immediately. Any incoming soldier who drew his identity from his hair style lost that identity when he got his first whitewall haircut. Some individuals claimed their identities through their clothing, so civilian clothing could no longer be worn. We all wore the Army olive drab uniform in boot camp—same pants, same shirts, same hats, same everything.

The only thing a person had left to separate himself from others was his personality, but the cadre (noncommissioned officers) took care of that, too. Hot tempers resulted in push-ups. Disobedience resulted in digging a hole and then filling it up again. Minor infractions resulted in KP. A poor shave resulted in a dry shave by the drill sergeant, who always had a disposable razor in his pocket and delighted in hacking away a troop's stubble, leaving plenty of bleeding cuts to display his art work.

Wrinkled clothing or missing buttons were not acceptable. The offending troop had to do 50 pushups and then go change clothes immediately. We ate what they put before us and were given a limited amount of time in which to eat it. We did everything in rank; we all barked "yes sir" in unison. We got up at the same time, ate the same things together, did all of our training side by side, and went to bed at the same time.

In short we were no longer individuals, but were a part of a platoon, company, or battalion. We became brainwashed to that culture and most of us expected that life in the Army would be that way forever.

So we had a pleasant surprise when we arrived in Okinawa and found that our cadre treated us like equals. According to them, we had paid our dues and were now respected dog handlers. We would be taught the fine art of dog handling. We would not go through degrading activities anymore. We could wear civilian clothing as long as we were not on duty. We would no longer have KP. We could let our hair grow and even have a mustache as long, as both were reasonable in presentation and were well trimmed.

Most of our cadre had been to Vietnam and all of them were lifers. We considered anyone who had enlisted voluntarily to be a lifer. Thus, no one in our cadre had been drafted, since a draftee would have had only a two-year enlistment, served his time in Vietnam, and then gone home. A lifer would have more time left to serve following his tour in Vietnam and, therefore, would be assigned to another duty station, like Okinawa. I'm sure the slant on conversation by our instructors would have been different had they been draftees rather than lifers, yet these guys treated us like regular human beings and that was so refreshing.

I happily listened to their propaganda.

They told us what we could expect in Vietnam and slanted it toward the Army's way of doing things. They told us that training in Okinawa would be sentry dog training. Sentry or guard dogs could smell an enemy trying to enter an area. We were to contact the infantry if the dog detected an enemy outside the perimeter, but if the intruder came inside the perimeter the dog would attack.

Later, the cadre told us, we might be training scout dogs to lead an infantry unit on patrol and provide early detection of the enemy. Also, they said we might be training dogs to detect drugs. For the latter, the handler would take the dogs through barracks to find drugs a soldier might have for personal use, or the dog might be taken into the Post Office to find drugs a soldier might be trying to send home.

"One thing's for sure," Sergeant Adams said. "Your dog is the best weapon you could possibly have in Vietnam. The jungle is thick and the Gooks fight at night, so you can't see them. You might miss a Gook with a rifle, but your dog will never miss. So, if you have to choose between your rifle or your dog, pick your dog every time."

Our squad leader, Karl, had just come back from Vietnam. We had just completed Basic Training and the drill instructors there had called us yo-yos when we botched an assignment. Karl would occasionally call me a yo-yo and it had a negative connotation with me because of how it was used in Basic. For that reason it grated on my nerves each time he called me by that name.

Life in Sioux Rapids had taught me to turn the other cheek or pay no attention. Life in the Army had taught me to fight back. So one day I doubled up my fists and confronted him. "Don't ever call me a yo-yo again," I said.

Why not?" Karl replied.

"Because that's what they called a screw-up in Basic and I'm not a screw-up."

Karl laughed and said "Hey! It's a compliment! I don't know anything about your Basic Training, but I call all my friends yo-yo. If I call you a yo-yo, it's because I like you."

I learned a good lesson there: It's good to talk before you take a swing at someone.

Our superiors treated us as peers, not as recruits. While we were not allowed any personal time when we were in Basic or AIT, on Okinawa we were left alone to do such things as write letters, read, play cards, and carry on conversations while we waited for the dogs to arrive.

Many of us just lay in our bunks thinking of home. I contemplated the fact that until recently I never had been farther than Des Moines, Iowa, about 150 miles from home. In the past few months I had gone to Fort Polk, Louisiana, for Basic Training and then Fort Gordon, Georgia, for AIT. And in the last few days I had flown to Oakland, seen Hawaii, Wake Island, and now Okinawa. I was halfway around the world from little Sioux Rapids, Iowa, and in another few weeks I'd be in a combat zone.

Life in the Army was so different from growing up. I never lacked something to do on the farm. When I finished one task, there'd always be another one waiting. Additionally, I didn't need someone to tell me that the shop needed to be cleaned up or that the tree damaged in the last storm needed to be trimmed. I made those decisions myself.

But nothing gets done in the Army unless a superior orders it done, and when that order is given everyone must be involved. Thus, individuality was lost and there were a lot of unproductive people with 20 men mostly standing around doing a two-man job.

Without dogs to train, the cadre had us doing make-work jobs to keep us occupied. My group of farm boys used plenty of elbow grease and we usually finished in a few hours a job that would take all day for other soldiers. Thus, we had a lot of time off in the afternoons. We usually spent that time by playing football or poker, reading books, writing letters, day dreaming, or just visiting.

Our barracks conversations usually centered on wives and girl friends. Hawk told us about his time on leave. He had come home to find his girl friend had shacked up with another guy while he was in Basic and AIT. That hurt him badly, but he didn't waste any time finding out from Charlie where the prostitutes were.

That was typical of most GIs. The barracks would be pretty empty on the weekends when we had time off. The guys were in town buying the girls their Saigon Tea and getting laid. Saigon Tea was just that: tea. The guys had to buy the girls drinks to get acquainted. The girls couldn't drink alcoholic beverages because they would get drunk and not be able to perform. Saigon Tea resolved that issue for both parties involved.

My family usually wrote once a week and I got a letter from Ginny almost every day. Ginny would often send cookies or brownies, and I'd share those with the rest of the guys, along with the latest news.

Edgar, one of the guys in my platoon, pulled me aside one day.

"What is it that you and Ginny have that we don't have?" he asked. "You never seem to worry about Ginny being out with another guy while you're gone. I worry constantly about my wife. She doesn't write many letters and never sends cookies the way Ginny does. I'm always worried that she's out having a good time with another guy and I can't seem to get that out of my mind."

I told him that the thought of Ginny being unfaithful just hadn't entered my mind. I told him that we both had faith and had centered our married life on God.

"One of the rituals we have when we're together is to hold hands during the Lord's Prayer," I told him. "So I go to chapel every Sunday and when we say the Lord's Prayer I just imagine in my mind that Ginny is sitting there, too, holding my hand. She's back home doing the same thing. So we're both looking up to God at the same time and that keeps us centered on the same thing."

I invited Edgar to come to chapel with me the next Sunday. He had never been to church before, but decided to come along. The timing couldn't have been more perfect.

The chaplain gave a sermon on how to make a happier marriage, suggesting the following:

(1) Show genuine concern for each other's problems and needs.

(2) Express appreciation for what your mate has done for you. It's not enough to have appreciation, you must express it.

(3) Be polite to your wife. Open doors for her, show good manners, and help her put her coat on.

(4) Be honest. Trust will never develop without honesty.

(5) Be tolerant. Neither you nor your mate is perfect. Learn to tolerate the imperfections in your mate.

(6) Exhibit mutual growth in your marriage. Rigidity, stagnation, and absence of change are the signs of death in a marriage. You must do new things together, go new places together, and learn new things together.

Edgar was a changed man after that clairvoyant sermon. I have always believed that God works in our lives if we let him.

A day or so later, we had morning mail call and, as often happened, I was the only one to receive anything. I'll never get over the dejected looks on other guy's faces when they didn't get a letter. It's a small thing to send a letter but it's a really big thing to receive one, especially when someone is a long way from home.

Nonetheless, the other guys knew that I got a letter almost every day and they seemed to enjoy my letters as much as I did. They were always anxious to hear the latest news from home: What's your Dad planting now? Has Ginny gotten a teaching job yet? When's she going to send more cookies? What has Emery been up to lately?

That day was different. I received a box rather than a letter and everyone gathered around, probably anticipating some of Ginny's chocolate chip cookies. However, when I opened the box we were all surprised at the contents. Neatly folded inside the box was a pair of orange boxer shorts with little yellow daisies printed on them!

"What the heck?" Smitty exclaimed. "That's the damndest pair of Cong Catchers I've ever seen!"

Everyone howled with laughter and the name "Cong Catcher" was born.

Then everyone listened eagerly as I read the accompanying letter:

Dear Lee,

I know that your groomsmen made fun of you at our wedding because of your Army-green boxer shorts. So I decided to make you a pair so no one would make fun of you anymore! I'll be making a pair every month for you and when you've got twelve pair, you'll be coming home.

Love, Ginny

"Hey Dad, make sure you show us your Cong Catchers next month!"

I was faithful to my wife. My friends knew that and, therefore, knew that I would be faithful to them. That's why they called me "Dad." If a man will cheat on his wife, would you expect him to be honest with you?

Ernie, another member of my platoon, came up afterward and said, "You're a lucky guy, Lee. I wish I had a girl like that at home."

I couldn't argue.

As I mentioned, we played a lot of football in our spare time. The monsoon presented a problem initially, but we soon adjusted and just went out in our shorts and played. We would be a muddy mess when we were done but that was no problem either. We just took a bar of soap out into the rain and showered there since there was more water in the monsoon than there was in the shower!

Getting tackled could be a problem because of all the snails in the grass. They had spiral-shaped shells with a point on top that could be up to five inches long. It hurt to land on them. There were smaller snails, about the size of a quarter, and they preferred to live on the buildings. When it was damp, the outside of the buildings would be covered with them.

Three-inch-long cockroaches were plentiful and everywhere. Boy, were they fast!

Bamboo spiders with a body the diameter of an orange liked to enter the barracks in the evenings to be where it was warm. Counting their legs, those spiders were the size of dinner plates and they, too, were very fast. I have trouble enough moving with two legs—I don't know how they could move so fast with eight!

Finally, the dogs would be arriving from Vietnam in a day or so. The only dogs already on the compound were mostly dogs that had washed out in previous classes. I had spent time visiting those dogs, wondering if I would like to save a washout or would I prefer to get an experienced dog arriving from Vietnam.

Shep had washed out six times and if he washed out again he would be put down. He was a large German shepherd weighing 90 to 100 pounds. He was friendly and that was his problem. He had been donated to the Army by a patriotic family back in the States. Thus, he had been taught to be friendly and had been punished when he got aggressive, just like any family dog. He had to be untrained from that friendly disposition and retrained to be mean. So far no one had been able to accomplish that, which made accepting Shep a real challenge for me.

I also liked a dog named Champ, absolutely the meanest dog I had ever seen in my life. When I'd go to his kennel to visit he would leap into the air, growling and snapping at me. The kennels were made of chain link fencing and he would try to bite me through the chain link, often bloodying his mouth in the process.

Champ probably didn't weigh more than 60 pounds, but his ferocious attitude made up for his lack of size. He had failed the school because he always attacked his trainer. His last handler had ended up in the hospital. Champ had turned on him during training exercises and had bitten him so badly that it took over 150 stitches to fix him up. A dog doesn't just bite, it also tears. Champ had bitten the guy in the calf and had pulled the muscle loose from his Achilles tendon. The poor handler required reconstructive surgery as well as sutures.

I told the cadre about my interest in those two dogs. Shep would be a real challenge and I would feel good to successfully train that dog when others had failed. I'm a bleeding heart to begin with and the thought of him getting put to sleep bothered me. Being realistic, I figured that if Shep couldn't be trained, I couldn't go wrong with Champ because he was naturally so aggressive. It might take a little time to make friends with him, but I believed I could do it.

The cadre listened politely to my request, but then advised, "We'll be assigning dogs to you."

I had nothing to do until the dogs arrived from Vietnam, when everyone would be assigned a dog and training would begin. All the guys were anxious for the dogs to come and were getting so antsy about it that they had lost interest in football and poker.

Thank goodness for mail call. I can't tell you how wonderful it was to get a letter from home. I got a letter from Mom, full of news that made me homesick. Here's part of it:

Dad is planting sweet corn down at the Brown farm today, the peas are getting ready to bloom, and the field corn [as opposed to sweet corn] *is peeking through the ground. Boyd is attending confirmation classes. He and Brian rode the bicycle built for two into class yesterday. Karen got a call from a boyfriend while she was making fudge—the fudge is a little on the hard side because she let it boil too long, but I guess we can forgive her for that.*

Gabe came up to visit Faith and stayed late into the night before he left as he had to be at work at seven the next morning. I'm so glad we went down to the airport to see you off. Ginny was a brave girl and so were you. We're proud of you both. God grant you a safe tour of duty and a happy homecoming.

Her letter felt like a warm blanket on a cold night.

A C-130 arrived at Kadena Airport. The plane held dogs, all housed in aluminum crates. The crates were about six feet long, three feet wide, and three feet high with plenty of holes in the aluminum to give them air. The barking was deafening, every dog was snarling and growling as if a prowler was at the front door.

We loaded the crates onto a deuce and a half for the trip to the kennels.

Once we were back at the compound, we carried each crate to a kennel, positioned it in such a way that the crate door could be opened, and the dog could move safely into the kennel through the open kennel gate. We were all warned that these dogs were dangerous and we should be careful to make sure they had no opportunity to go anywhere but into the kennel from the crate.

I raised the kennel gate and shoved the crate up to the kennel, thinking I could lean over the crate, open the door of the crate, and let the dog into the kennel. Then I could pull the crate back slightly, just far enough that I could close the kennel gate. It worked like a charm. As I closed the kennel gate the dog immediately sprang at me to attack, but the gate was shut and all he hit was cyclone fencing.

Once I had finished, I watched the other guys release their dogs.

Another guy in my platoon, Keith, had his crate too far away from the kennel leaving too much room between the crate and the kennel. There was enough room for the dog to get through the gap and that's just what happened. The dog attacked. Keith held his hands up to protect himself. The dog bit one hand and whipped his head back and forth, tearing the tissues of Keith's hand, until the cadre arrived and pulled the dog from him. Keith ended up in the hospital with 50 stitches.

I became a believer in the value of an attack dog, also called a sentry dog.

Finally, all the dogs had been moved into the kennels and the sound they made was incredible. All the dogs were mad and ready to attack. I don't mind saying I was scared to death. Those dogs indeed were mean and vicious, a force with which to contend.

Once everything settled down, the cadre told us that we were going to train the dogs. Our objective, we were told, was to make the dogs hate everyone but their handler. We were to do everything we could to make our dog mad at everyone else, and to make dogs belonging to other handlers hate us.

"Go to other kennels and shake the fence," we were told. "Yell at them and do anything you can to aggravate the hell out of them. Make them hate you!"

Smitty's eyes lit up like a Christmas tree. From that day on Smitty took pleasure in making every dog in the kennel area hate him to the core. He took a stick with him to every single kennel and whacked it against the kennel fence. He would snarl and growl at every dog. It wasn't long before every dog had a personal relationship with Smitty and simply hated his guts.

I've always had trouble getting out of bed in the morning; the covers feel so warm and the world outside so cold. The rare exception would be on a fishing trip with Ellis Brooks. On those occasions I would bounce out of bed at five a.m., ready to catch the biggest catfish in the Blue River up in Minnesota.

And that's the way agitating the dogs affected Smitty. He would bounce out of bed like a kid on a fishing trip, go to the door at the back of the barracks, and yell, "BAROOOOOO" at the top of his lungs.

Fifty dogs would go wild immediately. It wasn't long before the dogs got irate at just the sound of the back door opening, long before Smitty could yell his signature howl. Once he'd aggravated the dogs, Smitty would turn around with a satisfied smile on his face. He had found his niche in the United States Army.

Sergeant Yates, a member of the training cadre, announced, "OK. Listen up! Today is the first day of dog training. You'll be assigned a sentry dog and some of you will be assigned a backup dog as well. The objective of your training is to make your dog love and protect you, while hating and attacking anyone else. That's why we've asked you to agitate the dogs. Thanks to Private Smith, the dogs have learned to hate absolutely everyone!

"Your first assignment," Yates continued, "will be to make friends with your dog. You will feed him, water him, and talk to him. Under no conditions will you enter the kennel. These dogs have been taught to hate everyone but their handler, but they don't know that you are their new handler. They will attack you. I repeat: They *will* attack you. So take your time and let your dog get to know you. Now line up and you'll be assigned your dogs."

Grinning with pride that he had been recognized as the champion agitator of the group, Smitty joined me and we lined up for our assignments. Smitty got assigned Bullet, a seasoned dog that had returned from Vietnam. I got Shep, the dog that had flunked the school six times, and Champ, the dog that had chewed up a previous recruits and sent them to the hospital. I'm not sure why the cadre had assigned me the dogs I had requested, but I couldn't have been happier.

We went to the kennels to begin making friends with our dogs. Shep looked at me with what looked like a smile as I stuck the feed pan through the little door in his kennel. He happily began to eat his food, looking up from time to time to wag his tail and smile again. All around me the dogs were barking madly and biting the cyclone fencing trying to get at the person delivering their food.

Even after the harassment that Smitty had given every dog in the kennel, Shep still acted like someone's perfect little pet. *What have I gotten myself into?* I wondered.

Then I went to feed Champ, my backup dog. He amazed me at how high the little guy could jump, as he tried to attack me through the fence. The kennels were eight feet high and Champ could jump to the top trying to bite me. He bared his teeth and snarled as he jumped again and again. He bit into the fence as I leaned down to shove his food through a little door. His ferocity made my blood run cold.

"Good boy. You and I are going to become good friends," I said in the most soothing tones I could deliver, but my talk only seemed to make him madder.

I spent the rest of the day talking in friendly tones to both dogs. Shep wagged his tail and smiled at me. Champ seemed to hate me more at the end of the day than when I had begun.

"You can see why we assigned Shep to you," Sergeant Yates said as he came up behind me, scaring me out of my wits. "He's flunked the school six times and if he doesn't make it this time he'll be put to sleep. We figured if anybody can save him, it's you. If he doesn't make it, Champ is a good backup. He's naturally aggressive and will be a great guard dog if you can just gain his confidence."

I made up my mind that I would save Shep. No matter what it took, I would make that dog into a winner. Sergeant Yates and I stood there contemplating the dog when, all of a sudden, the entire kennel seemed to erupt with wild barking. Smitty had left Bullet and walked toward us. The rest of the dogs had gone absolutely wild as he walked by their kennels.

"Hey Dad, how's it going?"

Shep looked up at Smitty with loving eyes and wagged his tail in greeting.

It took a few days for anyone to get close to the dogs that had returned from Vietnam. They had been taught to be one-man dogs and they were simply doing what they had been taught to do: attack anyone other than their handler.

I felt sorry for those dogs because they were being true to their previous masters, who were now home in the United States. The dogs would never see them again. I imagined how frustrated they must be. They must have been thinking, *Where's Andy? Why isn't he here to pet me when I growl at someone?*

We were next instructed to hold the feeding bowls in our hands. We were not to feed the dogs unless they allowed us into the kennel without attacking. Thus, the dogs that continued to attack went hungry. After a few days without food, the desire to attack was overcome by the need to eat. The guys who had the least aggressive dogs were able to get into the kennel in just a few days. They spoke in soothing tones to the dogs and even petted them if the dog would allow it. The more aggressive dogs took longer, but hunger always prevailed.

Not only did Shep let me in the first day, he welcomed me! He wagged his tail and looked at me as if to say, *What took you so long?*

I petted him and talked to him as I had been instructed, but that didn't really accomplish anything. Shep would have welcomed Jack the Ripper into his kennel.

Champ was another matter altogether. I stood holding his feeding pan, speaking in soft, friendly tones. "Good boy, Champ. Good boy. You and I are going to be good friends. Soon you and I will be buddies and no one will be able to get near you but me! Good boy!"

But Champ wasn't buying it. He snarled and growled and leaped about his cage like a Tasmanian devil. Champ made it clear to me that he hadn't comprehended a single word I'd said! After four days, Champ had become weak with hunger and just couldn't stand it any longer. He allowed me to push his pan into the kennel without biting my hand and ate like the starving dog that he was. Yet he snarled and growled and looked at me with murder in his eyes all the time he gulped down his food.

Our relationship continued in that fashion for another week before Champ finally allowed me into the kennel. He didn't attack me but he didn't welcome me either. He glowered at me from the corner of his kennel as if to say, *All right. You can bring me food and I won't attack you because I want to eat again tomorrow. But if you get another step closer, I'll bite your hand off!*

Clearly, training Champ would take some time.

Meanwhile, Sergeant Yates reminded us to agitate other dogs while their new masters were making friends with them.

Smitty merrily went from kennel to kennel, yelling, "BAROOOOO," and the dogs barked and snapped at him as he went by.

While Smitty did this, the handlers patted their dogs on the head, saying, "Good boy, good boy!"

That had a miraculous effect. The more the new handler patted them when they barked at Smitty, the more aggressive the dogs became. The more aggressive the dogs became, the more praise their handlers gave them. The snowball effect worked, and in most cases the dogs loved their new handlers and grew to understand that they would be praised if they snarled and barked at anyone else.

And then there was Shep. Smitty came up to Shep's kennel with his typical call and Shep stood there with loving eyes, wagging his tail in response as if to say, *Aren't you going to come in and pet me?*

Smitty said, "Hey, Dad! Shep needs some extra agitation!"

He went and got his stick and scraped it across the cyclone fencing on Shep's kennel. That drove the other dogs into a wild frenzy, but Shep stood there drooling with his tongue hanging out, simply watching Smitty go through his theatrics.

Soon, Smitty got worn out from his antics. "Don't worry, Dad. I'll come up with something to get Shep going."

Once we had made friends with our dogs, we were issued dog training equipment. That consisted of a choke chain, a leather collar, a leather leash, and a leather muzzle. The collar, the leash, and the muzzle we kept in good condition using saddle soap.

We were told to muzzle our dogs at all times in the kennel area and to use the choke chain. If a dog tried to attack someone, a sharp pull on the leash would pull the choke chain tight and stop the dog. Once we were in the training area, we replaced the choke chain with the leather collar and removed the muzzle. We did that only when the dog was a safe distance from everyone else. That gave the dog a chance to play, smell the area, or find a proper place to relieve himself. The dogs soon learned that when the leather collar was on they could play, but when the choke chain was on it was all business.

Sergeant Yates taught us the basics in dog training. "When the leather collar is on the dog," Yates said, "he is free to do as he pleases. But when the choke chain is on, the dog must learn that you are the master. Most dogs will respond to a gentle yank on the choke chain. You do that to send a message to the dog that he is doing something wrong and his actions must change, or he will be punished by another yank on the choke chain. Some of your dogs will be hard-headed and a gentle yank on the choke chain won't register with them. If that happens, you must jerk the choke chain with all your strength.

"Don't worry about hurting the dog," he continued. "A dog has tremendous neck muscles. It's the strongest part of the dog. If the dog doesn't respond to a number of gentle yanks, I want you to jerk the choke chain so hard the dog does a summersault in the air. I repeat: This will not hurt him. In the event that a severe pull on the leash does not register with the dog, you must hang him. You must lift the leash into the air high enough to lift the dog from the ground so that he is suspended by the choke chain. Hang the dog until he passes out and releases his bladder."

Jeez, I thought. *That seems like a pretty severe way to treat man's best friend.*

I remembered Tippy, my dog at home while growing up, and knew how I would have felt if I had hung her until she passed out. She was such a good friend that I couldn't imagine treating her that way.

But Shep was an entirely different dog than Tippy. I placed the choke chain and the muzzle on Shep to take him to the obstacle course with everyone else. Shep pulled on the chain, anxious to go to the field and leave his kennel. I yanked the chain, but Shep continued to pull me to the course as if he were a Mack Truck.

I yelled "Heel," and yanked it again.

Shep continued to pull me. I yanked the chain harder with no change.

Gosh, how can he take that pain without any semblance of change at all? I thought. *He doesn't even seem to notice.*

I continued to yank the chain but made up my mind that I couldn't bear to pull it so hard that he would flip in the air. Hanging him was out of the question.

I noticed Dale with Rex. Rex heeled, meaning that he walked right beside Dale with his shoulder next to Dale's knee, the proper heeling position. Smitty came along with Bullet and Bullet heeled as well.

Damn, I thought. *Those guys got dogs from Vietnam that had been taught by others to heel and they have it easy. Here I am with this green dog and I'm darn near worn out from pulling on the choke chain.*

The first activity in training our dogs involved running the obstacle course. I watched as other guys took their experienced dogs through the course. The dogs knew exactly what they were doing since they had been through the course frequently with their past handlers. In fact the dogs went through the course without even thinking and their handlers raced to keep up.

The first obstacle was a window. The dog had to jump through the window and that made it difficult since the handler would have to let go of the leash on one side of the window and pick it up on the other side as the dog passed through. A handler had to move quickly to make the exchange from one hand to the other, and if that didn't take place the dog would race through the rest of the course while the handler raced wildly along trying to regain possession of the leash. We all laughed when that happened, which often did.

Sergeant Yates would say, "Intelligence can run up or down the leash!"

Once past the window, the remainder of the course could be covered while the handler held the leash, assuming he hadn't lost it in the first place. There was a catwalk, a teeter totter, a ramp with a platform that required the dog to jump six feet from the platform down to the ground, and a hurdle about four feet high. The dogs were supposed to heel through the whole course. The experienced dogs went first because they knew what they were doing and it gave the rest of us a chance to observe.

Then Sergeant Yates told Dale to run the obstacle course.

Dale said, "Heel" and Rex promptly ran at Dale's side as they went through the course. Dale didn't even need to hold the leash. Rex remained by him through the entire course. Smitty and Bullet took their turn with the same results.

Then it was my turn. "Heel," I shouted in my most commanding voice.

Shep immediately took off at a dead run. Some of the guys laughed. When he hit the end of the leash, all 100 pounds of him caught me off balance and down I went, flat on my face with him dragging me along as if he were a Belgian draft horse pulling a plow. Everyone howled with laughter as I regained my feet and headed to the window, trailing behind Shep.

I had rehearsed in my mind how smoothly I would trade the leash from my left hand to my right hand as Shep leaped through the window. I made the trade smoothly and inside I smiled. But then my plan made a sharp turn.

Shep stopped dead at the window. I didn't know he had stopped, so when the leash pulled tight there I was, flat on the ground to more gales of laughter. I coaxed and pleaded with Shep to jump through the window but to no avail. I finally had to lift him up and throw him through it.

More laughter.

Shep immediately took off through the rest of the course with me hanging onto the leash for dear life.

By that time, the entire platoon had cracked up. As if in chorus, everyone yelled, "Intelligence can run up or down the leash," and roared with laughter.

The remainder of the exercise went fairly well, although Shep pulled me all the way. Obviously he didn't understand the meaning of "heel" yet.

With the obstacle course over, I took my place in the ranks and heaved a sigh of relief. Underneath it all I thought, *You just got the biggest, dumbest dog in the whole kennel.*

I had started out with a goal of training Shep to save him from being destroyed, but he had embarrassed me in front of the rest of the platoon. He continued to act like a locomotive pulling 100 train cars full of coal as he dragged me along behind yelling, "Heel boy, heel!"

I could feel the heat in my cheeks as I flushed with embarrassment. This had become personal and my kindheartedness was about to end. The thought of hanging Shep sickened me, but so did the thought of him being put to sleep and so did the thought of being laughed at because he wasn't performing. In the final analysis, I had no choice. The only way I could save his life and my reputation was to train him. But before that could happen, my unit got assigned a special mission.

The United States occupied Okinawa after WWII. When I was there, the US dollar was the official currency and cars drove on the right side of the highway, American style, while cars in Japan drove on the left side. The dollar and the driving position were but a few of the messages the Okinawans sent to the Japanese government. Many Okinawans resented Japanese imperialism and the position Japan had placed them in during WWII.

President Richard Nixon met with Japanese Prime Minister Eisaku Sato in 1969 to discuss the possibility of Okinawa reverting to Japanese control. That understandably went against the grain of the Okinawan

117

people, who hated Japan. It resulted in massive demonstrations at both the American and Japanese Embassies. Okinawans threw Molotov cocktails, set fires, shot guns, and in general let it be known that they wanted their independence and didn't want to return to Japanese control.

In light of the demonstrations and fear that the crowds might get out of control, dogs were used to protect the US Embassy.

Our platoon got split into two groups. I was in the Monday, Wednesday, Friday group. The other half had Tuesday, Thursday, and Saturday. On our duty day, we trained in the mornings and stood guard at the embassy in the afternoon, since the demonstrations took place in the late afternoon or evening after people got off work.

We arose daily at 4 a.m. and ate breakfast. At 6 a.m. we trained with our dogs, doing the obstacle course, attack training, and basic commands. At 11 a.m. we'd put the dogs back in their kennels and go to lunch. Those who weren't on duty had the rest of the day off. Those who were on duty to guard the embassy would muzzle their dogs, put on riot gear (a helmet with a face guard, shin guards, and flak vest), and climb into the back of a deuce and a half for the ride to the embassy. Once we were there and had climbed from the truck, we were issued M14s. We then stood around the perimeter of the embassy with our rifles and our attack dogs prominently displayed, while thousands of Okinawans yelled at us, made obscene gestures, and threatened the safety of the embassy personnel.

I remember well the first day I had to stand guard. I got off the truck and stood there waiting for Sergeant Yates to give me my M14, as did all the other guys. Once we had our rifles, we waited for ammunition.

Finally, I asked Sergeant Yates, "Hey! Haven't you forgotten something? Where's our ammo?"

"You're not getting any ammunition," he replied. "We can't afford to have someone accidentally fire a round and kill someone. If that were to happen, the crowd could turn ugly and no telling how many people would be hurt or killed. The guns and the dogs are simply a deterrent to stop the crowd from advancing. They don't know you don't have a loaded gun."

Oh great, I thought, *here I am guarding an embassy with an empty gun and a dog that would lick the rioters to death.*

118

I remember one night in particular when the demonstrators really got ugly and began to advance. Some very bold leaders at the front of the pack got close enough for a dogs to bite one of them. The young man howled with pain and the group retreated. I made up my mind that night that I would have to recruit Smitty and his unique talent to turn Shep from a pet into an attack dog.

Meanwhile, Sergeant Yates was right. We must have looked fearsome standing there in our riot gear with our empty M-14s and our dogs, because we were never approached again.

I had written home about the social unrest in Okinawa and about how frustrated I was with Shep. He did alright in following commands, but just didn't seem to have a mean bone in his body. And if demonstrators had ever penetrated our perimeter, I would be in trouble because Shep offered no protection at all. Thank goodness the demonstrators didn't know what a Casper Milquetoast he was!

Mom wrote a newsy letter back to me, telling me that Dad and my Uncle Tubby were busy planting corn on the Zempke place. The peas were in full bloom and the fields looked beautiful. Everyone was doing fine, and they were all praying for my safe return.

And then she included something that was true to her nature. Mom constantly reminded us kids that there was a world bigger than the little one we experienced in Sioux Rapids. She bought us books about other places and other cultures, and made us read them. She always read without cease, but did not read love novels or westerns. She read literature, inspirational books, cookbooks, and gardening books.

That served her well because Mom could carry on a conversation with just about anyone from anywhere on any subject. She had never learned to cook when she was a little girl at home. But she made up her mind to be a good cook and, through her cookbooks, she became one of the best.

While others might have sympathized because I had been issued a dog that had failed training a number of times and probably would never become an attack dog, Mom went right to the heart of the problem and sent me the following:

Don't Quit

When things go wrong, as they sometimes will,
When the road you're trudging seems all up hill,
When the funds are low and the debts are high
And you want to smile, but have to sigh,
When care is pressing you down a bit,
Rest if you must, but don't you quit!

Life is strange with its twists and turns,
As every one of us sometimes learns,
And many a person turns about
When they might have won had they stuck it out.
Don't give up though the pace seems slow,
You may succeed with just one more blow.

Often strugglers have given up
When they might have captured the victor's cup;
And they learned too late when the night came down,
How close they were to the golden crown.
Success is failure turned inside out,
So stick to the fight when you're hardest hit-
It's when things seem worst that you mustn't quit.

That was good advice then and it's good advice now.

Holding a 100-pound dog in the air long enough for him to pass out takes a lot of strength. I remember when Mrs. Gray once made me hold a book over my head when I got out of line in junior high. That book got pretty heavy after a while, so you can imagine what it felt like to hang Shep.

I found a tree in the practice area that had a low-hanging branch. When I needed to hang him, I headed for that tree, threw the leash over the branch, and pulled Shep up into the air as far as I could. He gasped for breath as he hung there. His eyes began to bulge and I had mixed emotions: I hated to see him trying to breath and yet it was satisfying, too. *Take that for all the embarrassment you've caused me!*

120

Soon his legs began to quiver, and finally he'd release his bladder and pass out. I'd drop him to the ground and watch as he slowly got his breath back. He'd lay there for quite some time and finally he'd get to his legs, which were still shaking and quivering.

"Heel," I said, when I felt he had recovered enough to walk again.

He walked perfectly with his shoulder next to my knee, but it wasn't long before his nature came back and he pulled me once again. I determined that I'd rather punish him darn good a few times, instead of punishing him lightly a lot of times. So I hung him again.

He begrudgingly began to heel most of the time. I could see in his eyes when he thought about going out front again, and when he did I'd give him a sharp yank on the choke chain. That began to work with regularity, although once in a while he would lose his composure and jump out front. When he did that instead of heeling, I immediately hung him again.

He finally got the message. Whenever I headed for the tree, Shep would heel perfectly and watch me with a guilty look on his face. His look reminded me of years earlier when my Dad needed to give me a spanking. I'd straighten up, cover my buttocks with my hands, and say, "I'll be good. I'll never do it again."

Well, that didn't work for me then and it didn't work for Shep now.

When Shep heeled properly, I constantly patted him on the head and said, "Good boy, Shep. Good boy."

And that is the trick to training a dog: Dogs live to be praised. There is nothing that pleases a dog more than to make his master happy. As I praised Shep more, he became more adept at heeling and doing any other thing I wanted. He simply wanted more praise.

Hanging a dog is a very distasteful thing to do, but without it Shep never would have known that he had been doing anything wrong. Shep began to learn that if he didn't heel, he would be hung and hanging him sent a message that he understood.

He started obeying and that allowed me to give him praise. I could tell that praise was completely foreign to him. With previous handlers he had never been hung and yanking on the choke chain hadn't fazed him a bit. Consequently, Shep had never been praised before because he had never done the right thing. I praised him constantly for heeling, and he lavished each pat on the head and each kind word. Oh, how he loved it!

As I walked Shep back to the kennel with him obediently heeling at my side, I felt a pat on my shoulder. I turned and there was Sergeant Yates with a big grin on his face. "Looks like we have intelligence running down the leash instead of up!" he said.

I felt like I was on top of the world. That little bit of success made me hungry for more. I knew then that I could teach Shep anything because he would respond to praise and do anything to get it. I taught him to sit in no time at all. When I said, "Sit," Shep immediately would drop his haunches to the ground and look up at me with those loving eyes, yearning for a pat on the head and a "Good boy, Shep, good boy." Next came "Lay down." He would flop to the ground and again look at me for his reward. He learned to "stay." I could tell him to stay and walk all over the workout area. He stayed on the ground with his eyes constantly following me until I yelled, "Come," at which time he would race to my side to get his pat on the head.

Now I needed Shep to pass the obstacle course. I knew that the window would be the biggest test. Shep always halted at the window and I had been his victim a number of times. I took him to the window where he sat and then went to the other side. I told him to jump and then pulled him through the window with the leash. It was ugly at first, but as soon as he landed on the other side of the window I praised him abundantly. Before long he figured out that he could jump through the window on his own and would gladly do it to get praised.

I had been the brunt of much laughter in the past and wanted to run Shep successfully through the obstacle course in front of everyone. The day finally came and when it was my turn I ran with Shep to the window. Everyone expected Shep to stop and dig in his heels, refuse to jump through the window, and maybe slam me to the ground again. But this time Shep sailed through the window and I had to move quickly to pass the leash from one hand to the other in order to keep up with him. The crowd of onlookers murmured and some even started clapping!

The grin on Sergeant Yate's face told me that Shep had done well. "Way to go! I knew you could bring him through," he said.

Attack training was the nucleus of what our dogs needed. With Smitty's help, each of us trained our dogs to attack anyone else. When they did attack, we praised our dogs to high heaven. Once we had our attack dogs trained, it was time for a test.

A member of the cadre wore an arm sleeve made of heavily padded material. He waved his arm at each dog, daring the dog to attack. Most dogs would eagerly lunge at the sleeve and bite, then pull and tear at the sleeve. Another non-com followed the man with the sleeve, carrying a small tree branch and swatted any dog that didn't attack. Usually, the dog would growl and snap, and the handler would praise the dog for this action, reinforcing the fact that it was all right to snarl and bite an attacker.

But Shep didn't do so well during his first test. He just stood there as if in a trance instead of attacking the man with the sleeve. And when the other man swatted him with the tree branch, Shep simply retreated with a confused look on his face as if to say, *Why is that man hitting me?*

I drafted Smitty to help with Shep since every other dog in the kennel hated him. It made sense to me that if Smitty had successfully made all those dogs hate him when he wasn't even trying, what results could he get if he focused on one dog?

Smitty began by using a tree branch. He poked at Shep through the chain link fencing, growling and snarling in the process. That didn't work because Shep simply retreated into his kennel. That brought out the best in Smitty. He spent hours in his off time trying to agitate Shep, but with no success. And then he hit on something.

"Hey Dad, have you noticed that the only thing that Shep gets really excited about is eating?" Smitty asked. "He's done long before the other dogs. He eats that whole bowl in one giant gulp!"

And that's when the transformation began. Smitty got a hefty stick that resembled a pool cue and, whenever I fed Shep, Smitty was there. I'd remain in the kennel with Shep. As Shep tried to eat, Smitty would give him a sharp rap on the nose. Shep would back up and look at him. Then he would approach the bowl again and, RAP, right on the nose again. We repeated this process until finally (and miraculously, I might add) Shep snarled at Smitty!

I patted him on the head and said, "Good boy, Shep. Good boy!"

We did this at every feeding until Smitty didn't have to use the stick any more. Shep would snarl and bark as soon as Smitty approached the kennel. And I would praise him and praise him and praise him.

A couple of thoughts chased through my mind as Shep transformed into an attack dog: I had grown up with dogs and had been taught that a dog was man's best friend. Shep was a perfect example of that kind of dog; gentle, loving, and playful. While he had been praised for those traits by his original owners, I now praised him for being mean, hateful, and aggressive. The key to making all this happen was food. Nothing made Shep aggressive until he got deprived of his food.

I wondered to myself, *Would humans react the same way? Would we fight just like Shep if we were deprived of food?*

The final day of attack training came. Shep would either prove himself, or he would be deemed un-trainable and put to sleep.

Sergeant Yates asked for a volunteer to wear the sleeve and agitate the dogs. Smitty happily volunteered. Since all the dogs hated Smitty, they put on quite a show. As Smitty moved down the line of dogs, the barking crescendo increased as the dogs picked up his scent and knew he was coming.

I waited anxiously as Smitty came closer to Shep. When Shep picked up his scent, he went into an absolute frenzy. I had all I could do to hold his leash. When Smitty finally arrived, Shep attacked with a vengeance and sunk his teeth into the sleeve, pulling and tearing the whole time.

Smitty's typical smile disappeared and he yelled, "Ow!"

I got Shep away and Sergeant Gran pulled the sleeve from Smitty's arm. To our surprise we found blood trickling down his arm. Shep had bitten so hard that he had penetrated completely through the padded sleeve! It was the first time that had ever happened and Sergeant Yates couldn't believe his eyes.

Smitty just looked at me and smiled. "Hey Dad, we did it! Looks like you're stuck with that bone-headed dog!"

Our class had completed attack/sentry dog training two weeks ahead of schedule and the cadre decided that we should spend the extra time in scout dog training.

Let me explain the difference between the two. Attack dogs are trained to detect an enemy trying to penetrate the perimeter of a specific area. Generally, those areas are ammunition dumps, food yards, helicopter pads, hospitals, or headquarters companies. Those areas are surrounded with mine fields and rows of concertina wire. The concertina wire is laid out in a triangular shape with three coils tied together on the bottom, two more coils sitting on top of them, and one coil on top of those two. There may be anywhere from one row up to eight rows of these triangular shaped configurations spaced about ten feet apart around an area, depending on the importance of what's being guarded inside the wire. Ammunition dumps and food yards could have as many as eight rows, while a headquarters area might have only one or two. Guess we could spare officers more than we could spare ammo or food.

The attack dog and his handler move about inside the wire. Their objective is to detect the scent of an infiltrator and warn everyone long before the enemy gets inside the concertina wire. If an enemy penetrates the rows of concertina wire, the dog attacks to prevent him from stealing food or ammunition, or, worse, detonating the ammunition dump. Thus, the mission of a good sentry dog is to first of all pick up the scent, then to visually identify the intruder if he's close enough and finally to attack if the enemy penetrates the area.

Scout dogs, on the other hand, were used in infantry units. The handler and his dog were "on point" and led an infantry unit as it patrolled through the jungle. The dog's mission was to detect the enemy by scent, prior to engagement. Once the dog picked up the scent, the handler notified the leader of the unit that there may be enemy up ahead. Then the handler and dog would move to the back of the unit if possible. The infantry could then proceed, alert that there might be enemy contact soon. Obviously, a keen sense of smell is important for a scout dog.

I had settled on the fact that I'd be taking Shep to Vietnam. He had learned to take commands well. The fact that Shep had drawn blood when he attacked Smitty in the padded sleeve made him the poster-dog of the company.

However, I still had to care for Champ, my back up dog. He required attention, so I took Champ out for a good grooming. I had grown accustomed to Shep and had forgotten how aggressive Champ could be.

Grooming required Champ to stand still while I straddled him, using my fingertips to pull against the grain of the dog's coat. That pulled the dead hair from the coat and was very soothing to Champ. Afterward, I used a brush or comb to finish the coat, that time going with the grain of the hair. That removed all the dull hair and the brush brought out the shine and texture of the coat.

However, as I raked my fingers against the grain to pull out the dead hair, I got too low and touched Champ's flank, a very tender spot and one that dogs don't care to have touched. Champ turned around and snapped. His teeth settled on my hand. I lifted Champ into the air and shook him. He finally let go and fell to the ground.

I instantly snapped his choke chain and took him to his kennel thinking, *I've got to get rid of him before he attacks again. Then I've got to go to the doctor for stitches.*

One of the other guys, Bruce, came to mind. His dog had turned on him and, by the time the doctors were finished, he had to have over a 100 stitches. I wondered how many stitches my little ordeal would require.

With Champ safely locked in his kennel, I looked at my hand. No blood. Not even a scratch! But my wedding ring had been flattened on my finger and hurt like the dickens. I went back to the barracks and found Charlie, our Okinawan handyman. He found a pair of pliers and I soon had a round wedding ring again. I decided that I was darn glad to be married and that my ring would *never* come off!

I'd found another reason to be glad I had married to Ginny.

The next week was uneventful. We groomed the dogs and cleaned the kennels, but didn't have much else to do. We had plenty of down time after we finished our dog duties for the day. I had gotten used to taking Shep to the beach for a swim, but the waves were high and awash in brown snakes from the sea. Brown snakes are poisonous so it's a good idea to stay out of the water when they're around. I went down to the beach just to witness what it looked like and was amazed that the sea was covered with snakes. I wondered how they could survive in the sea.

Some of the guys went into town to lap up some libations and others tried to get lucky with the ladies. Neither of those activities interested me or several of my other buddies. We'd had our fill of football and cards and bull sessions were out since we all knew each other so well by this time. After writing letters, we had to find some other diversion.

Luckily, we heard of an orphanage nearby. Charley Peterson and I had become fast friends. Pete came from Austin, Minnesota. His father was a baker and a good family man who had brought his children up in the Christian faith. He didn't like to drink and carouse either. We both believed that what Jesus said made sense: "It's better to give than to receive." So we decided to go to an orphanage we had heard about and give the kids some candy.

Art stopped me as I was leaving my bunk. "I hear you're going to an orphanage to give the kids some candy. I'm headed down town but here's $5 for some extra candy." Six other guys stopped me before I got out the door, each giving me more money for candy. When I met Pete outside, he told me the same thing had happened to him. We had over $50 and that was a lot in those days. We filled the back seat of a taxi with boxes of Hershey bars, Milky Ways, Snickers, and Baby Ruths.

We arrived at the orphanage and unloaded our goods, only to find blank expressions on the faces of the kids. After questioning the adults in charge, we found that there was a very good reason: The kids had never eaten candy! They had no idea what it was. So I ate a Baby Ruth and a Snickers bar in front of everyone. Pete ate every kind of candy bar we had to show the kids how good they were. It was a dirty job, but someone had to do it

Pete would take a bite, smile, and say, "Mmmm."

Finally, a little boy named Skoshi, a common Oriental name meaning "small," took a candy bar and tried a taste. He smiled and then devoured the whole thing. Soon, all the kids dived in and ate like a bunch of hogs at a trough. We sat back and watched them..

Skoshi grabbed another candy bar in his left hand, then took my two smallest fingers in his right and began walking. He led me into a small cottage and leaned down at the foot of a bed. He jabbered something in his native tongue and two little boys crawled out from under the bed. He showed them the candy bar and explained what was going on. They smiled at me as Skoshi led me by the fingers to a refrigerator. He jabbered something again. Soon, a little girl appeared from behind the refrigerator. He pulled my two fingers to a closet. Skoshi opened the door and spoke again. This time a boy and a girl came out of nowhere into the room. Finally, Skoshi took me to a bedside table. He opened the little door on the table and curled up inside was the tiniest little girl. She uncurled herself from the meager confines of the table as Skoshi explained what was happening. Her name was Mary.

I picked Mary up to carry her because she was so tiny. The other kids were so much bigger I didn't think she could keep up with the pack. She raised an awful ruckus and I thought I had hurt her. I set her down and she scampered over to the closet and reached in to retrieve a little white hat, which she placed on her head. Then without a word she came over to me and raised her arms to be lifted into my embrace. She wasn't going anywhere without that little white hat. She looked into my eyes and, without saying a word, told me that she trusted me. She reminded me of my Grandma Brown who would never leave the house without "putting on her face" and putting on her earrings.

We went outside to the taxi where all the kids gorged themselves on candy.

I learned later that the children in the orphanage had been purchased from prostitutes. The children would mature in the orphanage and eventually be sold to work in fisheries, glass factories, or whore houses. A few lucky ones might be purchased by a family, but that wasn't likely. I still have their pictures. Once in a while I look at them and wonder where they are and what they are doing.

Jerry Isaacs approached me one day and asked, "How come you're so happy all the time?"

I wasn't sure where that came from so I asked him to explain himself.

Jerry told me that he had acquired a #1 nason, thinking that would make him happy but it hadn't.

A nason was an Okinawan girl who had become a GIs mistress. Okinawa was a very poor country and a young girl would try to attract a GI, hoping that he would marry her and take her back to the States. A soldier could rent an apartment for $20 a month, and a nason would stay there at the GIs beck and call.

GIs always wanted a cherry girl, a virgin, if they could find one. But once a cherry girl had given herself to a GI, she became damaged goods.

If the GI left without marrying her, she would be destined for the life of a whore since Okinawan men wouldn't marry a girl unless she was a virgin. Their culture and religion demanded that. The streets were full of damaged girls in their short skirts, low-cut halter tops, and high heels. They wore lots of make-up, including false eyelashes. They would bat their eyes at a GI, hoping to sell themselves for "$2.50 for a short time" or "$5 for a long time," the latter meaning the entire night.

Jerry also used drugs. Marijuana had grown in popularity. Stronger drugs were readily available, but marijuana was the extent of his drug usage. However, the thrill of that had worn off. I told him I was a Christian. I believed that a man should fall in love with a girl, marry, and "cleave unto her," as the scriptures say. Happiness is a product of giving love to someone else. Giving my love to Ginny was one of the things that made me happy. I explained that his nason wasn't love, just an attempt at happiness and a selfish one at that. He wasn't interested in her happiness. He was only interested in his own happiness and thought sex with her would accomplish that. The same could be said of his marijuana experience. He used it to hopefully gain pleasure and, therefore, happiness. But as the Bible says, it's better to give than to receive and what you give will come back to you tenfold.

I remember learning that from Mrs. Sieve Knutson. As I remember, her husband raised Hereford cattle north of Sioux Rapids. At any rate, she came to one of our junior class plays and we struck up a friendship. She always seemed so happy and I asked her why she was that way. She told me that every year she tried to find someone that needed her more than she needed herself. She helped young people who needed help and explained that making them happy was what made her happy.

So I told Jerry that it was time for him to make a paradigm shift. He needed to find happiness by giving it to someone else. I suggested that maybe we should buy more candy and take it to the orphanage. He agreed and we decided to go the next Saturday. Once more, the guys kicked in some extra bucks for the candy and Jerry had a ball handing out candy and mixing with the kids.

Jerry was excited about our visit to the orphanage and back at the barracks he told everyone that would listen about his experience there.

There's nothing like missionary zeal! One by one, the other guys came up and wanted to know if they could go to the orphanage, too.

At the time I didn't think too much about our growing orphanage project because our final test with our dogs would be the following day. The Inspector General would be there to observe, and he would make the final decision regarding which dogs had passed the test and be sent on to Vietnam.

I worried about Shep passing the test after all the work I'd put into him.

Other troops were worried about their own performances as handlers. The IG would decide which handlers were acceptable and which should be retrained. If he decided that a handler hadn't performed well enough to warrant retraining, the IG could have the handler stripped from the Military Police and sent to the Big Red One, where he'd become an infantryman.

The first test was a running attack. The handler muzzled his dog and held the leash tightly. As the attacker approached, a well-trained dog growled and acted in an aggressive fashion. At that point, the attacker turned and ran. The handler then released the leash and yelled, "Get him, boy!" Of course the dog ran after the attacker and knocked him down. He would also try to bite him, but with a muzzle in place the attacker was safe.

Shep strained at the leash when his turn came. He barked and snarled enough to curdle your blood. When the attacker turned and ran, I threw the leash and yelled, "Get him, boy!"

Shep caught up quickly, hit him in the back, and knocked the attacker to the ground. It surprised me how quickly a grown man could be knocked down by a dog. Shep then alternated between trying to bite the man and attempting to claw off his muzzle. When the man lay still, Shep would pull on his muzzle. But when the man moved, Shep would try to bite him.

The man lay still until I came and grabbed Shep's leash and said, "Out. Good boy."

During the second test, I tethered Shep to a cable about twenty feet long, attached to a wire strung between two poles. An attacker taunted him by running back and forth along the wire and then leaned in with the padded sleeve on his arm, daring the dog to bite the sleeve. Sergeant Yates played the attacker. He raced back and forth with Shep snarling and following him. He finally leaned in and Shep hit the sleeve with tremendous force.

"Ow!" yelled Sergeant Gran.

He pulled the sleeve off and, lo and behold, Shep had penetrated the thick padding and drawn blood, just like he had with Smitty.

The IG said, "That was very impressive and I'd like to see it again. Sergeant, would you mind?"

Sergeant Yates handed the sleeve to the IG and said, "If you liked it so much, do it yourself!"

Percy's dog failed the aggression test. He wouldn't chase the aggressor on the run and he didn't attack the aggressor when he came near the cable. We all knew what was coming.

After the exercise, we heard over the loudspeaker, "Percy and Lee come to the office."

Percy went into the commander's office first while I waited in the lobby. Percy came out later and confirmed my suspicions.

He was crying. "I'm being sent to the Big Red One, Dad," he said.

A million thoughts raced through my head. *Was I going to the Big Red One, too? Shep had done so well, hadn't he? Why had they called my name?*

I got summoned into the office where the IG waited for me.

"Halverson, we understand that you took Jerry Isaacs to an orphanage. Is that true?"

"Yes," I replied, wondering what could be wrong with that.

"Well, I'll be damned," he said. "Our biggest problems with men in the past have been boozing and whoring. Now we've got a brand new problem. Isaacs has been telling everyone what a great time he had there and everyone is asking if they can go to the orphanage, too. Jerry told them the place is run down and that a lot of fixing up needs to be done. It looks like the entire company wants to go to the orphanage to help out, instead of going downtown.

"So here's what we've decided to do," he declared. "We're going to give you a deuce and a half, tools, and lumber to go out there and make repairs. You'll be in charge."

Leaving the IG's office, I had torn feelings. I felt good about the orphanage arrangements but I felt bad for Percy.

The orphanage became a favorite spot for all the guys. Whenever we had time off, we rode out to help however we could. The facilities were run down and we needed to improve sewers, repair buildings, and paint, among other things.

Since I knew how to type, I spent a lot of time in the headquarters building doing paper work for officers who couldn't type. One day the officer-in-charge inquired about the orphanage, commenting on how it had made his life easier. He wasn't bailing men out of jail anymore because they weren't going downtown and getting drunk.

"I can't believe it," he said. "No drunks. No fights. No prostitutes calling. What's going on?"

I explained the orphanage to him. "The place really is run down and we're trying to repair it as best we can with what we've got. What we really need are things like lumber, tools, paint, QuickCrete, shovels, and pipe and tile for the sewer line. Besides that, the guys really are getting close to the kids."

"How about the Army donating materials and tools for this project?" he replied. "We've got plenty of tools and materials, and I could supply a driver and a deuce and a half to help out."

We now had the support of our CO *and* the IG.

We arranged for a three-day weekend so we could get as much done as possible. We filled the truck with supplies and sat down on the wooden benches in back for the ride to the orphanage. A car full of officers followed us in air-conditioned comfort while we rode in the ever-present sun.

When we got to the orphanage, the officers got out and called us into formation. We had to stand at attention while officers, who had never been there before, told us what we were going to do and how we were going to do it. They emphasized how they had taken time off for this project and we all had better toe the line. After they had given us our marching orders, they retired to the orphanage office with the orphanage officials for tea and crumpets! Pete's temperature was rising after this episode.

132

Meanwhile, we recruits went to work cutting boards, nailing, and painting. We repaired windows, fixed screens, replaced pipes under sinks and toilets, and made shelving in the kitchen to store food. We worked alongside the kids, who smiled incessantly and helped in any way they could. We passed out lots of candy in the process and I can still see Arturo Willimino Pollicelli, the Great American Wop, smiling as he watched his little charge eat a Baby Ruth.

"Ten Hut!"

Like all the others, I thought someone was pulling a joke and kept right on working.

Again someone yelled, "Ten Hut!" Only this time more emphatically.

I couldn't believe it. The officers were standing in the yard with the orphanage officials, calling another formation. When we finally arrived, the officers gave us another sermon about how they had taken time off from their busy schedules to help the orphanage project and if it wasn't for men like them, worthy projects such as this would never happen! The officers had stern looks on their faces while the orphanage officials smiled agreeably and nodded their heads approvingly.

Pete poked me in the side and said, *The officers never even knew the orphanage existed on this little island until we came along. A few good men donated their time and money and got a good thing going. Now the officers want to step in and take credit for the whole operation!*

That was our first real experience with a government bureaucracy!

Another weekend came and a bunch of us loaded up the deuce and a half to go to the orphanage. A number of the guys decided not to go because they were mad at Sergeant Yates for his display of "Army superiority" the previous weekend.

High on my list of projects was repairing the storm sewer. The concrete had broken up over the years, creating a small dam. More debris had piled up on the concrete so that when it rained the water backed up in the sewers and into the buildings. The inside of every cottage smelled of raw sewage. We cleaned all the concrete chunks and debris from the ditch, and then poured new concrete. We put new chains on a swing set and repainted it as well. While we did that, others painted the cottages. We spent a lot of time repairing floors, mopboards, and trim, which had deteriorated over the years and provided entry for rats. The living conditions were filthy enough without adding germ carriers like rats. We repaired windows and screens so outside germ carriers like mosquitoes could be controlled.

It felt good to do something for others. I think Jesus Christ was right: "Do unto others as you would have them do unto you." I have always believed that the best medicine for depression is to do something for someone who needs you more than you need yourself. First of all, I can always find others who have it worse than I do. Secondly, there's no feeling like the one I get when someone smiles with their eyes and says, "Thank you."

Sergeant Yates showed up late and immediately began to politic with the orphanage administrators. He expounded about how wonderful the Army was to contribute men, tools, and materials for the cause. "None of this could happen without the generous contributions of the United States Army," he proclaimed.

Then he began ordering the troops around and criticizing our work. Like the others who didn't come, we also were upset with Sergeant Yate's behavior but still came because we believed the orphanage work to be such a worthy cause.

Then Yates pulled me and Pete aside and quietly berated us for creating such a long list of needs for the orphanage. "Taxpayer dollars are paying for all of this," he said, "and we've got to be sure that they're getting a good bang for the buck!" Pete's temperature rose even more and I was beginning to match him.

"Why don't you just get the Hell out of here?" Pete demanded with fire in his eyes. "We were doing just fine without you!"

I thought of all the steaks and trimmings being served to the officers in their club. I thought of the pointless trips, golf outings, and personal amenities that Sergeant Yates enjoyed on the taxpayer's buck. I had had enough. I've got a long fuse but when it's burned long enough I can blow.

"Listen," I snarled. "We wanted to give and you said you wanted to help, so we let you have the list. Now you're chewing us out for doing what you asked us to do. Nobody asked the Army for anything. You *asked* to give. And as for the Army, if you want to advertise, buy a billboard! We're just individuals that want to help, not soldiers that want to advertise."

Everyone else cheered and Pete and I got a lot of handshakes all around. However, I couldn't help but think, *This is going to cost us later!* But it was worth it.

As we worked at the orphanage, everyone developed a close relationship with one or two of the orphans. For example, Arthur "Wop" Pollicelli became close with Charlie. Charlie had been in some kind of accident and his face had been horribly disfigured. Perhaps he felt that Art, who was six-foot-six and a muscular 250 pounds, could protect him from all the teasing other kids gave him.

All the kids considered Smitty to be a god. While the birthmark that covered the right side of his face might have been considered a disfigurement in America, the Okinawans believed that God had reached down from Heaven and placed the mark on Smitty's face to show His favor. Smitty relished that kind of treatment and entertained the kids tirelessly, one and all.

Dale befriended a little girl who always wore a purple dress. She would sit on his lap and he would tell her stories about growing up in Wisconsin. She didn't know what an apple was, so Dale brought her one from the mess hall. She loved it.

And my favorites were Mary with the little white hat and Skoshi, the little boy I'd met when Pete and I first brought all that candy to the orphanage.

And so it was with all the guys involved.

Our platoon had a few days off before we would have to pack up ourselves and our dogs and fly to Vietnam. The sea had been beckoning me for a long time. I thought, *What could be better than an afternoon in that beautiful, turquoise water?*

Our compound was situated about a half-mile from the beach I had seen from the plane when we arrived on Okinawa. It was the only spot on the island that wasn't a few hundred feet above the ocean. The land there sloped gently to the beach and the water was absolutely beautiful, with its blue and turquoise hues. Most of the island was rocky, but this area had finely-weathered soil dotted with palm trees and elephant grass.

The beach had light brown, fine sand. It was not a pretty beach in terms of what I had seen in pictures of other beaches, where the sand was white.

The surf was up, with waves topping out at about six feet. I watched as the native Okinawans bodysurfed. One could walk out into the water until it was chest high, swim like mad to catch the front of a wave, and then glide along on the wave for fifty yards or so until reaching shore. My buddies and I tried it, too, and soon learned to ditch the wave before it slammed us into the beach. The taste of the salt water was horrible and the coral, which I had never seen before, was sharp! Beneath the beauty of the sea were knife-like coral edges that could cut the skin.

Later we went into town to do some shopping and sightseeing. The colors and the beauty of the sewing, painting, and cabinetmaking the people there had for sale caught my attention immediately. The paints they used were shiny enamel that glittered in the light. Black, red, and gold seemed to be the craftsmen's preferred colors. Pictures of birds and flowers adorned vases and fabrics. Inlaid pearl adorned jewelry boxes, cabinets of all sorts and furniture. I bought pillows for Mom and Dad, Cleo and Emery, and Grandma and Grandpa Brown. I bought Ginny a jewelry box, a doll, and a see-through nightie that I hoped to see her in when we met in Hawaii for Rest and Relaxation, commonly called R & R.

The shops were the size of a large closet and were lined up side-by-side for blocks. Owners stood in front, hawking their wares to anyone who walked by. There were rolled-up pads, usually made of rice straw, hanging at the backs of the shops. I found out that at the end of the day the shop owners would roll out those pads on the floor of the shop to serve as beds for their family. Children, who had been roaming the streets during the day, would come back for supper and to sleep. An entire family lived in each small space.

I thought about home, where we had a kitchen, living room, several bedrooms, and a toilet, all under one roof. The efficiency with which those Okinawans lived their lives in such small spaces amazed me. I realized how lucky I had been to grow up somewhere that had such a high standard of living.

Rounding a corner, I noticed a carnival with rides, side shows, cotton candy, and everything else I'd found at fairs back home. I immediately thought of the kids at the orphanage and wondered, *Did they ever get to come to town and see a carnival?* I doubted they had.

I called Pete and said, "Look! I'll bet the kids at the orphanage have never been to a carnival."

Pete grinned and said, "Well, I guess it's about time they go to one!"

We made arrangements to have an Army bus pick the kids up at the orphanage and bring them to the carnival. When they arrived, we split the kids into small groups, one group for each soldier in attendance, and took our little groups through the gate. Two dollars got each child into the fair, and that covered all the rides and side shows. Eats were extra. I had six kids in my group, including Skoshi and Mary.

We rode the tilt-a-whirl, the Ferris wheel, and several others, until the kids tired of the rides. Then we went to the haunted house. The boys were pretty brave, until we got into the darkness and saw our first ghost. At that point I felt little hands grabbing my fingers for the rest of the journey.

When the carnival excursion ended, the children boarded the bus to leave. I can still picture Skoshi waving from the back window as we said good-bye. I realized that for the first time in my life I was saying good-bye for real. When I said good-bye to my family and Ginny, it was really more like, "See ya later." But this good-bye would be final and I would never see Skoshi again.

Al noticed that I wrote a letter to Ginny every day. "How do you do that?" he asked.

"Do what?" I replied.

"Write a letter. I've never written one and I probably should, but I don't know how."

"All you have to do is write your thoughts down on paper," I said. "It's easy."

"That's easy for you to say! You've done it so it's easy for you."

"Well, there's a first time for everything. You didn't know how to tie your shoes once upon a time, but you can do it now without even thinking. Writing a letter will be the same way."

"But I'm afraid they'll laugh at me," he said.

"Tell you what. Why don't you write a letter to Ginny? Then she will tell you if the letter is good or not. She's an English teacher so she may be able to help you. Once you're comfortable, you can write a letter to whomever you wish."

Here's the letter Al wrote to Ginny:

Dear Ginny,

I am about to go to a place that I call the unknown. I am an American soldier on my way to Vietnam. They say that is where future wars may be stopped and that is why I am here. In a few days I will put to use all I have been taught about killing to survive the coming year. Am I afraid? No, not really afraid, but cautious. I was called on as an American citizen to do my duty for my country. I did not hesitate about going. I am doing only what I feel is right. I am not growing long hair or attending any peace demonstrations. I am not going to any racial rallies. I am not protesting because I was called to serve, but I am praying that there will be peace in the world soon.

Right now my thoughts are on my loved ones at home. Home is a word that seems a million miles away right now. Of course, I know I can't be there just yet, but I long so much to be there right now because home is a beauty each and everyone knows. I have the longest year of my life ahead of me, but I know that in one year I will be home again and very proud to say that I defended our country. For this is my country and yours.

We, the fighting men of America know so well the worth of freedom because we see our buddies die beside us; we see hunger, poverty and sickness. I am happy to know I have so much to come home to, especially the girl that I love. I am also proud to know that I am a citizen of the greatest country ever, the good old United States of America.

Ginny gave her approval and Al joined the ranks of the letter writers.

We were coming to the end of our time in Okinawa. We had one final test for our dogs to take before we left for Vietnam.

Sergeant Yates took us to a remote part of Okinawa where there were no buildings or roads. The only thing visible was acres and acres of elephant grass. I remember thinking that this area would be heaven for a herd of cattle. Lush, green, tall grass grew as far as the eye could see.

"Muzzle your dogs," said Yates. "Your mission is to find the enemy, not to attack him. When you find the enemy, you will restrain your dog and return to this area. Someone is out there hiding in the grass and you are to find him."

Shep hated the muzzle, as did most dogs. Our muzzles were leather straps that covered the dog's mouth and prevented him from biting. I secured the muzzle on Shep and waited my turn.

"Halverson! You're first!" barked Gran.

Damn, I thought. *Why am I always the guinea pig?*

I wet my finger in my mouth and held it in the air to find the wind direction. The scent or our quarry would be carried by the wind. I then began to walk Shep on a line perpendicular to the wind. We walked about 50 yards to the right along the elephant grass with no success.

Surely Shep should have picked up the scent by now, I thought.

I turned and led Shep in the opposite direction. I didn't make eye contact with Sergeant Yates as we walked past him, but I knew he had a smirk on his face.

I had gone 20 yards past Yates when Shep raised his ears and started to sniff. He strained against the leash and, when he couldn't follow the scent as quickly as he wanted, he raised up on his back legs, using the leash for balance. He sniffed the air and pulled me as hard as he could through the elephant grass, which was a good three feet taller than I am. I couldn't see a thing, except Shep plowing through the grass ahead of me. I wondered if we were going to come upon some animal nesting in the grass, probably a skunk with my luck.

But after about 150 yards, Shep dove into a clump of the thick, green foliage and to my surprise there was a man! Shep tried desperately to bite him but the muzzle prevented that. He finally lay down on the ground and dug at the muzzle with his dew claws. When the man moved, Shep jumped on him and knocked him back to the ground, hovering over him and growling. When he was satisfied the man wouldn't move, Shep resumed trying to tear the muzzle from his face.

I yelled, "Out!" which is the command to quit attacking, but Shep would have none of that. He was in a rage because he couldn't get the muzzle off and bite the decoy.

We eventually made our way back to the staging area and another handler began his quest to locate another decoy.

I remember thinking, *How in the world did Shep smell that guy way out there in the middle of all that grass?*

Sergeant Yates looked at me and said, "When you get to 'Nam, your dog will find the enemy better at night than he will during the day. If you have to choose between your dog and an M-16, pick the dog every time!"

Hmm, I thought I had heard that somewhere before so it must be true! Maybe it's some sort of dog-handler credo.

Shep and I had done well, but we weren't quite through.

The field of elephant grass again served as the test site. Two men went out into the 10-foot-tall foliage and urinated in a spot, and then moved to another spot to hide. The objective was to see if the dog could distinguish between the weak scent left behind by an encampment and the strong scent of a live human being. Could the dog leave the weak scent of urine and focus on the newer and stronger scent of a man?

When my turn came, I again walked Shep perpendicular to the wind so he could pick up the scent. That scent could be a combination of soap, after shave, and body oils.

The wind caused a scent cone to be formed, emanating from the decoy person. Imagine a cone shape with a point that begins with the person and then widens out in the wind. The scent cone is wide if the wind is slow, but narrow if the wind is strong. The wind was strong that day so I knew the scent cone would be narrow. That meant I had to walk Shep slowly so he wouldn't miss it.

All of the sudden, Shep perked his ears up and directed them toward the interior of the field. He raised his head to sniff, and eventually dug his paws into the ground and pulled me into the grass. We went about 50 yards to a spot where he sniffed the ground with anticipation. That had to be where the decoy had urinated.

Soon Shep found the scent where the man had walked to his new location and he began pulling me again. How in the world a man could leave a scent as he walked through the grass was beyond me. He wore pants and boots, which would nullify any scent as far as I was concerned. Nonetheless, he had left a scent and Shep had identified it.

We went about 20 yards when Shep lunged into a hefty clump of grass, and there to my surprise was a man lying on the ground! Shep tried to bite him but the muzzle prevented it.

We escorted the man out to the gathering area and then found a scent cone for the second man. Shep entered the field at the same point we had entered before and I thought, *Oh boy, he's going after the old scent.* But half way to the previous area, he once again perked up his ears and began to pull me in another direction. We went another 30 yards before Shep lunged into another clump of grass with the same result.

Shep had found both men and had passed his final exam. Meanwhile, Champ would be held back for another handler—some newbie was going to get a great dog.

I lay back in the grass and daydreamed while the rest of the guys went through their tests, one by one. I dreamed of being back home with Ginny and wondered about her lot in life since she had married me. She'd have a teaching contract now if she hadn't married me. What a crummy deal.

**Cover photo
Me with Shep**

A well-organized footlocker.

Shep, my best friend.

Marker for our school in Okinawa.

Kennels in Okinawa.

Charlie the houseboy in Okinawa.

Obstacle course, Shep couldn't jump through
the window when we started.

Skoshi at the carnival.

Other boys from the orphanage.

Mary in her hat.

**Champ, the dog I didn't take with me.
He was vicious!**

Finally got my desk the way I wanted it
and then had to leave it behind.

Chain

Smitty with Brutus at Cam Ranh Bay.

Dale Bladorn

Charlie Peterson burning barrels from outhouse.

The guys wearing Cong Catchers for the officers.

Barracks in Pleiku

After a trip to the river for a water fight and jeep washing. We are wearing Ho Chi Minh sandals.

Charlie and me outside the bunker.

Charlie Butler, Ohara, Dan and me coming in off watch.

Me outside the bunker.

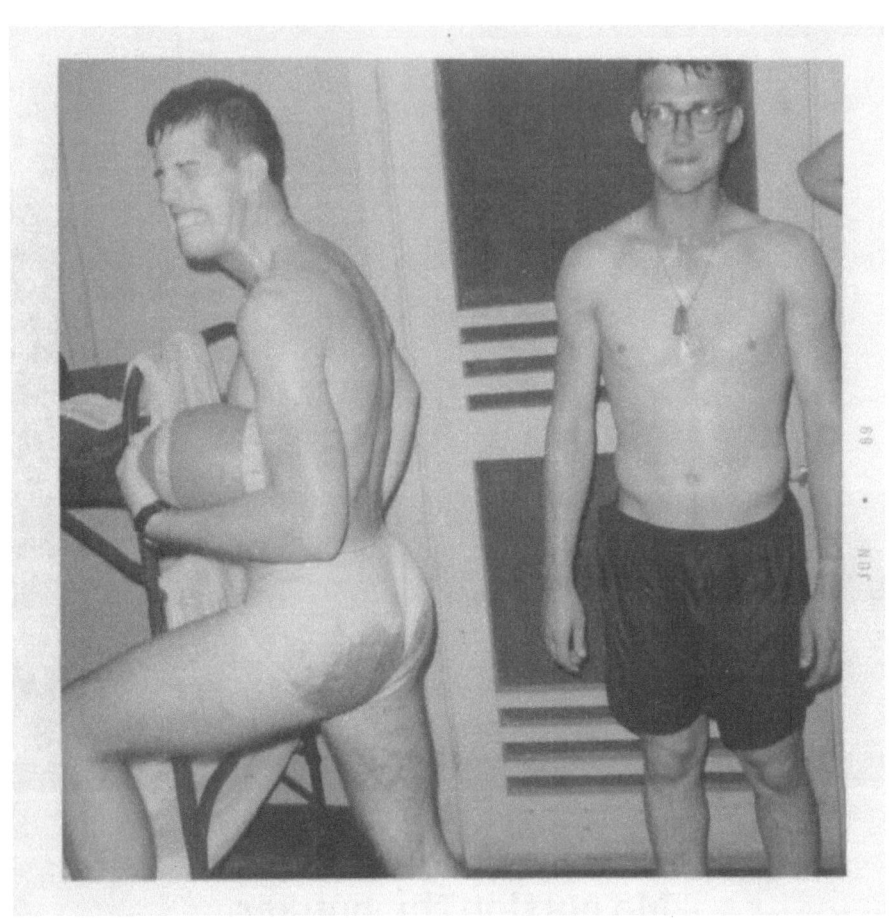

Skip Schaeffer. Football games in the monsoons were pretty rough.

I lifted some weights on my time off.

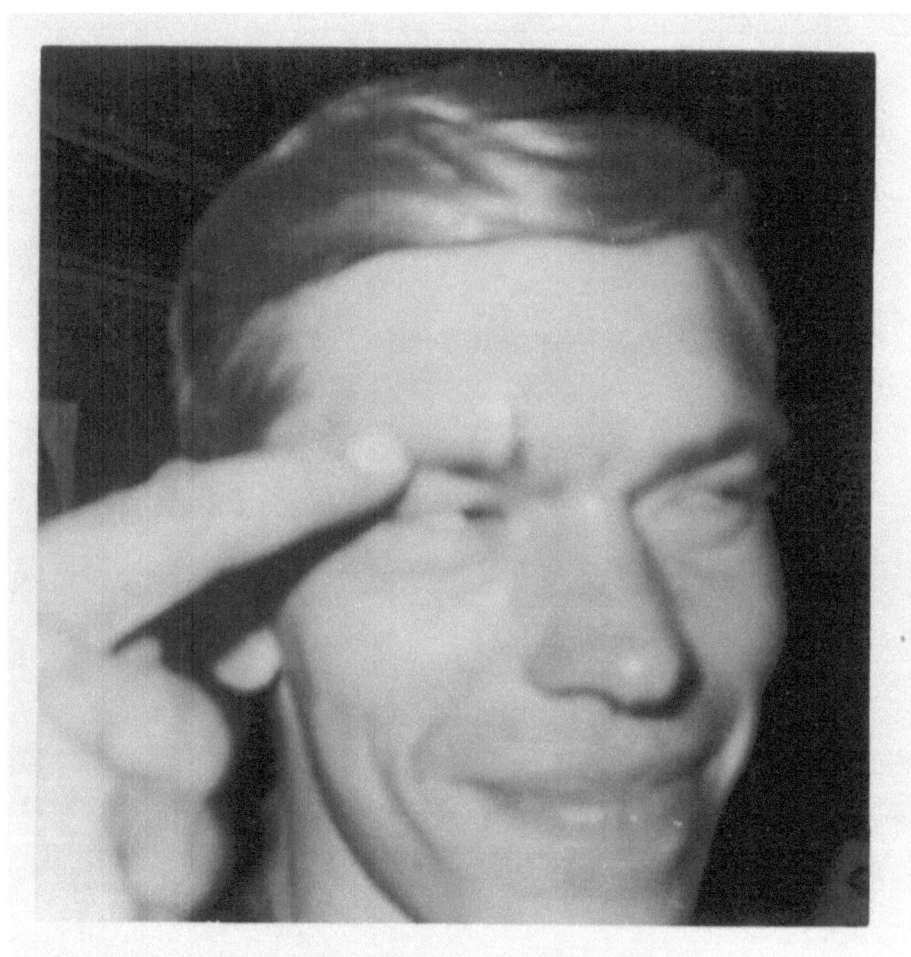

My three stitches

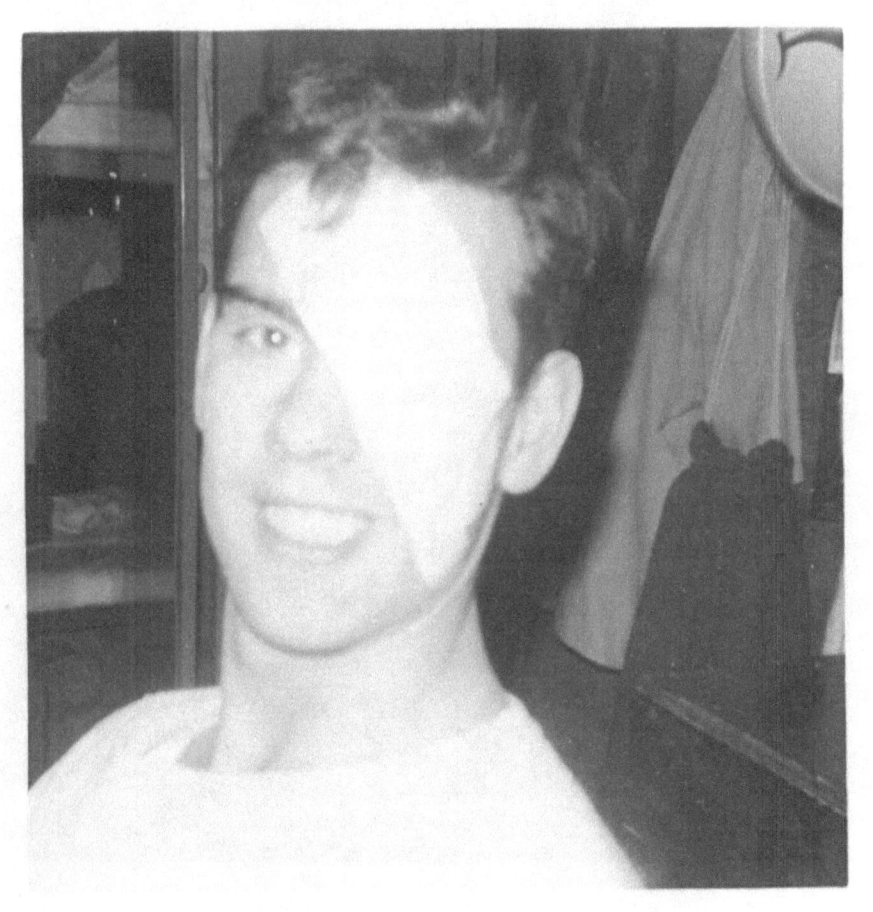

Mike's 32 stitches.

Mama San with picture of her husband.

Front of Card I sent Ginny.

Ever since I went away —
I have only memories ...
of the little silver stars ...
shining in the shadowed trees ...
All I ever think about ...
is the pallid moon on high ...
walking in his loneliness ...
on the empty, deep blue sky ...
and my eyes are always sad ...
when the winds at night will blow ...
in my winding garden lane ...
where the scented lilacs grow ...
and the clouds of angel hair ...
drifting through the silent night ...
are no longer growing dreams ...
that the dark will softly light ...
dearest, ever since the day ...
you and I have been apart ...
there has been a tiny tear ...
lying deep inside my heart.

James Metcalfe

Squeeze me, instead!

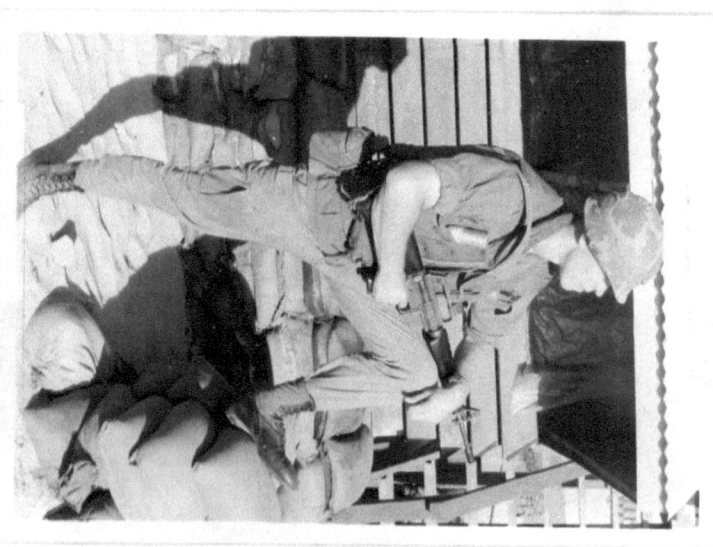

Inside of the card.

Me with the Christmas stockings Ginny sent
for my tree.
We still hang them every year.

Charlie Peterson and me.

Breakfast in the hotel in Hawaii.

Ginny in Hawaii after a day in the sun.

Bejerke and I expressing our feelings about re-upping.

Charlie Peterson and I manning a 50 caliber.

Mike Dunaway and I rebuilding fox holes and bunkers.

Ready for patrol. Magazine of rounds in helmet, flares in pockets, M16 rifle, and flak jacket.

Smitty, Me and Charlie Peterson
outside bunker.

Me with Dennis Pinkerton.
He kept Shep when I left.

Ginny doing her left-handed salute.

**May 10, 1969
Our Wedding.**

The pastor posted this sign after our wedding.

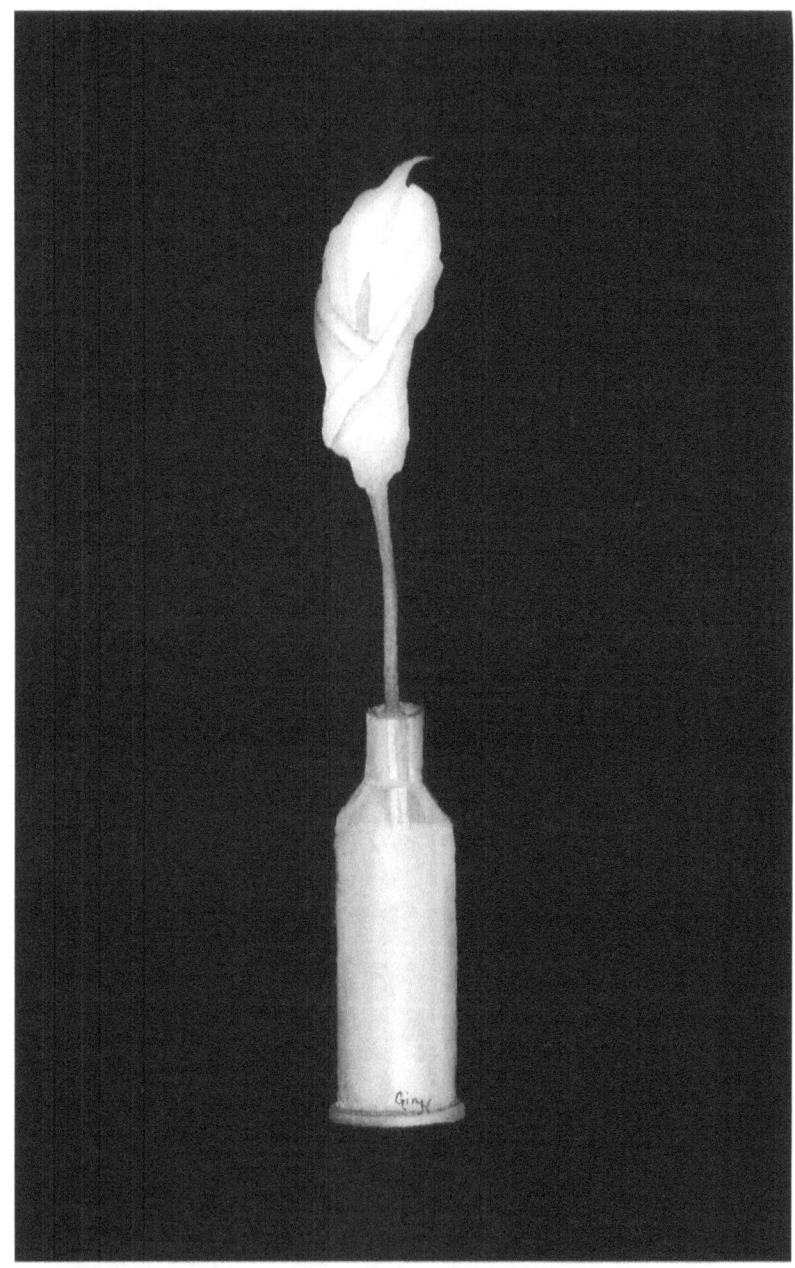

War and Peace Watercolor by Ginny Halverson.

CHAPTER 5
CAM RANH BAY

Jerry Sandine was our football coach in high school. He talked me into joining his typing class, a subject he taught when he wasn't on the gridiron. I thought, *Why should I take typing? I'm going to be a farmer, not a secretary*. But Jerry was my coach and I liked him, so I took typing. Doug Garringer joined me and the two of us pounded along on the typewriters like a couple of apes, while the girls in our class made their typewriters sing like musical instruments.

But typing came in handy in the Army. In my spare time, I used the typewriter in the office to write many of my letters home. Once the captain found out I could type faster than his clerk, he asked me to fill in. Being in the office gave me the opportunity to hear about things our cadre had planned, know when pay checks were ready, and see orders when they arrived. Knowing those things made me quite popular with the guys, who always wanted to know what was going on at the "head shed."

When orders arrived for Vietnam, I soon knew exactly where everyone would be stationed. The officers didn't issue the orders right away. They always had to have a formation to make it a formal occasion. So I took my notes back to the barracks and let everyone know where they would be going. Dale, Pete, Smitty, Art, and I would be going to Cam Ranh Bay. Hawk, Mike, Larry, and Kent would be going to Long Binh. We were all close friends and I hated to see the group split up.

I noticed that no orders had been cut for Smitty and Bullet. I immediately went to Sergeant Yates. "What the heck is going on here?" I asked.

He had a shocked look on his face and then said "Relax. Smitty may have helped every dog in the kennel; but he sure screwed up Bullet. He completely ruined that dog. We were going to send him to the Big Red 1 but we knew how close the two of you are so we cut orders for him to go to Cam Ranh Bay with you and he'll be issued another dog there."

Long Binh was close to Saigon and everyone dreaded going there because it had been attacked often by the North Vietnamese. Most of us had never heard of Cam Ranh Bay, but soon learned that it was a beautiful place, right on the South China Sea.

We loaded our dogs into aluminum kennels, maybe the same ones used to bring the dogs back from Vietnam to Okinawa. The kennels were then stacked into the cargo hold of a C-130. Nylon webbing held the kennels in place so they wouldn't shift in flight.

We soldiers then sat on fold-down seats along either side of the cargo hold and fastened our seat belts. I held my duffle bag between my legs and observed the inside of the plane. The floor was made of channeled aluminum. The channels allowed locking devices to be placed anywhere along the length of the plane so that webbing could be attached to hold things in place. The walls had D-rings for the same purpose. Our seats could be folded into the walls to allow more space for equipment. The hold was 12 feet wide, 40 feet long, and nine feet high. Wires and hydraulic lines ran everywhere. The plane could hold three V-100s, the army's new armor plated jeep, at once since it had a payload of 45,000 pounds and could fly at 300 mph. It truly was a flying machine shed!

The four turboprop engines began to howl, and down the runway we went on our journey from Okinawa to Vietnam. No one spoke. I'm sure they were thinking about what might lay ahead, just like I was. We landed at Clark Air Base on the island of Luzon in the Philippines. We had time to leave the plane and go to the rest room but that was about it. As soon as the plane refueled, we'd be back on our way.

I stepped off the plane into a sauna! I had never felt such heat and humidity. I looked at the gate of Clark Air Base and imagined the soldiers who had marched past it on the Bataan Death March. A few feet away and a few years ago men had marched by this very place, not knowing what their future had in store for them.

We boarded again and began the final leg of our trip. Soon we had gone far enough that the only thing visible in any direction was the ocean. I remember a time when I thought West Okoboji was a big body of water.

Soon, we began our descent into Cam Ranh Bay. The water was turquoise and the beaches looked like sugar. What a beautiful place! How could there be a war going on down there?

I watched the faces of the other guys. They were all quiet and deep in thought. We had all been brainwashed during Basic and Advanced Training into believing that we were all "John Waynes." We could walk straight and tall into a hail of bullets and take out the bad guys. Our weapons were superior, our cause was just, and our chaplains told us that God was on our side. How could anything go wrong?

The Domino Theory, so popular among our politicians, predicted that communism would take over the world if we didn't stop it in Vietnam. First they'd take South Vietnam, then Cambodia, and Laos. Those countries would all fall like dominoes if Vietnam was lost to the Commies. Who knew where it would end?

Despite all the training and hours of classes promoting the cause, I didn't see the look of confidence and resolve in the faces of my peers. Instead, I saw the look of fear.

While our politicians were promoting the war, the populace back in the States reacted in an entirely different way. Flower children demonstrated against the war. Huge anti-war demonstrations were taking place all over the country. Pictures of children maimed by napalm appeared in the papers, along with mothers hugging their children and pleading for their lives in front of an American soldier with an M-16. Vast areas of jungle, laid bare by Agent Orange, appeared in the backgrounds of the pictures.

Angel was a flower child who had been drafted. He was tall, blonde, and very athletic. I watched as he sat near the kennel with Butch, his attack dog. He flashed me the peace sign, grinned his gleaming white-toothed smile, and said, "It don't mean nothin'."

That saying was popular among the soldiers and became a common expression later when we faced unexplainable situations. For example, when Ginny sent me the Sunday edition of the *Des Moines Register* and the headlines read: "Americans are winning…4000 North Vietnamese killed in battle…American losses considered light," we would all say "It don't mean nothin'. What's light mean? 3999?"

Most of us were thinking of loved ones: wives, girl friends, Mom and Dad, siblings, and friends. Would we ever see them again? What if we get killed? Surprisingly, the prospect of dying didn't bother us much at all once we arrived in Vietnam. Dying would be clean and fast. Losing legs and arms concerned us much more. What would life be like if I lost both legs to a claymore mine? What if I lost a hand—would I have to wear a hook? What if I get hit in the head and become brain dead? Interestingly enough, once we were in 'Nam, the most common fear soldiers had was getting shot while on the toilet. "I don't want to die with my pants down around my ankles!"

Imaginings can be lethal. The human brain naturally focuses on fight-or-flight situations. It's perfectly natural to imagine a worst-case scenario. Whether thinking about business, love, friendship, or war, the natural tendency is to imagine what can go wrong. It's amazing how many situations the brain can come up with that predict a business will fail, this love affair or friendship will fall apart, or how quickly death will take place in war. That look was evident on every face.

I thought back to an incident that happened with my father. He needed an operation and was being readied by an anesthesiologist. The man had a limp and had obviously lost a portion of his face, yet he was cheerful and upbeat all the time he prepared Dad for the operation. Meanwhile, Dad imagined all the awful things that could go wrong while he was under the knife.

Dad finally asked, "What makes you so cheerful, especially when it's evident you've had some sort of serious injury?"

The man replied, "You have to keep an optimistic viewpoint in life. You see that I'm disfigured, but I see that God kept me alive so I could do good things, like I'm doing for you."

I determined that whatever happened, I would maintain an optimistic attitude.

The C-130 finally settled down on the airstrip at Cam Ranh Bay, Vietnam. We climbed down from the plane and looked over the area. The Army Corps of Engineers had built the airstrip some time ago and it was typical of airstrips throughout Vietnam. Sheets of metal roughly three feet wide and 10 feet long had been laid out side by side. One edge of the strip had holes that accepted fingers on the next strip so they would interlock. Once these strips are locked together, they made a surprisingly solid surface on which planes could land. I heard that the engineers could lay an entire strip on virgin ground in an afternoon.

Each strip had holes to promote drainage, the holes were about two inches in diameter on four-inch centers. Thus, when one viewed the airstrip from the side, all the holes lined up. Viewed from the end, the holes lined up. View the strips at a 45-degree angle and the holes still lined up. The airstrip reminded me of the wire-checked corn we used to plant on the farm and all the lines that the plants formed when being looked at from different angles.

Cargo planes landed and took off repeatedly. Conex containers were everywhere. Conex boxes are metal cargo containers that can be stacked side by side or on top of each other. They are roughly eight feet by eight feet and six feet tall. They had been filled in the States with things like clothing, food, and ammo, and then shipped or flown to Cam Ranh Bay. There the containers were offloaded and trucked to their final destinations.

It was hot! We were all sweating as we loaded our dogs and duffle bags into a deuce and a half to make our trip to the MP compound. Huey helicopters flew overhead and once in a while we saw a LOACH, a small helicopter used by high-ranking officers.

Our truck rattled down the road past rice paddies and I remember someone saying, "Hey look at her!"

A beautiful young Vietnamese girl was working in a rice paddy. We all gawked like a bunch of kids at a fair sideshow. She had our undivided attention and about that time she squatted to relieve herself right there in the field. We were silent as we beheld that sight. Soon we would learn that the culture in Vietnam was quite different from the culture in which we had grown up. The air smelled like the hog barn back home. That's because sewage flowed along the curbs of the streets. Gosh, they didn't even have outhouses!

Eventually, we saw the MP sign in front of the compound. It had two crossed pistols, the insignia for military police. Three Army insignias always stand out in my mind: crossed rifles for infantry, a parachute for airborne, and crossed pistols for MPs.

We spent our first day in Cam Ranh Bay setting up in the barracks and boarding our dogs. We unloaded our dogs into their kennels. The kennels' backs and sides were made of concrete and the fronts of cyclone fencing. Other dogs barked and snarled as we led in our dogs. There were roughly 80 dogs in all.

"Private Smith! Front and center!" a burly sergeant screamed. Smitty ambled over to him with the bill of his hat at a thirty degree angle as he usually wore it. He never wore it straight ahead like the rest of us or like the Army wanted it to be done. As usual, the sergeant who was ready to chastise him for the way he was wearing his hat, noticed Smitty's birth mark and forgot all about his hat. "Here's your new dog, Smith. His name is Brutus and he's about the best dog I've ever seen. You're one lucky boy to get him!" Smitty's guardian angel had come through again!

Then we took our duffle bags to the barracks. All the beds on the bottom floor were taken by the old timers, so we new guys had to claim unused beds upstairs. The two-story barracks were wooden structures with overhanging rooflines to protect us from the rain. The back walls were all screened to allow as much airflow as possible to relieve the heat and humidity in the building. That's right, no AC! I noticed a horseshoe pitching area outside the barracks and decided I would spend a lot of time there.

As darkness approached, we were called to stand mortar watch. I had learned a long time ago not to volunteer for anything, so I conveniently bent to tie my shoes as the man in charge picked people to go to the top of the building to watch for mortars. Those men climbed a ladder and took up positions on each corner of the roof with instructions to warn us if they saw any incoming mortars. Then I mixed with the others as they relaxed and laughed about the new guys standing mortar watch.

"Who's gonna see a mortar coming in?" one cackled. "Boy, are they dumb!"

That reminded me of entering high school, joining a fraternity, and any other event requiring a rite of passage. Every organization seems to have an initiation ritual of some sort.

The next morning everyone was in good cheer after initiating the guys who had been on mortar watch the night before. "Jeez, ya green horn. A mortar is a bullet. Did you really think you could see it coming and warn us?" The banter was all in good fun and other than some embarrassment no offense was taken over the incident.

Early the next morning we began our in-country training. We assembled in a classroom and awaited our first speaker. A master sergeant, an E-8, finally arrived at the front of the room and began his speech about the Vietnamese people, the Viet Cong, and the North Vietnamese Army. His speech was rambling and clumsy. We soon figured out that he was drunk! How in the world could a man be drunk first thing in the morning?

We soon found out that many officers and non-commissioned officers were alcoholics. The Army couldn't get rid of them so they were promoted into a position where they couldn't do any harm. Suddenly, the Peter Principle became real to all of us.

The Vietnamese people were at that time an agrarian people. They planted rice, cared for the rice, harvested the rice, and did it all over again the next year. They used water buffalo to pull plows to prepare their fields. They also raised chickens and vegetable gardens.

"Shooting a water buffalo can be very expensive," the master sergeant told us. "Uncle Sam has to pay for the water buffalo, the babies it would have had over its lifetime, and the crops that could have been grown had the buffalo remained alive to do its work.

"Likewise," he continued, "a chicken that you use for target practice can also cost Uncle Sam. He must pay for the chicken itself, the chicks that would have hatched over the life of the chicken, and the eggs that could have been produced by both the hen and her brood." The message here was simple: Don't use any animals for target practice because it's going to cost Uncle Sam big bucks.

He said nothing about the Vietnamese culture, religion, or mores.

We learned that the Viet Cong were local people who supported the North Vietnamese Army. They worked their normal jobs during the day and fought us at night. Hooch maids that cleaned our barracks and shined our shoes could be Viet Cong, and they could hide hand grenades in their body cavities and, once inside the compound, set them off in a group of soldiers. Children could ride bicycles crammed with plastic explosives into a group of soldiers and trigger the mechanism, blowing up themselves and the soldiers.

I wondered to myself, *Why do they fight us when we're here to save them? When do they get any sleep if they're working their fields by day and fighting us at night?*

Short arm inspections became a regular activity for us, black syphilis being prevalent in Vietnam. Black syphilis is incurable and results in the penis rotting away. Films we saw showed men who had black syphilis—their urine no longer ran in a stream, instead seeping from holes along their shafts.

"You'll be given a choice if you get black syph," we were told. "You can't go home because we don't want that disease in the US of A. We'll send a letter to your family telling them the truth, or telling them that you are missing in action—your choice. You will be sent to Hope Island (wherever that is) where you can spend the rest of your life hoping they find a cure." I didn't know how much of that was truth and how much was propaganda to keep us in line, but it didn't make any difference. I planned to be faithful to my wife so it wouldn't be a problem.

The North Vietnamese regulars were the most dangerous of the lot, we were told. They'd set booby traps, hide in spider holes, and when they came out in the open to fight they meant business. They were supplied by caravans of bicycles carrying food and ammunition down the Ho Chi Minh Trail from Hanoi. I looked around at all the planes, helicopters, trucks, supply depots, tanks, boats, and other equipment that we had and wondered, *How can soldiers with AK47s being supplied by a bicycle convoy stand up to all of this?*

Cam Ranh Bay has the most beautiful shoreline I've ever seen. The sand on the beaches looks just like granulated sugar and the depth of the water increases ever so gradually as one walks into the sea. I could easily go out a quarter-mile and only be up to my neck in water. That made for great body surfing on a windy day. I could catch a wave and body surf for the length of three football fields.

Salt water is a healing agent. Many of our dogs had cuts and scrapes from their kennels, so we were encouraged to take our dogs swimming. Shep thoroughly enjoyed his trips to the beach where he'd anxiously jump into the water to retrieve a stick.

Cam Ranh Bay was also the receiving area for shipments of ammunition, food, and clothing. There were huge warehouses of perishables and products that couldn't be exposed to the weather. The ammo dump was located on rolling ground at the edge of the city. Berms had been bulldozed into the jungle. Those berms, piles of dirt about eight feet high, surrounded an ammo pad. The purpose of the berms was to direct the blast straight up into the air in the event a pad of ammunition ever exploded. The jungle was between the berms and was dense, a good hiding place for the two-step viper, king cobra, spiders, orangutans, monkeys, wild hogs, birds of all descriptions, lizards, and other naturally occurring wild life.

I wasn't very worried about a two-step viper. It got its name because if it bit you, you wouldn't walk more than two steps before you died. It had extremely deadly venom. It's easily recognizable because it has beautiful bands of red, yellow, and black around its body. However, it's a very small snake and, consequently, it can only open its mouth far enough to bite your little finger.

The King Cobra is a different matter. It also has deadly venom and can open its mouth wide so it's fangs can penetrate your skin anywhere. There were no lights in the ammo dump, so we couldn't see the cobra ahead of us. But the dogs could smell a cobra before we got too close and they wouldn't get any closer than about six feet. We "Yankees" didn't know how to take care of a snake, but the "Rednecks" did and we soon learned how to take care of a cobra. They taught us to hold our M-16s a few feet away from the snake and wave the muzzle back and forth. The cobra would line himself up on the rifle so he could strike. All we had to do was to pull the trigger and nail him right between the eyes every time!

The orangutans would come out at night and give the most blood curdling screams to scare off intruders. The first time I heard an orangutan scream, I almost died of fright! Other soldiers told us about orangutan attacks. Supposedly, an orangutan would attack a soldier to protect its territory. There was a bounty of $2000 for anyone who shot one, and rumor had it that one orangutan had been shot eight times and still roamed the ammo dump!

I hate spiders! Vietnam was blessed with every spider in the book and, like the snakes, it seemed that every one of them was poisonous. The bamboo spider had a body about the size of a coffee cup, but with its legs it was more the size of a dinner plate. They could move surprisingly fast and loved a warm spot in which to sleep. Numerous times I woke up in the morning with a bamboo spider sleeping on my face! Thank goodness they weren't poisonous.

By far and away our favorite animal in Vietnam was the F-U lizard. They are a small, green lizard much like a chameleon that gets its name from its call. It used the four letter F-word to say "Fuck You!" They are absolutely everywhere and their call is as common as the ticking of a clock.

Most of us soldiers were draftees. We didn't like the war and didn't want to be in it. We had been drafted and were serving out of a sense of duty. "Lifers" is the term we used for career soldiers. We draftees hated lifers! Part of the reason we hated lifers is that they gave us our orders and we had to take them. You don't argue in the Army, so you can imagine the sheer joy that coursed through our veins when a lifer gave us an order in that gruff, Army voice, only to be followed by a lizard call saying, "Fuck You!"

Anything is scary the first time you have to do it. Whether it's learning how to ride a bike, how to handle yourself on your first date, or walking a guard post. It's scary the first time.

While stationed in Cam Ranh Bay, our sergeant gave me equipment and orders to walk the guard post around the ammunition dump. My equipment consisted of an M-16, a bandolier of M-16 clips, pen light flares, a radio, and my attack dog Shep. My orders were to walk the perimeter of the ammunition dump and protect it from sappers.

A sapper was a Viet Cong or North Vietnamese Regular with a backpack full of plastic explosives. He would try to penetrate the perimeter and throw his satchel charge into the dump and blow everything to kingdom come. In the event that I encountered the enemy, I was to fire a red penlight flare into the sky, command Shep to attack the enemy, and fire my weapon if needed.

Every hour I was supposed to call the command center and report. I was assigned the handle "Watchdog 1." If I had not encountered the enemy, my report would be, "Base, Base, this is Watchdog 1, over."

Base would reply, "Watchdog 1, Watchdog 1, this is Base, over."

I would then say, "Situation negative, over and out."

That conversation verified that I was still alive and that I had not encountered the enemy.

In the event that I did not report in at my designated time, base would assume that I was either in trouble or dead, and would send out a squad to investigate. If I reported, "Situation Positive" to Base, they would know that I had encountered a sapper and that they should send the squad to assist me.

Charley Butler was Watchdog 2. He called base to report in:

"Base, base. This is Watchdog 2, over."

"Watchdog 2, Watchdog 2, this is base, over." Came the reply.

The base's immediate reply shocked Charley and he couldn't think of the words he was supposed to say so he improvised. "Base, base, this is Watchdog 2. I can't remember those words we were supposed to say; but everything is nice and quiet out here!"

I also got green and white penlight flares. Those colors were to be fired if I encountered someone on my post and couldn't determine if it was another dog handler or the enemy. The color of the flare we fired would tell our compatriots if it was friend or foe. So, if we determined that a green flare should be used on this night, I would fire a green flare into the sky. That would tell other soldiers that it was a friend they were encountering and not the enemy.

We would alternate colors each night and did this because the enemy also had pen flares. They could fire a green penlight, too, and thereby get past us. By alternating colors, the enemy didn't know which color we would be using that night. The pen flares prevented us from getting killed by an enemy using penlight flares and also prevented us from getting killed by "friendly fire."

I walked my post regularly that first night and made my radio report on time. Before I knew it, the sun was beginning to rise and I thought I would take a rest. I sat down on my steel helmet and ordered Shep to sit.

A few minutes went by and I heard a foot step behind me. Shep's ears picked up.

I heard another step and froze with fear. Shep began to quiver with anticipation. He was ready to attack, but had been trained to remain immobile until I gave him a command.

I heard yet another step. I could tell that "Charley" was almost upon me and would probably slip a piano wire around my neck to finish me off. Shep was beside himself waiting for the command to attack.

I froze. I remember thinking to myself, *All you have to do is yell, "Kill him boy, kill him."*

But I was so frozen with fear I couldn't say anything.

Another step.

I thought to myself, *Your M-16 is on full automatic. All you have to do is spin around and blow him away.* But I was too frozen with fear to do it.

Another step.

Shep was delirious with anticipation.

I remember thinking to myself, *You're going to get your head popped off with piano wire and all because you're too scared to do anything.*

Another step, and this one was close!

And then … I heard a snort.

I thought to myself, *That's funny. Why would a Gook give himself away by making a sound like that?*

And then there was a squeal.

I turned around and discovered a wild pig and her six piglets rooting around in the ground behind me! I began laughing. My clothing was absolutely soaked with sweat, and that was the only time in my life that I can say I was glad to see a pig!

The ammo dump at Cam Ranh Bay was a big one. Supply and Transportation companies were based at Cam Ranh Bay and delivered supplies and ammunition by semi-trailer truck to outlying areas. Not only did the bay offer deep water for ship deliveries, but it was known as the "Jewel of Vietnam." Its turquoise water and sugary white sand beaches were breathtaking to behold.

Bunkers surrounded the ammo dump. Each bunker had three men and two of them had to be awake at all times while the third man catnapped. Each had a 50-caliber machine gun mounted on the top and there were two M-60s inside. Concertina wire surrounded the entire area encompassing the bunkers and the ammunition.

Outside the concertina wire were guard towers that resembled the old crow's nests that coaches sat in during football practice. The towers were mounted on telephone poles. Again, three men sat in the towers armed with an M-60 and two M-14s. Searchlights were pointed outward from the towers, lighting the entire area outside the perimeter. The searchlights not only lit the area for the guards but blinded anyone trying to enter.

We sentry dog handlers walked the area between the bunkers and the towers. Our job was to detect anyone who had gotten past the outside guards, through the concertina wire, and into the ammo dump. As I looked at the lighting, concertina wire, and armed guards, I wondered how anyone could possibly get through all that security. But sappers were very adept at snaking their way through the wire. Thus, ammo dumps were often blown up by the enemy.

Charlie, as we called the enemy, always fought at night so we walked the dogs in nightly shifts. The first shift was from six p.m. to midnight. The second shift was from midnight to six a.m. We all wanted the early shift because we'd be done at midnight and could get a good night's sleep before details in the morning. Late shift could be awful because we'd get back to the barracks at 7:30 in the morning. Details, such as cleaning kennels, feeding the dogs, cleaning the barracks and the surrounding area, and standing inspection, took place beginning at 8:30 a.m.

I remember walking my shift those first few nights. Being a powerful dog, Shep pulled me down one hill and up the next one. He never tired and always seemed anxious to see what was over the next hill. Those first nights were anxious for me because my imagination ran away with itself. I thought I saw Charlie around every corner.

During one of my shifts, Shep perked up his ears all at once and began to sniff the air, an indication that he had detected someone. He pulled at the leash and I held on for dear life. His paws dug into the ground as he pulled furiously to get to the man he smelled. A chill ran down my spine as I imagined what I might encounter. He dragged me to a tower guard who had climbed down to relieve himself in the elephant grass.

I gave a sigh of relief when I realized he wasn't a North Vietnamese with an AK47. I warned the guard never to come down from the tower again or I would turn my dog loose on him.

He asked, "What am I supposed to do when I have to go?"

I told him to do his business before he came to post or bring along a coffee can.

That may seem crass but I understood something that had been drilled into me during training: When a dog alerts, he needs to be rewarded for doing a good job. Shep's joy in training had been to attack any man he had detected. The man who served as the decoy in training had a padded suit, which allowed Shep to attack him, bite him, and tear at the suit. I would pet him afterward and praise him for doing a good job. Shep would smile and slobber with happiness. But this time Shep didn't get to attack and he didn't get praised. That can be destructive because the dog begins to wonder, *Why should I even try if I'm not going to get to attack and be praised?* Soon the dog becomes lazy and gives up working the way he's been trained. I wanted to get back home in one piece and that meant I needed Shep to work all the time. You can bet your boots that I would have turned him loose on that guard the next time he came down for a call of nature.

I told everybody back at the barracks what had happened. Everyone agreed that our dogs would become worthless if they found a person and couldn't attack. So it came as no surprise that the next night Smitty turned Brutus loose on a tower guard that was relieving himself in the elephant grass. The poor guy was squatting in the cover of the grass when he heard Smitty yell "Get 'im Boy!" Brutus took off on a dead run, the guy stood up and saw what was happening and tried to run to his tower with his pants still around his ankles. He was able to reach the ladder and grab a rung but with his pants around his ankles, he couldn't get his feet on the rungs of the ladder. So he went hand over hand up four rungs of the ladder before Brutus dove for the kill. Brutus got the guy's pants and hung on for dear life, growling and whipping his head back and forth. The guard must have had an enormous surge of adrenalin because he made it to the top of the ladder with Brutus hanging from his pants. And that was as far as he made it because he couldn't make it over the edge of the tower…he just helplessly hung there until Smitty came and got Brutus to let go of his pants. It must have been quite a sight to see that guy hanging to the ladder for dear life with his bare butt showing and a dog hanging from his pants!

"Hey Dad! You shoulda seen that guy run with his pants around his ankles! His eyes were as big as dinner plates! Bet we don't have trouble with tower gaurds coming down anymore!" And you know what? We didn't.

The master sergeant in charge of our unit in Cam Ranh Bay liked us. "Cleanest cut bunch of boys I've ever had," he said. "I'm going to try to keep all of you here and send the new guys north. Never seen a group that wants to help at an orphanage instead of getting drunk or getting laid, or so I hear. You treat the locals like they are good people instead of looking down your noses at them."

Our reputations had preceded us.

I've heard it said that war is 90% sheer boredom and 10% sheer hell . Cam Ranh Bay was the perfect setting for boredom. We had tight security and the enemy knew it, so they stayed away and attacked in other, more remote places.

The boredom was broken one afternoon when the sarge came running into our barracks and said "Load up your dogs….NOW!" We saw the expression on his face and knew that he meant business so we didn't ask why; we just got our dogs and ran for the deuce and a half. A whole barracks full of guys headed to the kennels. Charley Butler and I were the first to get on the truck and were waiting for others to arrive to make a full load. But the sarge threw the tail gate up when a few of us had gotten on and yelled at the driver to head to the Provost Marshall's Office. Other guys stood there with their dogs and watched as we roared off. There were four of us on the truck and as it bounced down the road we were all wondering what the big deal was. Did they want a dog show? An exhibition? We heard a rifle shot and then another and then another. The board I was resting my arm on exploded into splinters. "What the?"

"Down," I yelled. "They're shooting at us!" We all dived to the bed of the truck and listened as bullets flew over us. The driver wheeled into the Provost Marshall's area, ran around to the end gate and dropped it and yelled "Turn 'em loose!"

We didn't need any more coaxing. I tore the muzzle from Shep and yelled "Get 'em boy!" Charley and the others did the same. The shooting stopped and the yelling began.

"Help, help! Get him off me! Help."

We crawled out of the truck and found a group of African-Americans with dogs biting their arms and legs. The "Soul Brothers" had dropped their rifles when they saw the dogs coming and had tried to run, but that sure didn't work. We all commanded our dogs "OUT."

Once we had the dogs muzzled and back on their leashes, the Provost Marshall came out to thank us. "The soul brothers took over the office saying they didn't have any freedom at home so why should they fight for it here. I don't know what they were going to do with my office. I guess they just wanted to make a statement. Thanks for coming."

As we rode back to the barracks I said "Jeez. My first fire fight and it's with our own soldiers."

"Ya got that right," said Charley. "My own brothers."

Officers were everywhere, anxious to prove themselves and flaunt their authority. Spit-and-polish orders abounded. We had to stand formation while the officers checked the shine on our belt buckles and boots, checked for buttons and proper military dress, and issued make-work orders. Make-work orders consisted of policing the area for trash and cigarette butts, burning our excrement from the latrines, cleaning weapons, and checking the sandbag quality at the bunkers. It was all pointless activity and we knew it, as did the officers. But what else were we going to do when we had no battle to fight?

The boredom drove all of us to find activities to do in our off-time. The dopers made the most of it. While I didn't use drugs, some of my friends did. To them I became known as "The guy on the natural high!" They would take their marijuana to a remote bunker, turn their tape decks as high as they would go, and listen to music while they smoked pot. John Lennon's *Imagine* was high on their list of favored tunes. I found it incongruous to see a group of soldiers in uniform with steel pots on their heads and M-16s in their hands singing, "Imagine all the people living life in peace…"

Bob Dylan's *Blowing in the Wind* played on some decks while the same song by Peter, Paul and Mary played on others. Bruce Springsteen's *Born in the USA* was originally a song about the troubles of a working class man forced into the Vietnam War, and later became patriotic instead of an anti-war song. *Give Peace a Chance* by John Lennon was popular, especially in the States during the moratorium to end the war. Many liked the lines of *For What It's Worth* by Buffalo Springfield, saying, "There's battle lines being drawn, nobody's right is everybody's wrong, young people speaking their minds getting so much resistance from behind." The lyrics had been written by Stephen Stills of Crosby, Stills and Nash.

Edwin Starr sang, *War…What is it good for?* Barry McGuire's *Eve of Destruction* said "You're old enough to kill, but not for voting; you don't believe in war, but what's that gun you're toting?" Jim Morrison and the Doors gave us *The Unknown Soldier*.

REM sang *Orange Crush*, referring to our government's use of Agent Orange to defoliate trees and dense jungle. Later, after the war, many US soldiers suffered from diabetes, heart disease, Parkinson's, prostate cancer, leukemia, and lung cancer as a result of being exposed to that chemical.

All those songs, among others, were popular with almost every soldier, even though the dopers really identified with them. But there was one song that everyone accepted: *The I Feel Like I'm Fixing to Die Rag*, written by Joe McDonald and sung by Country Joe and the Fish. When that song played, everyone joined in for the chorus:

And it's one, two, three what are we fighting for?
Well, I don't give a damn, next stop is Vietnam.
And it's five, six, seven; open up the Pearly Gates.
Well, there ain't no time to wonder why
Whoopee, we're all gonna die!

We called our hooch maid "Mama-san." I didn't even know her real name; we just called her Mama-san. She washed our clothes, shined our shoes, and cleaned up around the barracks. All of us pitched money into a hat to pay her for her services and she always seemed happy with our freewill offering. Some of us gave her food, a precious commodity in a war zone. Ginny sent me chocolate chip cookies, and I gave Mama-san some to eat and take home to her family. I'll never forget the look of surprise on her face when she took a bite of one. She had never had a cookie in her life and the look of pleasure on her face was priceless.

Mama-san wore the typical black nightgown, as we called them. It's like a loose dress with slits on the sides up to the knee. She wore a conical, rice-straw hat to shield her from the sun. It hid her face down to her nose. Her husband had fought for the South Vietnamese Army and had been killed up north near Pleiku during the Tet Offensive of 1968. She had four children and no means of support, so she became our hooch maid in order to feed her family.

She was a devout Catholic and believed in the vows she had taken when she married her husband. So, despite the propositions of many soldiers, she remained faithful to her wedding vows. She didn't whore herself even though it would have meant more money to support her family.

She enjoyed our unit. "You go to chapel and believe in God," she said. "You are number one GIs, not number 10 like those other soldiers."

The Vietnamese judged everything and everyone on a numbered scale from one to 10. One meant very good and 10 meant very bad.

For some reason Mama-san and I had a remarkable relationship. One day she came to my bunk and cried. I didn't say anything because I didn't even know why she was crying, let alone what to say. So I just stood there with my hand on her shoulder. Finally, she held up a picture for me to see. It was a picture of her husband and her on their wedding day. This day happened to be their anniversary.

She asked me "What is the first thing you want to do when you get home?"

I told her the first thing would be to kiss Ginny. And the second thing: "I want to sit in a tub of hot water near the toilet and just reach over and flush it. Ahhh, the sound of a flushing toilet would be so nice."

She had never heard of a tub or a toilet, so I had to explain them to her.

"You mean it all goes away?" she asked.

"Yup, it sure does."

She thought our showers and outhouses were a step up from the way she lived. The Vietnamese bathed in a stream if they had one. Otherwise, a sponge bath had to do. And their toilets were simple holes in the ground with boards over them. The board had a hole in it, so aim had to be pretty good. Flies abounded. The sewage either sunk into the ground or ran down the gutters in the streets.

She thought our shower tanks on the roof were really something. We'd stand under the tank and pull a chain to release the water. We even had hot water if the sun shone enough to heat up the tank.

Our outhouses had the top or bottom half of a 55-gallon oil drum beneath the wooden seat. Every day we had to dump the barrel's contents into a hole in the ground and burn the material after dousing it with diesel fuel. That way the flies and the smell were minimal. Spiders liked to build their webs in the toilet seat hole because it was dark, moist and plenty of flies abounded there. Many a soldier had to be rushed to the dispensary with a spider bite in a very tender spot. To this day I still check the toilet for spiders.

One day the Mail Officer came down the aisle to my bunk. "Halverson, we're going to have mail call, and I want you front and center! There's a box from your wife and I'm guessing it's another pair of those fancy boxer shorts she makes for you. It's been about a month since you got the last pair. There's been too much boredom, so the guys need a pick-me-up and I think it will give them a charge if they can see your new Cong Catchers."

Here's how mail call worked: The Mail Officer might yell, "Perkins, Johnson, Bladorn, Peterson." Perkins, Johnson, Bladorn, and Peterson would run forward anxiously to receive their mail. Then he would announce: "That is all." And the bulk of the guys would look at the ground, so hurt because they hadn't gotten any mail. I wish I could convey that look in words, but I can't.

On this particular day, the two of us walked up the stairs to a small balcony overlooking the formation grounds. There the Mail Officer stood with a sack of mail and announced the names of the recipients of letters and packages. Then he held up my box. "Halverson, or Dad as you like to call him, got another package with those fancy drawers inside and I thought you'd all like to see them."

I opened the box and pulled out the boxers. It was October and Ginny had made black boxers with a pumpkin on the back, a cat on the front, and orange fringe all the way around. Everyone cheered and whistled as I held them up for everyone to see.

The note on top said, "Seven more pair and you'll be coming home."

And that's how I counted my time in Vietnam. I knew I'd been gone for 5 months because I had now had 5 pair of shorts and that meant I had 7 more to go.

I got another care package from Ginny one day. I opened it and found a nice, shriveled-up potato lying on the top! No question where that came from: Ginny's father, Emery, was quite a prankster. I could just see him giggling as he sneaked it into the box.

Of course, I got another pair of boxer shorts. These were made from Chicago Bear material, my favorite football team.

"You're gonna have to get up on the balcony and show everyone your new Cong Catchers," Smitty said with a laugh.

Then there were cookies, brownies, and other edibles all packed in popcorn. The popcorn kept everything from getting broken and made a great snack, even though it was old and stale. Why did they ever change to bubble wrap? And on the bottom was a package of Cracker Jacks. I hadn't had them in a while and drooled at the thought of the caramel and nuts.

"I get the prize," Smitty chimed in.

The boxers came in pretty handy and made a reputation for me as someone who stood up to the officers. While we were in Cam Ranh Bay, the officers had a standing order that no civilian clothing could be worn on post. Underwear was the only exception to the "no civilian clothes" rule. Many people preferred jockey shorts to the olive drab boxer shorts that were Army issue. I suspect that was also true of officers and that might have been why they made the exception. As I said earlier, Cam

Ranh Bay was a peaceful, well protected compound, so officers made up stupid rules to exert their authority since they weren't involved in anything important, like combat.

The vast majority of us had been drafted, didn't want to be in the military, and wore civilian clothing at every opportunity just to show that we hated the Army. At any rate, back at the barracks I called Smitty and Pete over to my bunk and said, "Here, each of you put on a pair of my boxers and let's go parading around the headquarters building."

Officers noticed us as soon as we arrived. Smitty had on orange ones with yellow flowers, Pete had pink ones with white trim, and I had the Chicago Bears boxers. The officers stood in front of their office and scowled at us, but there was absolutely nothing they could do because of their exception rule. A crowd had followed us as we left the barracks and, when they saw the officers standing there dumbfounded, they cheered and howled with pleasure.

Smitty looked over at a second lieutenant that we all disliked and said, "What do you think of my Cong Catchers?"

The lieutenant scowled and Smitty roared with laughter.

That was one of the true triumphs of my tour in Vietnam!

Getting back to my mail, Ginny's letters hadn't told me about going to the Clay County Fair, seeing a show, riding the Ferris wheel, eating a foot-long hot dog, or anything like that. She knew telling me things like that would make me homesick. Instead, her letters said, "I love you. You're important to me."

Not everyone got letters like that, and I'm sure that's why a lot of the guys used drugs and drank.

I remember a cute card I sent her and want to share it with you: The front of the card showed a man with his hair singed, his clothing mostly burned off, and his eyes blackened. Wisps of smoke rose above him. On the front of the card he was saying, "I got to thinking about you yesterday." The message inside the card said, "And I got hit by a heat-seeking missile!"

"Halverson! Front and center!" boomed a voice one day.

Sergeant Pepper waited for me as I responded and walked to the front of the barracks.

"Straighten up your uniform, put on your MP helmet, strap on your.45, and follow me," he said. "They just brought in a prisoner and they need someone to guard him while Intelligence changes shifts and processes his information. They had a B-52 raid on the Cambodian border a few days ago. Recon went in to gather information and they found this guy huddled near a weapons cache. Guess he was nearly deaf and out of his mind—imagine being in the middle with all those 800-pounders going off? The noise would blow your ear drums out and the shock of all those explosions would drive you batty! Anyway, you need to keep him safe and secure until Intelligence is done with him and they can put him in the brig."

We went to the Provost Marshall's office and they ushered me into a conference room. There sat a young man who didn't look to be over 16 years of age. Fear was written all over his face. I made a showing of my.45 to make sure he understood that I meant business and sat down near the door. He seemed so young, so helpless, so lost. And yet, that was typical of most of the men we were fighting. The Vietnamese, in comparison to Americans, are smaller in stature, partly due to genetics and partly due to diet.

So many of them were just boys, not only boys but girls, too. Guys in the infantry told me about going out on body counts and finding dead women with AK47s in their hands. I thought about the soldiers in WWII. They knew who the enemy was simply because of their uniforms. The NVA regulars had uniforms but most of the people we were fighting had none at all. The young man I was guarding was a good example. He wore shorts, a shirt, no hat, and a pair of Ho Chi Minhs...sandals made from old tire casings and strips of inner tube left behind by the French and, now, the Americans. They took our junk and made shoes—and booby traps—and trinkets that we could buy to send home to our loved ones. I've got a pool cue that a Vietnamese made from our junk. The tip on the cue is a shell casing stuffed with felt. The rubber tip on the other end, to protect it when set on the floor, is made from melted rubber from inner tubes. The stick itself is made of monkey pod, a tree that grows there, and it's decorated with rings made from melted brass from shell casings.

Meanwhile, this young man and I were in the middle of a war, just like a lot of other young men from both our countries, poor kids fighting a rich man's war.

Smitty, Pete and I got orders to go to Pleiku, along with several others in the platoon.

Darn! I had just finished making myself a proper desk. Most of us used the boxes mortar rounds came in as desks. We'd nail a box to the wall so the lid swung down to make a writing surface. When we were done, we could swing the lid up and lock it in place. The lid was only a foot or so wide and about three feet long, not much room to work on.

But I wanted something more conducive to letter writing and reading, so I scrounged up some plywood, nails, saw, and hammer and made a real desk. I'm an avid reader, so the desk had a place for my books. My book ends were Coke cans filled with sand. I had a sign on my desk saying, "Put the coffee on, I'll be right there." The sign reminded me of home, where Mom always had the coffee on for the neighbors.

Pleiku is up north in the Central Highlands. It's colder and has more Viet Cong and North Vietnamese regulars than points farther south. We were nervous about the move.

I had read a quote by Ho Chi Minh:

The rice grain suffers under the blows of the pestle;
But admire its whiteness once the ordeal is over.
Thus it is with men in the world we live in;
To be a man one must suffer the blows of misfortune.

His soldiers took those words to heart and reveled in their misfortune, believing they would be better in the end because of any misfortune they might suffer. That's not much different than we felt ourselves and they are pretty wise words, even if they came from the leader of the opposition.

I didn't have any choice about moving to Pleiku, so I grasped the necklace that Ginny had given me. I can't tell you how many times I gripped that medallion and drew strength from it. I always believed that

I would come home safely because of what it represented: our love, our faith and our prayers.

I have always felt that when things get depressing, it's time to laugh. So my letter to Gin that day ended with the story of a farm dog that went to town. He walked up to a parking meter and said, "Jeez. Pay toilets!" Well, he did his business anyway and the parking meter dinged and up popped a sign that said "Violation!"

I laughed as I wrote it and that made me feel better. Laughter is good medicine. Like the Bible says: A cheerful heart is like a good medicine.

While in 'Nam, I only had the US mail with which to stay in touch with my friends and loved ones. They wrote often and I'm thankful for that, but gosh, I'd have given anything for a visit from one of them.

Mama-san was sorry that I'd be leaving for Pleiku. We were close friends. She and Ginny had gotten close as well. Ginny sent cookies and perfume to her, and Mama-san sent little trinkets to her. Mama-san said that Ginny and I reminded her of the marriage she and her husband had had. Her husband had been drafted as well.

She sat me down and wrote something on a piece of paper, and then asked me to read it. I couldn't because it was written in Vietnamese. She coached me and wouldn't quit until I had mastered the saying.

Finally, she nodded and told me I was saying the phrase correctly. "Now, here's what it means," she said. "'I have a wife at home that I love very much. I am not looking for a girlfriend in Vietnam but I would like you to be my friend.'"

She told me that many women had lost their husbands at Pleiku, and that some had become whores in order to support themselves and feed their children. "They will understand if you tell them what I have taught you and you will make many new friends in Pleiku," she said.

The emotional weight of getting orders to Pleiku weighed heavily on many of the guys. Loomis had gone to the bar and gotten royally drunk, and Loomis got mean when he got drunk. He came into the barracks looking for a fight. The first guy he saw was Smitty. "Hey," Lommis said as he looked at Smitty. "Did you get the license plate number?"

"What license plate number?" Smitty asked.

"The one on the truck that hit your face!" Loomis replied.

Smitty looked destroyed with the reference to his birth mark. Now I like to get along with people and tell jokes instead of fighting, but nobody was going to insult my friend like that.

"You apologize," I ordered Loomis.

Loomis made a fist, which he shook in my face, and said, "Oh yah, Dad. What are you going to do about it?"

I turned and walked away, figuring he'd leave me alone and pick on someone else. However, Loomis jumped me from behind. One thing I had excelled at in Military Police training was judo. In an instant I had Loomis flat on his face and in a hammerlock.

He grunted "You'd better not let me go or I'll get my M-16. You can't outrun that!"

I let him go and walked off saying, "You don't scare me, Loomis."

I had decided it was over, but learned that Smitty reported Loomis to our CO.

I knew the MPs would be coming soon. I went to Loomis and told him that Smitty had reported him. "Let's get this behind us and I won't press charges," I told him.

Loomis began to cry. "First of all, we get orders for Pleiku," he said. "Then I get a letter from my sister. She says my wife is shacking up with my so-called best friend back home. I guess I had too much to drink and wanted to take it out on somebody. Smitty just happened to be the first guy I saw. I didn't mean what I said to him or to you. I'm sorry."

When the MPs arrived I told them that we had just had a misunderstanding and that everything was OK.

Loomis looked at me and said, "You just go with the flow and nothing seems to bother you. How do you do that?"

I told him that I was a Christian. "I believe that the Bible tells us how to live a happy life. One of my favorite stories in the Bible is about Joseph. Joseph was the last son of Jacob and was Jacob's favorite. Jacob gave Joseph a coat of many colors, which must have been beautiful. The problem is that it made his other brothers jealous. One night the brothers took Joseph and threw him into a well. A group of Egyptian traders came along and the brothers sold Joseph into slavery. Joseph was sold to a very rich man and worked in his master's household. Everything he did was successful and his master began to notice Joseph. Eventually, Joseph was promoted into a position as administrator over the entire household and all business affairs. Then his master's wife fell in love with Joseph and invited him to go to bed with her. He refused saying it was against his Christian beliefs and she retaliated by accusing him of raping her. Joseph was thrown into jail and once again, he excelled at doing the right thing. The jailer noticed Joseph's actions and began to give him responsibilities. Joseph did all of them well and eventually the jailer made Joseph the administrator of the jail! His reputation grew and the Pharaoh, who was like the president of the United States, heard about him. So the Pharaoh took Joseph out of jail and put him in charge of his farm program. They had famines back in those days and it was very important to save food for the future in case another famine came along. Well, Joseph did a tremendous job and a famine did arrive. Not only did the Egyptians have food for their people; but people from other countries came to Egypt for food too. And guess who came to Joseph for food. His father and his brothers! Now here's the kicker: Joseph was the second most powerful man in Egypt next to the Pharaoh and he could have put all of them in jail. But you know what he did? He fed them and forgave them! Imagine that! Being sold into slavery and then forgiving the very people that sold you! What Joseph did was make the best of every situation he was in. He didn't feel sorry for himself. He just made up his mind to do the best with what he had. And that's what I try to do…make the best of every situation I'm in.

Loomis and I became great friends that night.

My last walk on the ammo dump at Cam Ranh Bay was a memorable one. I had the midnight shift and Loomis had gotten drunk again. He was in no condition to walk his dog and, since we had become such good friends after our dustup, I told him that I would walk his post and mine, too. There were eight posts around the perimeter with six other guys and their dogs out there.

I usually walked the length of the perimeter watching Shep's ears and nose. His ears would perk up if he heard something unusual. An unusual smell would cause him to lift his head high and sniff the air. I had learned long ago that he would pick up a sound or a smell long before he had visual contact. So, as long as he didn't do either of these things, I figured things were peaceful. A handler who depended on the dog's sight and growl usually had the enemy in his lap before he knew it. But Shep could detect a man half a mile away by picking up his scent. That gave me time to prepare and call in a search unit long before the enemy got close.

After walking the length of the post, I picked out a spot that provided cover and good sight lines. That particular post had a fallen log about three feet in diameter, which happened to be on a small hill. So I sat down behind the log for protection from snipers and allowed Shep to look over the log so he could smell and watch to his heart's content.

It was a gorgeous night, not a cloud in the sky. The full moon allowed me to see way past the perimeter. There were no farmyard lights or street lights to pollute the sky, so every star in the sky stood out. I had never realized how many stars were lost to my sight back on the farm because of our yard light. At night, shooting stars were common in Vietnam. Once I tried to see how far I could count before I saw another shooting star. Thirty-five was the furthest I ever got.

The sounds from the jungle were deafening. I imagined that lots of animals were foraging and hunting in the light of the full moon. An orangutan's shriek occasionally scared the bejeezuz out of me. Big cats growled once in a while. Small animals and birds all had their sounds to contribute.

While I sat lost in the stars and the jungle, Shep stiffened and perked his ears straight up. He had definitely focused on something near the perimeter. I grabbed his leash and we made our way to the perimeter, near the jungle. I heard some hissing. The hiss wasn't from a man; it was an animal hiss, so I hollered to the tower guard to set off a flare.

Each tower had phosphorus flares which were about three feet long, composed of a metal tube inside another metal tube. The inside tube held the phosphorus. When one held the outside tube and rammed the inside tube into it, a triggering mechanism shot the flare about a hundred feet into the sky. The phosphorus would burn brightly and turn night into day. The flare hung from a parachute that was maybe four feet wide. The heat from the burning phosphorus filled the parachute, keeping it up in the sky. Thus, the flare provided light in the middle of the night for about five minutes, allowing us to see what the heck was out there and provided the opportunity to zero in on a target if we needed to shoot.

BANG!

The flare shot off into the sky, the light shone down on my area and there in front of my eyes was a big, black jaguar! The bang startled him and the light blinded him until his eyes adjusted. And then he ran! What a magnificent animal, such fluid motion.

And then I heard another BANG!

Smitty always pirated things and he had pilfered a flare for his own use. He rammed the cylinder down and the flare discharged just as his dog, Brutus, jumped up. The flare burned a nice furrow along Brutus' back and left a singed trail right between his ears. The flare rammed into a tree and sat there smoldering while Brutus hid behind Smitty, scared to death.

CHAPTER 6
PLEIKU

When we arrived at Pleiku and Sergeant Panky along with other veterans who had been there for some time filled us in on what to expect. Here's the orientation they gave, as well as I can remember it:

Don't shine your shoes or your belt buckle anymore. They'll glint in the sun and make wonderful targets for snipers. Scuff your shoes up real good and then turn your belt buckle backwards. This ain't no place for spit and shine like it was down south. The name of the game is to lay low and stay alive for a year, and then de-de-mow [Vietnamese for leave or go away] back to The World. Don't worry about officers. They aren't going to gig you for your shoes or belt buckle up here. They want you to stay alive so you can shoot! Besides that, officers are afraid of dogs. They don't mess with us at all and just let us do our thing. You can be happy you're a dog handler.

VC are everywhere and you won't know who's who. A South Vietnamese looks just like a North Vietnamese and there aren't any uniforms or flags. We went on a body count of VC after a raid a while back and I found my own barber lying dead with an AK47 in his hands. Man, he'd been cutting my hair during the day and shooting at me at night! So don't trust anybody and, above all, don't go downtown alone. Always make sure there's a group of you so you can protect each other. And watch out for kids! Last week there was a kid riding a bike and he rode it near a group of GIs, rang the bell, and blew himself and the bike and the GIs to kingdom come. The bike had been packed with plastic explosives and wired to the bell. Kid never had a chance. Women are just as

214

bad. They can hide a razor blade in their private parts. You mess with them and you'll slice your Johnson right down the middle!

The ammo dump is big. We run two shifts and you'll have one of them. Just walk your dog between the towers and keep moving. If you do that, you won't have any trouble. Just don't sit down at the end of your post and start jawing with the guy next to you. That's when Charlie will sneak in and blow you and everyone else to kingdom come. And don't think he won't find out. There's a Charlie out there in the elephant grass sitting stone-cold still, just watching you every night. He'll figure out your patterns, your height, your dog, when you walk, when you talk, how you walk, when you take a rest, everything you do. He'll figure out if you have a weakness and then he'll strike. Kit Carson scouts (VC that changed sides and advised our soldiers.) have told us that when they were VC, they sometimes sat on a perimeter for two weeks, never moving, to scout out a weak spot.

And don't let the tower guards out of their towers. They like to go into the weeds to take a dump. When your dog smells that, he won't be any good for the rest of the night. You see a tower guard on the ground, muzzle your dog and turn him loose. That usually scares the Hell out of them and they'll never do it again.

Do not—and I repeat—do not follow any internal alerts. You are to guard the perimeter and the perimeter alone. You are to prevent a Gook from getting into the ammo dump. We have our own men working inside the dump getting rounds ready for Arty Hill and the choppers, and we don't want you to be sic-ing your dogs on them!

That was our orientation, short and sweet. As usual, I tended to focus on the positive: No more shining shoes or belt buckles!

Pleiku was a whole different ball game from Cam Ranh Bay. Cam Ranh was a heavily-fortified port of entry. It had an abundance of artillery batteries, gobs of helicopters and fighter planes, Navy boats patrolling the water, Military Police walking and riding the streets, infantry units surrounding the area, and operations working to protect all the food, ammunition, supplies, materials, and people in the area. Cam

Ranh Bay was an example of the ratios I had heard about: For every guy in the field there are 20 in the rear area supporting him.

Cam Ranh Bay was a very safe and secure area. As a result, peacetime rules applied. Everyone had to shine their shoes and belt buckles. Our uniforms were inspected regularly and had to conform to military standards. Weapons were kept in the armory under lock and key. One had to sign for a rifle when going on post.

People walked freely up and down the streets, shopping in stores. American businesses had representatives with store fronts where we could buy jewelry, new cars for when we got home, life insurance, electronics, and gifts of all kinds for our loved ones. Walking down the street in Cam Ranh Bay was like walking down the street in Spencer, Iowa, except that everyone wore the same clothes: military issue. Officers had to justify their existence, so they made rules about everything. Rules had to be enforced and the officers got to enforce them, giving them job justification. We had noise rules, smoking rules, drug rules, intoxication rules, need-to-know rules for classified information, security rules, and so on.

But Pleiku was a war zone. People died there. They only cared that you were able to shoot and that when you did, you shot in the same direction as they did.

We saw choppers bringing in wounded and dead soldiers. After a battle we saw the bodies of NVA piled like cordwood. We looked for a buddy we saw just yesterday, only to learn that he had been "wasted" last night. As a result, we were cautious about getting too close to anyone. Closeness meant a lot of hurt, should that buddy get killed. That was a big reason we used nicknames. We didn't want to know the next guy's real name and all of his history because we would get too close to him and if he died; it would hurt. So we kept relationships shallow and on the surface.

Men who faced death every day defied meaningless rules. "You mean you don't want me to smoke here after I've been laying in mud all night with mortars falling all around me? Fuck you! What are you going to do…put me in jail?"

Rules that made a society comfortable for everyone fell by the wayside in Pleiku. Men carried their M16s everywhere they went. We didn't shine shoes and belt buckles because they reflected the sun's rays and made perfect targets. Uniforms no longer needed to meet code. "Hey, if I want to carry extra magazines in a claymore bag and it gets hot, I'll ditch my shirt before I'll ditch my ammo."

We had no bowling alleys or theaters. After a patrol, men would unwind with booze or drugs. "You wanna throw me in the slammer for being drunk? Go ahead. Then I won't have to hump the boonies tomorrow and you'll have one less gun shooting the same direction you're shooting!"

A large percentage of soldiers used things like marijuana, hashish, opium, and LSD. Those guys got a tremendous amount of pleasure from music, and the louder the better. Consequently, one could hardly hear himself think in the barracks. I didn't use drugs nor did I drink while I was in Vietnam. I vowed that I would never let anything interfere with my brain functions while I was there because I wanted to come home to Ginny. I had a hard time finding a place I could relax and get away from the racket.

I spent a lot of my free time in either the craft center or the library. A very nice lady ran the craft center. Her children were grown and had moved on with their lives. Her husband had passed away and, rather than sit in the corner and feel sorry for herself, she had volunteered to go to Vietnam and run a craft center for those young boys who were fighting there. She always had freshly-baked cookies ready for us and always had time to listen. She became our "grandmother" while we were there.

She taught me the art of decoupage. She showed me how to burn the edges of a picture—I wanted to make it look weathered. Then I'd put a rough edge on a piece of plywood and burn that edge with a small propane torch. When that was done I glued the picture to the board and applied two coats of polyurethane. The finished product was a wanted poster for Butch Cassidy and the Sundance Kid that looked like I had taken it from a tree trunk in Dodge City. It really looked old!

She told me that I had done such a good job that she'd let me make a purse for Ginny. She had a little wooden purse kit. Holly Hobby was popular back then and I found a picture of her on some wrapping paper that I applied to some thin pasteboard with glue. I cut her out with an X-acto Knife and then applied her to the outside of the purse. The inside of the purse was covered with the wrapping paper. Edna showed me how to use different stain colors to give the purse an antiqued look, and after a few coats of polyurethane it looked perfect!

Ginny still has it.

One day I noticed a water tower at the edge of the compound. It was about 40 feet tall, had a ladder to the top, and a walkway all around it. Perfect! I often climbed to my safe haven at the top of the water tower to read and write letters, read books, pray, and contemplate.

One of my mother's favorite sayings was, "Sometimes, the best companion is solitude."

One night Loomis came over to my table during dinner and sat down. The mess sergeant had received a shipment of fresh lettuce and I was enjoying a crisp, cold salad with French dressing for the first time in a long while. I mentioned how nice it was to have a good salad for a change, but I may as well have been talking to the wall. He hadn't heard a word I'd said, just looked past me at something far, far away.

"Here, read this," Loomis finally said and then resumed his faraway gaze.

I opened the envelope and noticed the heading: "Dear John." It was a letter from his wife. She went on to say that she had grown tired of waiting for him. Two old friends who were in the Navy were home on leave and she was sleeping with both of them at the same time.

Jeez, I thought. *What do you say to a guy whose wife sends him a Dear John and tells him she's sleeping with two guys?*

I finished my salad in silence and when I got done, Loomis said "We need to talk, but somewhere private. I don't want anyone else to know."

Loomis had come from a wealthy family in Boston and had been a big man on campus in college. He was president of his fraternity and had married the president of some sorority, a match seemingly made in heaven.

There aren't many places where one can find privacy on an Army compound, but I thought about my water tower. "You might think this is a little off the wall, but I know a place where we can have complete privacy," I said. "Follow me."

He followed me to the back of the compound and we climbed the ladder onto the catwalk that surrounded the tower. We sat down with our legs hanging over the side. I just sat there waiting. I figured when he was ready to talk, he would do so and I'd just wait and let him gather his thoughts.

"That's why I wanted to kill you," he said finally. "You get letters every day from Ginny, homemade cookies, those fancy boxer shorts. Everything is so perfect for you. Meanwhile, I'm getting nasty letters from my wife. It just made me so mad I wanted to kill you. How come everything works out for you and not for me?"

"Well," I said. "First of all, we are Christians and our marriage isn't just Ginny and me. It's Ginny and *God* and me. We pray for each other. I pray for her success as a teacher and ask that God make me a good husband for her. She prays for my safety and asks God to help her be a good wife to me. We believe that God works in our lives."

"I've never been much of a church-goer," Loomis admitted.

"Church has little to do with it," I said. "After all, we don't even have a church here. But God is still in my heart no matter where I am or who I'm with."

"I've always been told that absence makes the heart go wander," Loomis said. "And I guess that's what's happened to me and Linda."

"And I've always believed that absence makes the heart grow *fonder*," I said. "I grow in my love for Ginny every single day, even while I'm here in Vietnam."

Suddenly, we both saw the truth of the matter: Life is what you choose it to be. Loomis had chosen to believe that absence makes the heart go wander—I believed that absence makes the heart grow fonder. He agreed that he had chosen that approach. As a result, he didn't see anything wrong in sleeping with a whore, and he judged his wife the same way. He assumed that she would wander as well and he treated her that way. As a result of my choice, I didn't cheat on Ginny and never once believed that she would cheat on me, and I treated her accordingly.

Life is a choice. We can choose to be happy or we can choose to be grumpy. We can choose to see the storm or we can choose to see the rainbow. We can choose to be judgmental or we can choose to be accepting. But it's all a choice. One thing's for sure: Life will treat you the same way you choose.

Loomis and I became fast friends and I was reminded of the scripture I Peter 3:16: Do what is right; then if men speak against you, calling you evil names, they will become ashamed of themselves for falsely accusing you when you have only done what is good.

I was guarding the food yard. The sun had been down for a while and there was barely enough light to see. My dog's ears pricked up and I knew someone was coming through the concertina wire. Each storage yard whether it was food, ammunition or helicopter had eight rows of concertina wire stacked into the shape of a pyramid. Each row had three coils on the bottom, two coils lying on top of the lower three and one coil lying on top of those two. Each coil was about three feet in diameter with razor sharp teeth interspersed along the wire. It made barbed wire from the farm look anemic. Thus, each pyramid of wire was about nine feet wide at the base and nine feet tall. The rows were spaced 10 feet apart. Anyone trying to penetrate a perimeter had 80 feet of razor sharp wire to come through.

As the sounds grew louder, Shep was beside himself with desire to attack. He was a trained attack dog and his mission was to kill anyone that came through the wire. Any farm boy who's had to kill a dog because it had killed a chicken knows how the taste of blood can turn an otherwise friendly dog into a killer. Shep knew the taste of blood and was anxious for more.

Normally, the intruder would be a sapper, a North Vietnamese soldier carrying plastic explosives. He would throw the plastic explosives into the small arms ammunition pad where it would set off a chain reaction of explosives that would eventually blow the whole ammunition dump into the wild, blue yonder.

That's what troubled me: why would a sapper try to blow up a food yard?

I held on to Shep and watched. Imagine my surprise when a small boy entered through the concertina wire, went to a garbage barrel, and grabbed a rotten apple. He shoved the apple into his mouth and started to swallow without even chewing. Had anyone seen me not turn my dog loose, I could have been arrested. But how could I turn Shep loose to kill an obviously starving little boy?

I knew a little Vietnamese, so when I got to him I asked for his name and the location of his home. His name was Dinh. He lived in a hamlet near the food yard. I told him to leave immediately and never come back. When I got done with my watch for that night, I loaded a loaf of bread, a can of peaches, and a can of tuna into the Jeep . As I drove back to my barracks, I drove by his home and shoved the food out of the side of the Jeep . Each night I would inconspicuously drop off another batch of food.

It wasn't long after I had been dropping the food that Dinh came to my barracks and announced, "GI be in bunker at eight o'clock tonight," and then disappeared as quickly as he had appeared.

I wasn't sure what to make of this announcement until at exactly eight o'clock we started to get attacked with mortars and rockets. From that night on I knew of an attack long before Intelligence knew. Dinh took care of me because I took care of him.

At the ammunition dump the deuce and a half, the name given to the two-and-a-half ton truck that the Army had would come to pick us up in the morning. We noticed the guard's deuce and a half stopped at a corner tower. All we could hear was crying. It turned out that a sapper had somehow figured out that all the guards were asleep, climbed up their ladder, popped the heads off two guards, and left the other one asleep. They used piano wire with a stick handle on each end. They would make a loop in the wire, place it over the soldier's head, and pull on the handles to decapitate the soldier. That was a powerful psychological tool that the North Vietnamese used, since it would drive the man left alive berserk.

That sort of thing happened frequently and showed everyone that falling asleep was like signing our own death warrant. The most popular solution for staying awake was to take "speed." A person on speed could stay awake for a week if he wanted to. The problem with speed is that it usually led to harder drugs.

I had worked as an orderly in a hospital when I went to college and had seen what drugs could do to people So I chose to smoke cigarettes to stay awake. I smoked at least three packs of Camel straights a day. Believe me, it kept me awake!

My smoking habit has led to great difficulty in the politically correct world I live in today. I do believe people would rather sit with a killer-rapist than a smoker! But whether they like it or not, cigarettes kept me alive.

At least in my case, there came a time when I had seen so much killing and pain that I got sick of war. Naturally, when someone shot at me, I had to defend myself to stay alive but there certainly wasn't any joy in it. I was working as a scout dog at the time. A scout dog leads a combat unit into the field. He sniffs the air and, when he smells the enemy and gives his alert, the handler tells the commander of the combat unit that the enemy is near. The scout dog is invaluable in bamboo jungles. The bamboo grows so thick and tall that it's like dusk at high noon. Thus, someone could be a few feet away and you wouldn't even see him until you almost ran into him.

It's difficult to make a path through bamboo because it's so thick. Consequently, soldiers tended to follow paths that someone had previously chopped with a machete. Once in a while, you came to a dead end in one of those paths. A dead end occurred when whoever had chopped the path decided the bamboo was just too thick and gave up. As I came around a corner in the path, Shep alerted and I saw before me a North Vietnamese regular who had just run into a dead end in the path. I normally would have given my dog the command to attack and then dived for cover. The soldier had an AK47 in his hand and, as he turned and looked into my eyes, something told me he wouldn't shoot. I held onto Shep's leash and walked toward the North Vietnamese soldier and held my hand out. Our eyes never parted.

He gave me his AK47 and I took him prisoner. We went back to base camp where I turned him over to Intelligence. I told the officer there that I wanted to interview him later. That look in the eye of the prisoner haunted me. He could have killed me. I should have turned my dog on him, in which case he would have been killed.

Later, through an interpreter I asked him, "Why are you fighting?"

He replied, "I was drafted."

I had been, too.

I asked him, "How can you justify what you are doing?"

He replied, "Our chaplains tell us that God is on our side."

Our chaplains told us that God was on our side.

I inquired, "If you could leave here right now, what would you do?"

He said, "I had just gotten married when I was drafted. I'd like to go home to my wife, raise a family, and be left alone."

Ginny and I had been married for 3 weeks before I left for Vietnam. All I wanted to do was go home to her, raise a family and be left alone.

There was no difference between the prisoner and me but our place of birth.

He volunteered to become a "Kit Carson" scout. That's a VC or NVA that comes over to the other side and works for us. We remained close and I asked him one day, "How can you get through all that concertina wire?"

Dung looked at me a laughed. We went to the ammo dump where there were three rows of pyramid concertina wire. He put on a back pack and picked up an AK-47. "Time me," he said. Taking the AK in both hands and using it as a tool, he put the butt of the rifle against a strip of concertina wire and shoved it to his left. This created a hole large enough for him to sashay into the concertina wire. He then used the sight on the barrel to catch another strand of the concertina wire and shove it to his right. Once again, he dodged into the coils of wire without touching. He repeated these actions and all but ran through the coils of co0ncertina wire. It took him twenty seconds to go through three sets of coils. We could just as well have strung a rope around our perimeter!

I had just finished telling a joke to Pete. It was about the drunk that had been picked up by a police officer. The officer asked him what he was doing and the drunk stuck a car key in the officer's face and said "Offisher, ya gotta help me find my car. It was right on the end of this key!"

The officer said "We'll go down to the station and find your car right away, but don't you think you should pull up your fly before we go?"

The drunk looked down at his open fly and replied "Oh Jeesh, they took my girlfriend too!"

We were laughing when the first mortar hit. They attacked outside the opposite side of the ammo dump. Mortars, rockets and small arms fire went on for about two hours while Pete and I hunkered down in a reventment. When the battle is going on far enough away, it is actually a thing of beauty…like a fourth of July on steroids. Tracers (Every seventh bullet is coated with phosphorus so it burns white hot when it is flying through the air.) fly in every direction and when they ricochet they bounce every which way. Flares light up the sky and float lazily along as they hang from their little, white parachutes. The bright light they throw off makes crazy patterns in the trees and smoke. The smoke of cordite and phosphorus burning is as thick as a heavy fog. Choppers and planes fly in and out of the smoke either to pick up the dead and wounded or zero in on the enemy. They disappear into the smoke and reappear later as they make their turns.

When it was over, we could hear the wounded crying to their mothers, begging for help and shouting "Over here. Over here." People were shouting directions. Rifles rang out. I could only imagine the dilemma of someone trying to help others while at the same time fearing for his own life.

It moved me to put my thoughts down in the form of a poem just like Mrs. Fortune told me I would do back in English class in Sioux Rapids.

If peace were only the silenced cries of those who suffer,
Then where would there be peace?
Beneath the protective roar of the crowd that cries
My country right or wrong.
Is the crowd that screams
My country is wrong.
Peace is too honest to hide.
And it's too big to be hidden by flags
Or screams or even tears.
Peace is only the simple things
Like that green meadow that knew dew drops
Before it knew tear drops.
The place that was someone's home
Before it was distorted into a shapeless, shameful battlefield.
By a thousand blind and blood stained boots
Or like that silent blue bird that graced a clear sky.
A sky so blue, it had to be free.
Free to have as many stars as it damned well pleased.

A bird so strong it caught sun light on its wings
And cast its shadow on the people below.
Wingless souls who could only look up
Squint their eyes in the sun and gaze in awe
Just in time to see the hawk expel its explosive feces
That brutal bomb that turned the bluest blue into black.
If peace is too big to hide
Why is it so hard to find?
People don't understand big words like peace.
How many will have to die trying?

The North Vietnamese had hit us with mortars and rockets for three solid days and two nights. Thankfully, I had spent this time in a bunker and had been safe. Our bunker had double rows of sandbags for walls and four layers of sandbags on the roof. The roof had more thickness to protect us from a direct hit. The walls didn't need to be as thick because they only had to protect us from shrapnel.

I went out to survey the damage after it was all over. The supply warehouse had taken a number of direct hits. There were gas masks, clothing, and parts spread all over the place.

A number of businesses in Pleiku had been hit as well. Most businesses were frame buildings with tin siding. Tin sheeting lay all over the place and bare studs stood pointing at the sky. The property of the businesses had been blown away and littered the streets: shoes, clothing, pool cues, crossbows, statues of Buddha, paintings, dolls, long range patrol rations, C-Rations, and so on.

I came upon an area I had not visited before. There were a few adults and a number of children sifting through the debris. I asked a few questions and found out that it was an orphanage. Their little huts had been damaged and were no longer habitable. Each hut housed a pair of adults and four children. I spent the rest of the day helping them clean up their mess.

When I went back to the barracks, I told the other guys about what I had seen and that I planned to go back. Of course, Pete was rearing to go as well. We thought it would be nice to go to the PX and buy the kids some candy, just as we had done on Okinawa. As we prepared to go on our next day off, we had a number of other soldiers approach us and give us money.

They said, "Buy a little extra candy for the kids."

We ended up with $75, went to the PX, and spent it all on candy. It filled a Lambretta, a three-wheeled Cushman motor scooter with a bed on the back for carrying things. The Lambretta was the favored mode of trucking and traveling in Viet Nam. Usually a Lambretta had a driver with a rider in the front and six people in the back holding vegetables, chickens, pigs or anything else to sell at the farmers market. There usually was a huge load of charcoal strapped on the top.

We arrived at the orphanage and unloaded the candy, thinking the kids really would be surprised and happy. However, the kids just looked at us questioningly. One of the adults could speak English and told me that the Viet Cong had told the children that American GIs would bring them food that had been poisoned. He told us we would have to eat samples of the candy to prove that it had not been poisoned. So we opened each box of candy and ate part of each type of candy bar. Finally, one of the kids grabbed a Baby Ruth and devoured it immediately. Then the others all joined in.

On the following days off we took hammers, nails, and lumber with us and began to repair the huts. Other soldiers soon joined in. Eventually, everyone in the company spent their time off at the orphanage. We built a merry-go-round, a swing set, a jungle gym, and other playground equipment. Each soldier fell in love with one or two of the children.

One day we held a dog show for the kids. We ran some of the dogs through the obstacle course and gave them an "attack dog" show that they'll never forget. The company commander provided hot dogs, potato chips, pop, and did the cooking himself.

I became friends with a number of Buddhists while I was in Vietnam. I went with one of them to decorate the grave of one of his friends who had been killed in action. He placed food on the grave.

I asked him "When do you expect him to come up and eat the food?"

He replied "At the same time your friends and loved ones come up to smell the flowers you leave on their graves."

Buddhists have a sort of shrine at the end of their lane much like we have a mail box at the end of ours. They put flowers and food in the shrine every day. That was done so that the needy could go out in the dark of night and get food to eat and flowers to decorate their homes.

"If they want to eat and decorate their homes with flowers," my friend explained, "they have to go out on their own and get them. We'll provide for them but we're not going to hand it to them. They must show the initiative to go out on their own and get it."

I had to admit that their method made sense. Anyone who is poor would be humiliated by taking a donation in person. But they could pick up the donation in the dark of night and remain anonymous. By the same token, the giver received no public recognition for giving. It's all done at night when no one can see who the giver or who the receiver might be.

I helped him deliver a load of lumber and nails to the site of a business that had been ruined by mortar fire. We delivered at night. He explained to me that his faith requires him to supply re-building materials to his neighbors. But it's the neighbor's responsibility to take the materials that have been given him and put them to use rebuilding his store. "As long as he uses the material that we bring, we will continue to supply them until his business is re-built. On the other hand, if he doesn't get to work restoring his business with the materials we bring, we will pick them up at night and that will be the end of it."

I thought of the old saying, *The Lord helps those who help themselves.*

We had all been conditioned for what happens when a mortar round falls: Hit the dirt because there will be more. We didn't even have to think. When a mortar hit, we automatically hit the dirt and began digging a hole to get lower. That's because a mortar crew will "walk" their mortars to hit a target. The first mortar is intentionally sent long. The second mortar is intentionally sent short. That gives the team an approximate idea of where next to aim their mortar tube to hit the intended target.

A mortar round has a compression head on it that triggers the explosion. A round that hits granite will go off immediately and the shrapnel will spray out horizontally. A round that hits mud will go three feet deep before there is enough compression to fire. In that case the shrapnel will blow straight up. We worked in an area that had clay soil and we usually had rain. So the shrapnel would blow straight up into the air and we would be safe if we were flat on the ground. Well, as safe as you can be with a mortar round going off. What we feared most was a direct hit.

Smitty and I had just been dropped off at the ammunition dump. The sun was just setting, giving us just enough light to walk to our individual posts. Smitty said, "Wait up Dad. I've got to take a leak."

I stood in the road with Shep, admiring the sunset when, WHOOMP, a mortar round came in! I immediately hit the ground and pulled Shep in close to me. I listened for the familiar sound of another mortar leaving the tube but all I heard was screaming.

Oh no! I thought. Smitty got hit!

"Smitty, Are you OK?" I yelled.

"No! I'm hurt bad!" Smitty yelled back.

After I low-crawled over to Smitty, I grabbed the package of gauze out of my helmet band, figuring I'd have to put compression on his wound. Smitty was writhing in pain and holding his groin.

Oh God, no, I thought. *How am I going to put compression on that?*

"How bad is it?" I asked.

"Oh, it's bad, Dad. It hurts like Hell ."

"Well, let me see it and I'll do the best I can."

Smitty took his hands away from his injury. I had expected to see blood and tissue damage but there wasn't any at all. The only thing I saw was a small amount of skin protruding from his zipper. *What the…?*

"When the first mortar hit, I zipped up as fast as I could and hit the dirt," Smitty said. "I zipped myself into my zipper."

I had all I could do to keep from laughing, but the mortars were still coming and it was far too serious a time to laugh. We were shelled for three hours and Smitty groaned and moaned the entire time.

When it finally ended, I borrowed a Jeep from the ammo dump and took Smitty and the dogs to the dispensary. I tied the dogs to the Jeep and took Smitty into the lobby where a nurse approached us. "How can I help you?" she asked.

Smitty's face reddened and he said, "I need to see a doctor."

"I can't bring a doctor unless I can tell him what the problem is," she replied. "So, what's wrong?"

Smitty continued to cover his groin area with his hands as he said, "I have my penis caught in my zipper."

I was surprised! I didn't think Smitty had that term in his vocabulary.

"I'll be right back," the nurse said.

Shortly she returned with three more nurses who all inspected Smitty's injury with obvious delight. It was evident that each of them had a huge laugh welling up inside but none of them surrendered more than a slight smile. It reminded me of myself holding back a laugh in church when someone passed gas. It's all about control!

Two doctors finally entered the room and walked around Smitty, inspecting him as if he were a new car they were thinking about buying. "Hmm," one said. "Uh huh," the other said.

Finally, one of the doctors reached over and grabbed Smitty's zipper. With a violent pull, he yanked the zipper down. Blood flew everywhere, but the zipper was down and Smitty was once again a free man.

Dale Bladorn and I met on the flight from the States and became fast friends after making a bet on a Green Bay Packers-Chicago Bears game. I had been a Chicago Bears fan since I was a little boy. Dale had grown up in Janesville, Wisconsin, and had been a Packer backer since he was a little boy. The Bears' quarterback threw a last-minute, winning touchdown pass that put $20 in my pocket.

It was only natural that we should become friends. We grew up as farm boys, played football, loved sports of any kind, had loving families back home, and took pride in our work. I had just married Ginny before leaving for Vietnam and Dale had just become engaged to Judy. When we pulled guard duty together we would walk our posts and meet in the middle to talk. Of course Ginny and Judy were almost always the topics of our conversations.

We shared our dreams of what life would be like once we returned home to them. How nice it would be to wake up in the morning and have the warmth of Ginny's body next to mine. Wouldn't it be great to have a good job, a cozy little home, a dinner together, and go on a walk without being shot at? We'd go bowling and have picnics and go swimming and go fishing and camp out under the stars. The list was endless.

We often got paperwork for what we called "suicide missions" from Headquarters. Those were extremely dangerous assignments that we could volunteer for. Most of us steered clear of them, but there were plenty of "gung-ho" nuts who would volunteer for those missions. They rarely came back.

It surprised me when I looked at the roster one day and found Dale's name assigned to one of the orders. I went to his bunk to talk to him about it and found him crying. He pointed at the local home town newspaper lying on his bunk. The front page had a picture of Judy's wedding. She had married another man.

Thankfully, Dale returned from that mission. I told Dale that he needed to talk to someone and get his troubles off his chest. "Why don't you write a letter to Ginny"? I asked. "She'll listen to you and I'll bet she'll write back. She's a woman, so she'll understand and maybe that will help you get over Judy."

A few weeks later Dale came down to my bunk area with a little box in his hand. "Hey Halverson," he said. "Ya want a cookie? Your wife sent me cookies!"

Ginny and Dale corresponded with each other for the duration of our tour in Viet Nam.

A while later another guy got jilted by his girlfriend. Dale said, "Why don't you write to Ginny. She'll write back to you." Before my tour was over in Vietnam Ginny wrote to six other men besides me!

Ginny got the idea that we could also send audio letters to each other. We both got little cassette recorders with four-inch tape reels for that purpose. It brought us closer together because we could hear each other's voices. A letter provided only words, but a tape gave us the words along with the voice, the inflection, the tone, and the laugh. I can't tell you how homesick I'd get when I heard Ginny's laugh on that tape.

When we were dating, Ginny and I went to church regularly. For some reason Ginny grabbed my hand when we said the Lord's Prayer on our first "church date." It became our habit and to this day we hold hands during the Lord's Prayer. The Lord's Prayer also became an important part of our audio tapes and the very end of the tape was always reserved for the Lord's Prayer. We would both let friends and family listen to our tapes when they arrived, but the final part of the tape was private. We would both turn off the tape and ask whoever was listening with us to depart, at which time we would say the Lord's Prayer together via the tape.

Once, I was recording a letter to Ginny when we got attacked. I abandoned the recorder to grab my M16 and return fire. The entire attack got recorded because the tape kept running. The sounds of mortars and rockets falling and exploding, the howitzers, and the banter between us troops all got recorded. Ginny said that everyone sat in absolute silence after she played that tape.

A few weeks after Ginny started corresponding with Dale and the other guys that had gotten "Dear John" letters I opened my letter of the day. I pulled the letter out of its envelope and read the salutation that usually read "Sweetheart" or "Dearest Lee." I was completely shocked when I read "Dear John!" I couldn't believe my eyes! Hadn't we given each other our word that we would be true to one another? Hadn't we given each other vows at our wedding? How could she do this to me? I thought that perhaps she was pulling a joke on me and read the first page of the letter. She wrote that I was a really good guy and would make any woman happy, including her. But life goes on and things change including our relationship. She had simply fallen in love with another and couldn't help herself.

I screamed and threw the letter. I had lost the one thing that was the anchor in my life. How could she do this to me? Well, I reasoned, "If she doesn't care for me anymore; what's the sense of going on?" I determined that I would go to the volunteer board and pick the most dangerous mission available. "With a little luck, maybe some Gook will shoot me and put an end to this misery. There's no reason to go on."

I was standing at the volunteer board researching the missions when Pete came up to me. I was waiting for him to give me some friendly advice like "She isn't the only fish in the sea. There are plenty of other girls out there that would really appreciate a guy like you. Now pull it together and go on with your life!"

But instead, Pete held the letter out to me and said, "I think you'd better read the entire letter." I wanted to tell him to go to Hell, but I noticed the warm look in Pete's eyes. So I took the letter and began reading.

Ginny explained that she had married a young man. Being in the Army and in Viet Nam had changed that young man into another man. And that is the new man she had fallen in love with. She went on to say that she felt sorry for me because so many of my friends had received "Dear John" letters and I hadn't. So she decided that I should have one too!

Pete put his arm around my shoulder and walked me back to my bunk. All I could think was "What a good friend."

Pleiku was a battle zone and the landscape proved it. What once had been jungle was nothing but a vast wasteland. All the trees had been defoliated by spraying them with Agent Orange. The defoliation allowed anyone in a helicopter or scout plane to see any NVA on the ground. The trees reminded me of zombies. The shape was of a tree, but without any leaves they looked like the living dead. Trees that had been in the middle of a firefight looked like the trees after a tornado, nothing left but a trunk and the only branches larger than six inches in diameter remaining. The ground was bare—no grass, no flowers, no weeds—just bare. Lakes and rivers should have had abundant greenery along their banks, but didn't. Somehow, the birds survived and their songs were the only pleasant things to enjoy.

Snipers were always present, despite the lack of cover. I couldn't comprehend how they found a place to hide and take a shot at someone. I had a post to walk with Shep and I always had a tough decision as to whether I should walk the whole post or position myself in cover and use Shep's ability to smell and hear and see to my advantage. Walking the post meant that I'd be an easy target. Sitting in cover meant that I'd get sleepy.

So I alternated between the two: When I got sleepy, we would walk. Then I would take cover and let Shep do his work until I got sleepy again. When the wind came from the right direction, I could position myself downwind where I had some sort of cover and could let Shep sniff for the scent of someone trying to enter the ammo dump. He had a magnificent sense of smell!

On a good night, I could tell if someone was out there from a half mile away, and I could tell if they were North Vietnamese, South Vietnamese, black or white. North and South Vietnamese had different diets with different spices and, therefore, their body odor was different. Shep would react differently to each of those smells. Our black and white soldiers were on the same diet, but their bodies exuded different oils and Shep could tell the difference between them, too.

When an infiltrator got within quarter mile, I could tell where to shoot a grenade and get him. Within a hundred yards, I could tell you where to aim a rifle. My goal was to detect someone approaching the ammo dump when they were still far away.

The dopers did not share that goal. Often, they would get together on someone's post and smoke OJs, marijuana joints that have been painted with a smear of opium. They had a great time together, but their posts were neglected in the process. Sappers figured out which posts weren't being walked and tried to enter the dump at that point. When a sapper got that close, the dogs went berserk and even a doper could figure out something was wrong. They would turn their dogs loose to get the sapper. The dogs always won. I can tell you this: When a dog tasted blood, he really loved it; couldn't get enough of it. A dog that had killed a sapper became a vicious animal indeed.

WHOOMP!

I knew immediately that was not the sound of the howitzers on Arty Hill sending an outgoing barrage, nor was it anything coming from the helicopter pad. No, this was different. There was normally a lot of banter among the guys in the barracks, but they were all silent too, realizing that we were hearing an unusual explosion.

WHOOOMP!

It happened again and I knew that it was the sound of a rocket exploding. I had never heard a rocket explode, but somehow I knew what it was. I grabbed my flack vest, M-16 and steel pot and headed for the door.

WHOOMP!

Another one hit and it was very close to our barracks. I dived into one of the foxholes just outside the barracks because it was closer than the bunker. This foxhole was about six feet in diameter and three feet deep with sandbags piled two feet deep around the outside. Thus, I had five feet of protection around me unless there was a direct hit, in which case it wouldn't make any difference how deep I was.

Others came running from the barracks, hurriedly putting on their flack vests and juggling their helmets on the way. There were six foxholes and a large bunker near our barracks. The foxholes could each hold about eight men comfortably and the bunker could hold 40 or so. The bunker was like a small garage in size. It had sandbag walls and a sandbag roof. Rifle slots were the only openings in the walls, other than the doorway.

Men peered through the rifle slots and the doorway to get a view of the explosions, while those of us in the foxholes simply lay on our backs and looked upward. I remember seeing what looked like a sparkler from the Fourth of July, just floating along about 10 feet above me. Looking closer, I could see the outline of the rocket and what appeared to be the sparkler was the last of the fuel being burned before the rocket slammed into something and detonated. The funny thing is that it all seemed to be happening in slow motion. The rocket appeared to be going so slowly that I think I could have reached up and grabbed it. That's what happens when a body is pumped full of adrenaline. People think and react so fast that they are capable of doing impossible things, things they could never do normally.

Mortar rounds began falling, too. The Gooks were softening up the area with rockets, which could be fired from quite a distance away in the hopes that all of us would run for cover. That would allow mortar teams to creep in closer, set up their tubes, and shoot off their inventory.

It was a good plan, too. We were all hunkered down in the foxholes and bunkers limited in delivering defensive fire because most of us had left our rifles in the barracks in our rush to head for cover. We were shelled for about four hours.

Rockets are expensive, so there weren't many of them. They fly parallel to the ground. Thus, they slam into the side of a building, explode, and the shrapnel flies horizontally from the explosion. Mortar rounds fly in a more vertical path, sort of like the flight of a golf ball when hit with a pitching wedge. Mortar damage is downward and upward. So a foxhole is good cover since there is very little horizontal flight from the shrapnel. That is, unless one lands right on top of you.

I prayed. But then, I pray a lot anyway. The thing is that everyone begins praying when they are under attack. I could hear others who had a church background saying the Lord's Prayer and the 23rd Psalm that starts, "The Lord is my Shepherd…" But I could also hear the praying of those who had no church affiliation. "Dear God, don't let it hit me!" "Dear God, make it stop." "Dear God, keep me alive and I promise I'll be good!"

We had a lot of converts that night.

It was ten o'clock another night when the barracks shook as if an earthquake had just hit the place. The sound of a tremendous explosion followed almost immediately and most of us jumped from our beds wondering what was going on.

Some stayed in their beds saying, "It's nothing. Go back to sleep."

Others yelled "We're under attack!"

It seemed almost comical to watch the different reactions of people as their imaginations ran wild. I saw a few guys crying. While they cried and others remained in their beds, I grabbed Pete and said, "Come on. We're heading for the bunker." We grabbed our steel pots, flak jackets, M16s, and ammo clips.

The bunker walls were all made of a double thickness of sand bags, piled eight feet high. Beams lay across the top of the walls with a double layer of sand bags on top of the boards, making the roof of the bunker. We crawled up onto the roof and manned a.50-caliber machine gun. I remember looking at that cartridge belt and wondered what kind of damage a bullet as big as my thumb would do.

The air filled with Hueys, each with a door gunner and his M60 machine gun hanging out from the side. Cobra gunships with their rockets and miniguns flew by. The Cobra was as narrow as a canoe making it very hard to hit with a rifle, while the Huey was as big as a barn. Maintenance personnel used duct tape, which was unknown at that time except to the military, to repair bullet holes in the skin of a Huey.

Flares lit the sky about a mile away from us and most of the activity seemed to be in that area. More guys came from the barracks and entered the bunker. Some cried, some hunkered down in the remotest corner of the bunker, and some gawked around to see what was going on, as if they were watching a parade on Main Street in Sioux Rapids. You really could tell what men were made of when under attack. Some big, strong bully types cried, while some squirrelly, little banker types efficiently did their jobs. Many had no clue and just watched in anticipation without taking cover. There was no way to predict how a person would handle such danger.

We watched the activity as it unfolded. The gunships were concentrating on a helicopter pad, which we found out later had been the target. North Vietnamese sappers had penetrated the perimeter and planted satchel charges loaded with C-4 plastic explosive. The charges had damaged a number of helicopters as well as the airstrip itself.

Jeeps with M60s mounted on them patrolled the area around us, and everything seemed to be relatively peaceful and quiet. Then we heard nearby small arms fire. Flares went up immediately and night turned into day in our little compound. I could see everybody as I turned the.50-caliber right and left looking for the enemy. I realized at that point that our lives hung in the balance. Anyone outside a bunker could be mistaken for the enemy. I watched guys outside the bunker straining to see what was going on. A gook could have walked into all that activity and never been noticed.

What do you do when someone comes around the corner? Ask to see their I.D.?

When someone is scared to death, they shoot first and ask questions later.

One night we heard rifle fire nearby and immediately went on alert, arming ourselves and watching for enemy soldiers. After an hour or so of utter quiet, we went back to our bunks. As we learned later, it turned out that the rifle shots we had heard were made by a trooper who had been fast asleep in the corner of his bunker. His best friend had shaken him awake. He woke with a start, grabbed his M16, and shot his best friend.

We all learned a new phrase that night: "Killed by friendly fire."

Basic Training drove home the importance of following orders. Anyone not following orders could put the entire group in danger, assuming that the orders are sensible. Anyone who didn't follow orders could be given an Article 15 if the offense was minor, or be court-martialed for insubordination or even treason for more serious offenses.

The key word above is "sensible." Generally speaking, officers who had been promoted through the ranks knew from experience what was sensible. Such an officer usually gained the respect of those beneath him. He made no hasty decisions. He balanced his orders by weighing the chance of gaining a military victory against the danger he'd be putting his men through to get it. His men knew that he wouldn't put them in danger unless he had thought it over and considered the advantages and disadvantages beforehand. When such a man gave an order, his troops followed it in good faith.

The problem in Vietnam was simply this: Good officers were killed at an alarming rate. Lieutenant Colonel Eli P. Howard, Jr. was one such case. His helicopter got shot down and he died, along with seven others.

His replacement was a lieutenant. He had no combat experience, had not been promoted through the ranks, and had received his rank simply by graduating from an ROTC program. Soon after arriving, his superiors had told the young officer over the radio to kick some ass. He ordered his men to retrieve two bodies from a battlefield. His unit had been fighting for five days without food or water. At night they had been bombarded by 82 mm mortar fire, followed by a small arms barrage the next morning. The men were thirsty, hungry, sleep-deprived, and scared to death. They requested a helicopter in order to go see the Inspector General and complain about the lieutenant's unreasonable order. That was their right.

And there you have it. A young, inexperienced officer torn between doing the right thing for his men, or pleasing his superior officers. Officers like that lieutenant had no combat experience whatsoever. Thus, they were prone to make snap decisions based on their book-learning in college. They were often anxious to establish their authority and had no goal beyond proving that they out-ranked others. Some couldn't wait to win medals and notoriety by having their units win battles, no matter what the price. Woe be it to the young officer who said, "I'm a lieutenant and you're a non-com. You *will* do as I say."

To be fair, some ROTC officers told their sergeants, "You've been here longer than I have. Just tell me what to do and I'll give the order."

Officers like that usually gained the respect of their people over time and did well.

I had a friend in the 4th Infantry Division. He told me of a 2nd lieutenant replacing an officer who had been killed. The lieutenant's squad was on patrol when they were confronted by an NVA unit and had to call for howitzer bombardment. The 2nd looey got confused in all the action, looked at the map, and called in his squad's location instead of the NVA location. The squad got shelled by their own howitzers for two hours before someone realized the mistake and silenced the howitzers.

That's one reason some G.I.s carried AK47s. We couldn't afford to have our lives hang in the balance because a 2nd looey called in the wrong coordinates and brought down fire on us from our own guns. If that happened, one of his own men might shoot him and claim the lieutenant got hit by a sniper, since snipers used AK47s and not M-16s.

Many of the infantry guys I talked to bragged on the AK47. *You could tie it on the end of a rope and drag it along behind you, pick it up and it would fire every single time! Look at an M-16 cross eyed and it will jam!*

The infantry barracks were next door to us. I enjoyed talking to the guys who humped the boonies and hearing their stories. They told stories of firefights, search and destroy missions, recons, bombing runs, death, and injury, along with a mix of sheer boredom at times and overwhelming fear at others. They truly were the ones who faced death every day.

Generally, they went out into the bush for a two-week stint, and then came back for rest and relaxation before they went out again. Their work was dangerous. They lost men and they lost officers. Second lieutenants arrived regularly to replace those officers who had been wounded or killed.

Those infantrymen faced danger all the time and it took its toll on them. Eighteen year-old soldiers looked like old men in just a few weeks. In their faces you could see the pain and misery they had experienced.

When they got back to base camp, they needed to unwind. They needed to forget. They needed peace. Booze and drugs were not just a form of recreation for those guys. They were tools that helped them to unwind, forget, and have a little peace…at least for a little while.

Booze has always been a part of the Army. Clubs existed for officers, non-coms, and enlisted men to provide alcohol and entertainment. The Army condoned it and provided it. Drugs, on the other hand, were not condoned by the Army. They were illegal, so drugs were purchased through the black market. They were available wherever soldiers were present. They were cheap and plentiful in every imaginable variety and form. Right or wrong, soldiers found release, peace, and relaxation with their drug of choice.

The infantry guys told me of 2nd looeys who came in and made the decision that they were going to clean drugs out of their companies. The guys told stories of how they dealt with those officers. "Put 'em on point," one laughed. "They usually die of a sniper's shot out there!" They claimed that every outfit had someone who carried an AK47 for just that purpose, and laughed at this or similar comments. I never knew if they were joking or telling the truth, so I just nodded my head and laughed along.

One time a new 2nd looey arrived. I had the chance to meet him and found him to be a very likable guy. He was the son of a Baptist minister and lived the kind of life you would expect of such a man. He did everything by the book and one of the things he intended to do was rid his company of drugs. He met with me to discuss using a dog to smell out drugs in the barracks. He had heard that I had trained Shep to scent them.

"Maybe we can give Shep a try somewhere down the road," he said.

He began his leadership by holding an inspection. Every troop had to stand by his bunk while the 2nd looey checked his locker, foot locker, and bunk. He found caches of marijuana and OJs (opium joints) during that inspection and came down hard on the offenders.

A few days later, he had to take a trip and stopped to fill his Jeep with gas. He left the compound and got a few miles down the road before his Jeep blew up and killed him. The official word was that he had hit a mine. But my infantry friends told me that when he stopped to fill up with gas, the attendant placed a grenade in his tank. The grenade had been wrapped with black tape and the pin had been pulled. It took a while for the gasoline to dissolve the glue on the tape, but when it did, the grenade exploded, turning his Jeep into a fireball.

My infantry friend didn't laugh when he told me about the grenade and I could tell he was dead serious. I also knew that if I took Shep into a barracks and he found drugs, I would probably get similar treatment.

The brass took the death of the young officer seriously. They couldn't prove he had been fragged instead of hitting a mine, but they were sure that was the case. He had planted the seed that dogs could sniff out drugs and so they came a callin'.

They wanted to see just what a dog could do so Shep and I were taken to the post office where they told me that they had hidden some marijuana. I knew immediately that drugs were present just by Shep's reaction when we walked into the room. His ears pricked up and he raised his head to get a better scent. The room was full of hundreds of boxes destined to go back to family and friends in the U.S. We slowly moved box after box out of the way and followed Shep's nose. Finally, he zeroed in on a rather large box. They unwrapped the box and found a suitcase inside. The suitcase had trinkets and clothing that the soldier had purchased on the streets of Pleiku. We found Ho Chi Minh sandals, oriental dresses, the familiar black plaques with inlaid pearl, Montagnard bracelets and a Kodak Instamatic camera. Shep alerted on the camera. An officer opened the camera and it was stuffed with marijuana. He gasped as he realized what was in it and looked at Shep as though he had seen a magician make the Statue of Liberty disappear.

I had mixed emotions as the event took place. I was proud that Shep could accomplish such a seemingly impossible task. I was fearful about what would happen next. Shep had just proven that finding a stash in someone's foot locker would be a piece of cake compared to what he had just done.

A few days later I was called to headquarters. I was told that the brass were impressed with what Shep had done and that he would be used to detect drugs in the infantry barracks. "Drugs are illegal and are not acceptable in this man's army," the Colonel stated. The accompanying officers all nodded their heads in approval and I thought about the bobble head dog in the back window of my Grandpa's car back home.

War is a serious business and no one knows it better than a ground pounder. Those guys live in fear every second they are out in the bush. They see people die…both friend and foe. I heard stories of guys that held a friends guts inside so they wouldn't spill out as they were dying. Imagine holding a guy's guts inside a wound and saying the Lord's Prayer with him while he's dying? Snipers experience a relatively short career for the most part. True, some really enjoy sniping, but most fall apart after pulling the trigger and watching the guy's head explode as they watch through their scope. Even though he was the enemy he was still a human being. A steady regimen of that kind of experience can cause a guy to come apart at the seams. Imagine the steady pressure of looking for trip wires every step you take. Imagine the sheer terror of being in a fire fight…tracers ricocheting so thickly it looks like the Fourth of July, mortars exploding nearby, cordite so thick it looks like a heavy fog, men screaming from their wounds and hoping the next mortar doesn't land on you.

This isn't a John Wayne movie where you walk away unscathed. This is real. These men came over as boys, but they grew old real fast as a result of these experiences and they need release whether it's alcohol, religion or drugs. Try to take that release mechanism away from them and you're asking for trouble with a capital T.

I knew that I was being placed in that position and that if Shep found drugs, I would be the next fragging victim. "How do I get out of this mess?" I wondered. "I'm damned if I do and damned if I don't."

The infantry barracks were right next door to us. I was good friends with Jimmy because we pitched horse shoes together after supper each night that he was back from patrol. I told Jimmy that the brass had intentions of going after drugs in the infantry barracks. I also told him about finding the stash in the post office. The color drained from his face.

"Man, if you do that; you're a dead man," he said.

"I know. Now what are we going to do about it?" I asked.

"I don't know. Let me talk to the guys and see what we can come up with."

Just as I had expected, I was called to headquarters where a group of officers were meeting to stamp out drugs from within our ranks. They were all chattering about article so and so within the uniform code of military justice. "Drugs are a bane to this man's army," one of them said with a sneering grin on his face.

They were all smiling and patting each other on the back as they discussed their plan of action. I was reminded of them later when I saw the movie "Animal House." These were fraternity types that were drunk with the idea of strutting their position and power in front of their underlings. They were ROTC graduates that had studied war in a text book but had no combat experience whatsoever. They were more interested in enforcing some rule than in keeping their men safe and alive.

Finally, I was given the date and destination of the search. "Thank goodness," I thought. "I have a few days to prepare and they're searching the infantry barracks right next to ours where I have some friends.

That night Smitty and I went to the horse shoe pitching pits and stood a Jimmy and one of his infantry friends. It was the "Puppy Pushers" against the "Ground Pounders."

"Jimmy," I said. "The brass want me to take Shep into your barracks and search for drugs."

"If you know what's good for you; you won't do it," Jimmy replied.

"I don't have a choice," I said. These guys are ROTC Jockeys and they're in a position of power. They have ordered me to do it and if I decline I'll get an Article 15 and they'll just find someone else to do it. You're better off having someone who is sympathetic with your situation than possibly getting a *lifer* who's looking for a medal."

"Well, I can have the guys clean all their stashes and get the stuff out of the barracks," Jimmy said.

"That won't work," I said. "Shep will detect traces and there's going to be somebody that forgot he had a stash in his footlocker or up in the rafters. We've got three days so we can do some experimenting. Here's what I want you to do: Soak marijuana in some water and the fill a squirt gun with the water. Go around the barracks and squirt a number of places. I'll bring Shep down tomorrow night and we'll see what happens."

Jerry did his job and the next night I took Shep into the barracks. He alerted on every spot they had squirted. "That's it," I said. "Now Shep will find Mary Jane everywhere and there won't be anything there."

The day finally came and the ROTC Jockeys led me to the barracks and announced their "Surprise Search." Meanwhile, I saw Jerry and his friends reach for their squirt guns. They were very casual and straight faced as they inconspicuously aimed their guns here and there throughout the barracks.

The brass led Shep and I through the door and stood aside like conquering generals. Shep immediately alerted on a foot locker. One of the 2nd looeys dived at the foot locker. After tearing it apart and finding nothing he dejectedly stood aside. The scene was to repeat itself a number of times before one of the officers said, "Get that damn dog out of here!" I heard comments about a dog being worthless and how I must have been damn lucky in the post office. I knew then that I would never be called to do this again.

The "Ground Pounders" knew that I didn't use drugs and were amazed and pleased that I had protected them. That night I earned a new nickname: "Dad. The guy on the natural high."

The officers were apparently mad that their "surprise attack"" for drugs had gone badly. They decided to hold an I.G. inspection of the dog handler's barracks to get revenge. We hadn't had an inspection since Cam Ranh Bay and the guys were just as mad about it as the officers were of their failed drug search. Nonetheless, we straightened up our beds, footlockers and wall lockers. Some shined their belt buckles and shined their boots, but most of us didn't. We stood at attention at the foot of our bunks while the general and his entourage came through. The general didn't waste any time stopping and inspecting each soldier. He just walked along like he was on a mandatory mission that he didn't believe in himself. His face had the look of "All right, let's get this little game over with and get back to business."

That is; until he got to my bunk. He stopped. When he stopped, I heard Pete gasp. I looked at Pete and he pointed to my wall locker. "Oh my gosh," I thought. "I'd completely forgotten about that."

The general and the first looey at his side were looking at the sign on my wall locker. The sign had a fly circling a cow pie and underneath it said: "Officers are like flies. They eat shit and bother people."

The first looey had a look on his face that said, "I've gotcha! Next stop…Long Binh Jail!" I swallowed hard and concentrated on standing at attention.

And then the general laughed! And this wasn't a giggle. It was a belly laugh that built force with time. He erupted into gales of laughter. The poor first looey had no choice but to laugh along with the general. His face looked like he'd swallowed part of that cow pie, but he laughed right along with his general. The entire barracks began to laugh along in unison.

The general finally stopped laughing and looked at me. "You'd better take that sign down, son," he said as he winked at me.

I had made friends with a number of soldiers from the Republic of Korea. We called them "ROKs" and, boy, were they good soldiers. They operated with different rules than we did. Once they had a certain number of kills, they got a leave to go home. So they were anxious to get out in the bush and earn their leave. When we sent a squad out into the bush, everyone gathered together in a group and set up perimeter guards. The squad would remain in the perimeter area until it was time to go back to base camp. The ROKs, on the other hand, would go out a few miles and drop off one guy. With nothing but a knife, he would enter the jungle looking for the enemy. The truck would continue on for another few miles and drop off another soldier. A few weeks or so later the ROKs would come out of the jungle with strings of ears hanging from their belts. That was how they measured their kills and earned their leaves.

As you can well imagine, the North Vietnamese were scared to death of the ROKs and usually would leave any area in which the Koreans operated.

Ginny always sent me the Sunday edition of the *Des Moines Register* so I could keep up on events back home. The paper a few weeks earlier announced a large troop pull-out from Vietnam. We were all anxious to hear if we would be going home. Little did we know that the politicians were playing with the figures in order to appease anti-war groups.

Sixteen thousand were to be pulled out, the war was winding down, and soon it would all be over, the paper said. The truth we would later find out was that the 16,000 were due to go back home within a month anyway. The government pulled them out early to make it look good. While those 16,000 were coming home a month early, 18,000 replacements arrived. So, after the pullout we had 2000 more soldiers than before!

We grew up being taught to trust our leaders but that trust had dwindled away, not only with us soldiers in Vietnam, but also with the citizenry back home who sooner or later learned the truth. There's nothing like having hopes dashed on the rocks to send people into hopelessness and despair. And that's what happened when we all found out that we wouldn't be going home until our tour was over. The vast majority of the troops resorted to booze, drugs, and visits to the dispensary for medication and counseling.

Pete and I ended up walking extra posts for guys who were either too impaired to walk their own posts or held from their posts by doctor's orders. The doctors thought the worst thing to give a suicidal patient was an M-16. The dopers, at least, reported for duty. They could be under the influence but the symptoms were not as noticeable as they were with a falling-down drunk.

During the Vietnam conflict there were no telephones available for soldiers to call friends and family back home. The Internet hadn't been invented yet and we sure didn't have cell phones! To address that problem, United States MARS stations from all branches of the service were deployed throughout Vietnam. The MARS system offered soldiers a way to communicate with loved ones back home via a telephone connection over shortwave radio. Once per month MARS stations would allow each solder a free five-minute personal radio-telephone call home to the United States.

So, I could go to the MARS station once a month and request a call to a specific phone number, usually Ginny's. The MARS operator had a shortwave radio and would call a Ham radio operator in the United States. That Ham radio operator would then place a long distance telephone call to the requested number. They always paid for the long distance call! What a great group of people those Ham operators were.

(Ham radio operators are another story all by themselves. "Ham" is the name given to amateur radio operators. The Federal Communications Commission requires an exam that amateurs must take. Once they pass, they are given a license to operate on frequencies known as amateur bands. In the early days of Ham radio, some of the radios used on those bands were very powerful and jammed up adjacent commercial frequencies. The commercial operators called the amateurs "Hams.")

So when I called Ginny, I first spoke over a radio to a stateside Ham operator and told him which number to call. Once he'd made the telephone connection, he held his handset to his radio speaker so Ginny could hear me. When Ginny spoke back, the reverse was true. Now this presented a few problems.

Number one, the radio operators had to key their microphones to transmit a message, but they didn't know when we were done. Consequently, Ginny would respond to my "I love you," but if I hadn't said "Over" the radio operator on my end would still have his mike keyed. Thus, the radio on my end would be in the "send" mode and we couldn't "receive" Ginny's response. So the first few minutes of any conversation meant that my MARS operator would look at me and say, "You've got to say 'over' when you're done talking." And on the other end, the Ham operator would tell Ginny to say "over" when she finished.

So the first few times we made the calls, we spent most of the time hearing, "You've got to say 'over,'" and not much else got said.

Number two, there could be a lot of static in the radio transmission. So even if we got the "overs" done properly, the static destroyed the transmission. Then we had to repeat the message and hope the static didn't interfere.

And number three, carrying on a personal conversation with two perfect strangers listening could be difficult. There were a lot of things I would have liked to say, but it just wasn't appropriate in the company of strangers.

There'd be a long line of guys at the MARS station, at least there was every time I went. I could see the anxiety on the faces of each guy as he waited to talk to his loved ones back home. And I could see the tears running down a fellow's cheeks as he left the station, always looking down and never making eye contact because his little five-minute conversation had been so meaningful.

Many of us wondered, *Will this be the last time I'll ever talk to them?*

Such is the life of soldiers at war, never knowing if we'd make it safely to the end of our tour. Despite all the "overs" and the static, hearing that voice on the other end of the line saying, "I love you" made it worth all the trouble. And I'll never be able to thank those wonderful Ham radio operators for the magnificent service they so unselfishly provided.

It had been quiet for too long. Some of the dog handlers were beginning to sleep on their posts, as were some of the tower guards. The dopers were getting together at one post and having parties, leaving their assigned posts unguarded. I remembered the quote General George Patton made to a soldier who had been caught asleep: "You had better stay awake, troop, or some Nazi SOB is going to sneak up on you and beat you to death with a sock full of shit!"

I had just reached the end of my post and turned around to walk Shep the other direction when Shep alerted. The alert was inside the perimeter wire rather than outside where one would normally get an alert.

I knelt down and rubbed Shep's neck, saying, "Watch him, boy, watch him."

Shep was beside himself in his desire to attack, but I held him close. Tower guards sometimes came down from the towers to relieve themselves and I didn't want to turn him loose on one of my own people. I heard footsteps and knew it couldn't be an NVA sapper since they wore sandals and were all but silent when they walked. Shep was standing on his hind feet now, balanced against the leash I held, and trying to get loose to attack. Suddenly, out of the darkness Pete appeared with Gus. Gus was a seasoned old dog and knew my scent, so he wasn't the least bit aggressive. Shep, being on his first tour, hadn't learned to accept others yet. He just wanted to attack anyone else.

I calmed Shep down so we could have a conversation.

"There's nobody on the four posts between us," Pete said. "They're all down on Kentuck's post having a pot party."

Kentuck was a redneck from Kentucky, as you might imagine. He'd never heard of pot until he got to Vietnam. But he had been talked into trying pot and he absolutely loved it. His easy going style made him the perfect host for a party.

Pete said, "I ought to go down there and turn Gus loose on all of them."

Pete and I were good together. Pete had a short fuse. I had a long fuse. Together, we could reason things out, usually for the best. Without me, Pete would have been in a fight every day. Without him, I would have let people run all over me.

"Let's just split the posts for now," I said. "I'll walk mine and the two next to me. You walk yours and the two next to you. That will get us through the night and then we'll talk more tomorrow."

We both walked the posts for the rest of the night. The sun was coming up and the deuce and a half pulled into the ammo dump to pick us up. Shep jumped the four feet up into the back and I admired how easily he did that, considering that when I first started working with him in Okinawa he couldn't jump through a window whose bottom was only two feet above the ground.

I climbed up into the truck and sat down. We picked up more dog handlers and met the security truck at a corner tower. Men were getting off the truck and milling about, which was unusual. It turned out that the Gooks had figured out the tower guards were asleep and had popped the heads of all of them.

We all learned a lesson from the guards who got killed. You might be beheaded yourself if you fell asleep on post. Smitty had been a habitual abuser of this practice. When he took his sentry dog to his post, he also took a sleeping bag and a pillow! But he decided to do things differently in the future.

"Hey Dad, what are we going to do to stay awake on post? A lot of the guys are going to take speed. They say a guy can stay awake for a week and then crash. What do you think?"

I had worked as an orderly at the hospital at Iowa State University and had seen plenty of students who had taken speed to stay awake in order to study for finals. They were thin as rails and their bodies were exhausted from being up for so long. Many of them had gone on to harder drugs. They were a real mess and I didn't want any part of that.

"No," I said. "I smoke cigarettes and they keep me awake. I've never fallen asleep yet, so I know they work."

"What kind do you smoke?" Smitty asked.

"Camel straights. Once in a while I switch to Luckies, but Camels are smooth and they stimulate me enough that I stay awake."

Cigarettes were acceptable in society in those days. There were none of the punitive taxes on them like there are today. One could buy a carton at the PX for $2, so they were quite cheap. I suppose we all knew that lung cancer was a possibility if we smoked. On the other hand, falling asleep was a sure way to die very quickly and we were willing to take our chances on the cigarettes.

Smitty spoke to everyone to get their opinions on the subject. "Hey Dad, most everybody is using speed. They say it works just fine, and it's fun!"

"Go ahead," I said, "but count me out. I'm sticking to my Camels."

Pete came along about that time, brandishing a pack of Marlboro Reds. "No speed for me," he said. "I'm going with Marlboro Reds; just call me the Marlboro man!"

That got Smitty's attention because he respected Pete as well. "That looks good to me," Smitty said. "I think a filtered cigarette will be easier to handle, at least at the beginning."

Smitty and Pete headed off to the PX arm-in-arm. They bonded because they were both smoking the same brand and decided to walk adjacent posts that night.

The deuce and a half dropped them off at the point where their posts met and I got off later. My post was at the other end of Pete's because we both wanted to walk near the small arms pad, the best one for the enemy to set off with a satchel charge.

A monsoon set in and it rained night and day. Smitty said it was like walking in a river. Everything got wet no matter how well protected. We could put on rain suits, but after a few minutes even our underwear got soaked. The nice thing about a monsoon is that it was just as miserable for the North Vietnamese as it was for us, so there wasn't much combat during that time.

My escape during off time had been the water tower. It was the only place where I had peace of mind to think, read, and write letters. Going to the water tower was out of the question during the monsoon.

But then Charlie Butler came to me and said, "Hey Dad. I need some extra money. Want to buy my hammock?"

I bought Butler's hammock for $3.

No one ever went into the bunker unless we were being attacked and I thought, *What a perfect place to have some peace and quiet, and in a hammock to boot!*

It was so peaceful and quiet the first time I tried that hammock that I fell asleep and missed dinner!

Butler was from Mississippi and was black, not just African-American but really, really black. He had a big advantage over us because you could never see him at night, which is when we had our duty. But when he smiled, those brilliant, white teeth gave him away. Smitty once told Butler, "That smile of yours makes you stand out like a tree in the middle of the desert!"

Charlie and I, along with the other handlers on duty were once pinned down by rockets and mortars for a night. When the deuce and a half picked us up the next morning it was still dark. All of a sudden I noticed that white smile of his glowing from the front of the truck.

"Somebody done crapped their pants," Charlie giggled. Then just as quickly his smile disappeared and he said, "It was me!"

He didn't need to feel embarrassed—all of us had.

The Army did its best at Thanksgiving. The Mess Hall sergeant worked around the clock for three days in preparation. He ordered fresh turkeys, cranberry sauce, green beans, corn, yams, potatoes, and all the other fixings to make a great Thanksgiving dinner for all the troops. He made cornbread muffins, cornbread stuffing for the southern boys, and typical bread stuffing for all of us from the north. He even put raisins in the stuffing, a favorite with me.

I went to chapel that morning to thank God for my life, family, and friends. As I sat in the chapel I thought of home, as I'm sure every other troop did. I thought how Dad and I would go out and do chores early in the morning, giving extra feed to the cattle and cleaning up the feed lots so we wouldn't have to do chores in the afternoon. That way Dad could have his nap and I could watch the big football game.

When we had finished chores, we'd race into the house for breakfast, normally about the same time that church started. We wolfed down our breakfast, dressed in a flash, and then raced to First Lutheran, all of us except Mom—she stayed home to cook. We'd walk into the service, already in progress. Most people didn't even turn around to see who it was because they knew that the Bendix Halverson family always came in late.

After the service, we kids waited anxiously while Dad chatted with his brothers and friends. That usually took about half an hour.

C'mon Dad, let's go home! I thought to myself. *The game will be on soon!*

Walking in the front door at home, we could smell the turkey. Somehow the smell I remembered from home seemed so much better than the smell of turkey in the mess hall.

Mom would be busy making creamed corn, fresh rolls, her green salad with olives and a dab of mayo on top, cherry salad, mashed potatoes with gravy, and sweet potatoes with melted marshmallows on top. She also had a relish dish with pickles, ripe and green olives, carrot sticks, and celery sticks. All this she served on Candlewick china, which we only used for special occasions. I always tried to sneak a piece of turkey or sample a roll, but Mom would slap my hand and tell me to wait. Dad would try to sneak a sample, too, and would also get a slap and a sermon. How I missed sneaking a sample…it just tasted so good!

Grandma and Grandpa Brown would arrive shortly before noon. Grandma always brought her creamed onions, which are a favorite in our family to this day. And she brought her signature custard pie and pumpkin pie. We had pumpkin pie with our Army meal, too, but how I missed that custard pie. We kids always fought over it and that always brought a satisfied smile to Grandma's face.

Our portions were served by Mess Hall personnel, so servings were limited.

But at home we could pile our plates to overflowing! Looking back, I don't understand why we did that. We could have taken smaller portions and gone back for more as many times as we wanted. But there's just something about having food piled to the point of almost falling over the edge of the plate that made the meal taste just that much better.

Dad would say a prayer before the meal and then we would all dive in. Poor Karen always seemed to be in the middle of the table and spent most of her time passing the relish dish to our sister Faith, the mashed potatoes to our brother Boyd, or the creamed onions to me. Karen's food would be cold by the time she got done passing food to everyone else and her temper would be just as hot as her food was cold.

Conversation around the table usually involved the weather, the crops, and the latest gossip from town. I missed those comments, such as how the weather soon would turn cold and how the corn had yielded better than expected.

Army conversation centered on the same old topics: "Where are you being ordered to go?" "I'll never wear olive drab again!"

All in all, I realized that Thanksgiving isn't about turkey and the trimmings. It's about family and those wonderful, simple moments that remain in your brain for a lifetime.

Ginny sent me a small Christmas tree which I placed on my foot locker. It was about two feet tall with balls and tinsel and a star at the top. She made two little stockings that had our names in glitter on them. We hang those stockings on our tree to this day and remember what it was like to be so far apart. Many times I would come back from a mission to find other soldiers sitting on my bunk staring at that little tree with tears in their eyes. They would look up at me apologetically and say "Sorry. It just reminds me of home."

Pete and I exchanged letters with a seventh grade class in Ohio. The kids would send us letters and we would write them letters about our experiences in Viet Nam. Shortly before Christmas we got two large Charmin toilet tissue boxes full of presents…books, tooth paste, Bibles, soap, candy and decks of cards. Pete and I went to the chapel for

Christmas Eve service and when we got back, the barracks were empty. We decided to play Santa Claus and took our boxes of presents and laid presents on everybody's bunks. The next morning was quite a shock. The barracks were silent except for the sound of a whimper now and again. Soldiers were holding their little presents close to their chests and were crying. "This was the only present I got for Christmas," was the common remark.

Imagine that! They all had family and friends and yet; the only thing they got for Christmas were little presents from complete strangers in the seventh grade somewhere in Ohio.

Our families sent us plenty of gifts for Christmas, but Pete's grandmother took the prize. "Hey, Dad." Pete said. "Come here and look what Grandma Peterson sent me for Christmas!" He displayed a nice little white box filled with donuts. "Look closer," He said. And there in the holes of the donuts were little airline bottles of booze! All kinds of it! Imagine that little gray haired old lady smiling as she stuck bottles of booze into her Christmas present for her grandson?

Our base often came under attack at night, but the shelling usually ended about the time the sun came up. The Viet Cong were sympathizers with the Communist movement, or else had been forced into helping the North Vietnamese in order to protect their families. For instance; we had a VC that stood in the elephant grass at the end of the air strip in Pleiku and shot at every plane that went over. I wondered why no one ever shot him. I found out that the NVA had given him an AK47 and ammunition. They told him they would be back in a week with more ammo and if the ammunition wasn't gone, they would kill his wife and kids. It was made clear that they would be watching. So the poor man had no choice but to do what they had commanded in order to protect his loved ones. So far, he had never hit a plane! It was made clear that we should just leave him be because if he was shot, he might be replaced with someone who could shoot straight!

At sunup, they had to get back to their day jobs so their anonymity would be protected. They were barbers, shoe shiners, yard landscapers, construction workers, and shop owners. We worked alongside the Viet

Cong every day and they shot at us at night. I wonder when they got their sleep!

The NVA regulars also had to hide during the day. When the sun was up, our light scout planes and helicopters would be up looking for them. So they scurried to their tunnels and remained there until night.

It always amazed me that we had jets, tanks, gunships, all the food we could eat, plenty of ammunition, Navy ships just off the coast with 16-inch guns, fuel, helicopters, mini-guns, boots, helmets, flak jackets, and medical facilities. Whatever we needed for war, we had it. The Gooks, on the other hand, wore Ho Chi Minh sandals made from the scraps of inner tubes and tire casings, carried AK47s, had straw hats on their heads, and that was about it. Their supplies came down the Ho Chi Minh trail on bicycles! They hid in their tunnels during the day, re-supplying themselves from the rice and ammunition caches they had there.

They took our junk (dud bombs, hand grenades, bullets) and made booby traps. Those were effective both physically and psychologically. You didn't dare kick a can lying in the path like you would have at home. It might dislodge a hand grenade hidden inside. Walking in the jungle was dangerous. Trigger wires to booby trap bombs were the thickness of a spider's silk. You had to take your time and really look for them.

We had a devil of a time fighting them even though we had superior machinery, weapons, supply, and technology. I am convinced that the reason was simple: Most of us had been drafted and our only mission in Vietnam was to stay alive for the year we had to be there and then go back home. The Vietnamese were fighting for the land where they lived. They figured we would leave sooner or later, just like the French had, and they wanted to control their own destiny.

An enemy attack hit the transportation company and the headquarters company. The transportation company had experienced a lot of damage and quite a few of their men had been killed or wounded, ditto for the headquarters company.

We had suffered little damage, but it was a wakeup call for us. Our bunkers and foxhole entrenchments were decayed. The sandbags were weathered and were leaking sand. They were like the old machine shed back home. It had a few shingles that needed to be replaced but we were too busy with other things to tackle the job. Slowly, more shingles deteriorated until the shop was drenched every time it rained. By then, it wasn't a simple job of replacing a few bad shingles…we had to replace the whole roof! This wasn't a matter of getting wet. It was a matter of losing a life if we didn't fix our protective structures.

Sergeant Panky wanted the sandbags repaired and picked Mike Dunaway and myself to repair them.

"Take as much time as you need," he said. "Just tear them all apart, remove the damaged bags, and replace them with good ones. You won't pull any guard duty until you're done."

I had been getting up at 11 p.m. and pulling guard duty until sunup for so long I had forgotten what a pleasant thing it was to go to bed at a decent time! To this day I thank God that I can go to bed and sleep all night long.

When our little vacation rebuilding the bunkers and foxholes finally ended, Mike and I had to go back to walking our dogs on the ammunition dump and the food yard. Once again, the wonderful feeling of a good night's sleep went away. We worked first shift from sundown to midnight, and slept after we got back to the barracks and half the next morning. Then, just when we had gotten used to that regimen, we worked midnight to sunup, sleeping afternoons and evenings. Our body clocks went completely haywire.

The soul brothers picked New Year's Eve as a good time to hold another demonstration. They refused to follow orders, saying that they had been drafted into a white man's war. They felt the Army wanted them to fight for rights they didn't have at home.

"So why fight? Why put our lives on the line?" they declared.

Since we were technically military police, we were called to quell the demonstration. The officers in charge were no fools. They had heard what happened when we showed up with our dogs when the soul brothers had tried to take over Military Police Headquarters a few months earlier in Cam Ranh Bay. Needless to say, the demonstration was over as soon as we showed up and took the muzzles off our dogs. Shep snarled, as did Brutus and Gus. It was enough to make one's blood curdle. We had to remain and guard the area even though the demonstration was over. All in all, most of us had walked the ammo dump all night long and now we were standing guard when all of us wanted to be in bed sleeping. None of us felt sympathetic with the blacks' plight back home.

We finally got back to the barracks in the early evening.

Smitty said, "Hey, Dad! Let's go to the club! They have Filipino dancing girls tonight."

"Man, I'm beat, Smitty. I'm just gonna hit the sack."

"Oh, come on Dad! It'll be fun! Besides, I might need someone to carry me back. I feel like getting wasted tonight."

We all went to the club. The Filipinos provided entertainment for the troops in Vietnam. The girls they provided looked like they were 14 years old and were all very pretty. They took turns dancing on the stage while soldiers hooted and hollered. The soldiers stood up to stuff bills into the skimpy outfits the girls wore, and the girls did their level best to maintain a friendly smile through it all.

It was the first time in a long while that I had seen an almost naked woman's body and it made me all the more homesick to see Ginny. I sat at the periphery of the group and dreamed of seeing Ginny in Hawaii. I gazed around the room and could easily identify the married guys. They were there in body but they were somewhere else in their minds, all thinking about that someone special back home.

As the night wore on, more and more guys were getting really happy or really drunk. The club manager brought in guards to stand by the stage and hold back fellows who had become too aggressive in their appreciation of the dancing girls.

Smitty had a crew of friends with him and joined me at the table. Smitty was his usual self—it was hard to detect if he was drunk or just being normal. "What are we going to do to bring in the New Year?" he asked.

Some suggestions offered were just going to bed, shooting off a couple clips of M-16 ammo, singing Auld Lang Syne, and so on.

"Hey, I've got it," Smitty announced! "Let's take over Arty Hill, aim the mini-guns straight up into the air, and turn them on!" Smitty would have made a great evangelist, because everyone bought into his idea immediately.

"Are you nuts?" I asked. "They'll have you in Long Binh Jail (affectionately called "LBJ," after our president) before morning."

"Aw, come on Dad! Everyone's scared of our dogs; you know that. We can take it over in no time, and when they see those tracers going straight up into the sky they'll love it. It'll be the best New Year's Eve they've ever had in Vietnam!"

I watched at the gate as Smitty led his group of drunken buddies onto Artillery Hill. The artillery guys scattered as soon as they saw the dogs.

It wasn't long till the RRRRRRRRRRRRR sound of mini-guns echoed from the hillsides and solid, white lines of tracers shot straight up into the sky.

After expending a fair amount of ammunition, Smitty and his, by then, fairly sober crew arrived back at the gate and we headed for the barracks before anyone could recognize us.

"Hey Dad, wasn't that beautiful? Best New Year's Eve ever!"

Sergeant Becker came to see me, saying he had to deliver some classified information to our headquarters in Nha Trang, a village about thirty miles away. I grabbed my.45 pistol and M-16 rifle, and agreed to ride shotgun for him. We got about 10 miles north of camp and suddenly there was a big explosion right beside the Jeep, then another, and another. Small arms fire erupted and more explosions.

I sprayed the area with the M16 and yelled at Becker, "Get this thing into road gear!" That's farm boy talk, road gear being the fastest gear on a tractor.

We arrived safely in Nha Trang and delivered the documents.

Aside from the gunfight, the country on the way to Nha Trang was beautiful. The rice fields looked like a giant pool table stretching off to the horizon, as far as the eye could see. Farmers were irrigating their fields with a contraption that looked like a bunch of huge ice cream sugar cones lined up on a cart, the cart being on rails. The farmer backed the cart into a canal to fill the cones with water. Then he pulled it out of the water and pushed the rig up the rails. Once the rig cleared the dike around his rice paddy, the rails dipped allowing the cones to dump their water into his rice paddy. That process continued until he had the whole field covered with water. I could only imagine how long he had to work to get that field completely flooded.

We drove by banana groves, coconut groves, and a rubber tree plantation. We drew more fire from the rubber tree plantation but continued safely on our journey. The groves were beautiful! The large trunks supported limbs full of large, green leaves.

We saw a large Buddhist temple on a mountain peak, Buddhism being the predominant religion in Vietnam. The shrine was pure white and had to be at least 30 feet tall. Each of the homes we saw along the way, most made of rice straw or mud stucco bricks, had a small Buddhist altar in front. Each altar resembled an open-front, martin birdhouse in size and appearance. The Vietnamese placed offerings of food, flowers, and incense on those altars every day. In the dark of night, the poor could go to those altars for food, flowers, and incense. No one knows who gave it or who got it, all completely anonymous. I liked that.

The people were very poor, as their homes and dress revealed. I often saw people defecating in their yards or fields. Most of the children wore T-shirts. Some also wore shorts but most were completely naked beneath their T-shirt.

The American dollar had changed the culture there. Children were selling monkeys, pigeons, and trinkets made from war waste, along with anything else they could get their hands on that a GI might want to buy. Food stands stood in front of every home, with bananas, coconuts, crabs, and shrimp displayed. Other homes had a bar set up. Old military ice chests displayed pop, all kinds of beer, European and French wines, and even the Vietnamese version of moonshine.

Young women in revealing clothing marketed themselves. The older women who had lost their beauty operated steam baths for a gentleman's pleasure.

All in all, it was a shame to have a war in such a pretty place.

Claymore mines dotted the perimeter. Claymores are about as big as a dictionary. The back is solid metal and the front is plastic. Behind the plastic were thousands of ball bearings and behind the bearings were explosives. The claymores were triggered by either electricity or a trip wire. Thus, one of our guys could set off a claymore by throwing a switch or an enemy combatant could trigger it by tripping a wire. Once triggered or tripped, the mechanism explodes and the ball bearings fly straight out in an ever-widening pattern. A person hit by a claymore is unrecognizable; they look like hamburger.

The Gooks were very good at penetrating a perimeter, turning the claymores around, and then triggering them to explode when a GI came in the vicinity. I wondered how in the world they got through all that concertina wire to turn them around in the first place.

Sappers were our biggest fear. They were usually North Vietnamese regulars carrying a backpack full of plastic explosives. Sneaking through the concertina wire and the perimeter, they'd approach a small arms ammo pad and throw their backpacks into the middle of it. The satchel charge would blow up, igniting the ammunition, which would potentially set off all the other pads. A satchel charge probably wouldn't set off a 600-pound bomb or other large ordnance, but an exploding pad of small arms ammo could ignite the larger stuff if the soil berms weren't effective.

Thus, the small arms ammo pad was the most critical part of the ammo dump. Some hated to walk it for that reason. But Charley Peterson and I regularly volunteered for the small arms pad. We knew that if the whole ammo dump got blown, it would begin at the small arms pad and we wanted to be there. We both wanted to come home safely, so we took the small arms ammo pad out of the equation.

Our perimeter began where we walked, the roadway inside the perimeter providing access to all the ammunition pads. Each of us had to patrol the length of that road between the towers that lined the outermost fence of the ammo dump. Towers ranged from 100 yards to 300 yards apart and surrounded the entire dump. Between the towers and our road was a ditch.

Back in Sioux Rapids the roads had ditches for rain drainage in the summer and snow collection in the winter, but the ditches near the towers in 'Nam had only one purpose: protection. If a firefight broke out or if mortar rounds came in, the ditch was a safe place to be. Just like during a tornado: Get low and stay below the things that are flying around.

The most dangerous times for any of us walking dogs were at evening drop-off and morning pick-up. Both of these events happened during twilight. It's the same time of day when you wonder if you should turn on the headlights on your car. It's light enough to see to drive, but dark is coming and other cars have their lights on so maybe you should turn yours on, too. As for us, the snipers could see us at twilight. Later, the spotlights would come on and shine out into the jungle, blinding anyone looking in. But at dusk and dawn, there were no blinding lights and we were highly visible.

I always took Shep right to the deepest part of the ditch on my post and laid down to watch the sun set. We didn't move from that area until the spotlights came on. Then I felt safe moving around on my post.

The days were short since it was Vietnam's winter season and it was almost dark when we were dropped off. I heard a rifle crack. The distinctive sound of an AK47 rang through the air.

They're out there, I thought to myself.

"Dad! Come here quick!" someone yelled.

I ran with Shep in the direction of the yelling, and found Pete and Smitty standing together. Smitty looked white as a sheet and Pete was his normal, excitable self and it had been he who yelled.

"Those SOBs almost got us," Pete told me. "Smitty and I were having a smoke and, BANG! Just look at Smitty's helmet!"

I looked and saw a small hole in the front of Smitty's helmet.

"Darn bullet went in, made a circle around the inside of his helmet, and went right back out the same hole," Pete said.

I took off Smitty's helmet and sure enough, I could see the track the bullet had left as it made its circle around his head.

Smitty still had not said a word. The smell of singed hair was overwhelming after the helmet came off and I could see the circle of singed hair around Smitty's scalp. Smitty's color had started coming back and I'm sure he finally realized that he wasn't dead after all, even though he had thought differently earlier.

"Hey Dad," he said. "Now I know why the movies always talk about not being the second guy to light a cigarette from the same match!" Striking that match had alerted the sniper and by the time they were lighting the second cigarette he'd had enough time to zero in and shoot.

We had been told that a flame from a lighter or the glow of a cigarette can be seen from a mile away. So it's important to never light more than one cigarette at a time to prevent a sniper from drawing a bead on you and your companion. And always smoke under cover.

A few days later, the singed hair fell out and we had fun calling Smitty "Monk." Both guys had been a little lax that night and it almost cost them. We all agreed that Smitty's guardian angel had come through again!

Later that night there was a firefight about a 1000 yards from the dump. I marveled at the beauty made by the tracers bouncing into the air and the explosions made by the mortars. Flares hung in the air, lighting up the landscape with an eerie glow. Smoke grenades left clouds of various colors floating in the light of the flares. If it hadn't been such a serious a thing, I would have been glad to buy tickets just to see it.

One day Captain Morgan approached me in the barracks. "The commanding officer of the transportation company and I have made a little bet on a football game," he said. "I want you to organize a team and be ready to show those truck drivers what the game of football is all about!"

"I can't," I said. "I had brain concussions playing high school football and the doctors told me not to play again."

"I really need you to organize this, Halverson. It'll be good for the morale of the troops, to say nothing of how happy I will be with that bottle of Jim Beam I've got bet with the transportation commander. You're smart enough not to get hurt. Play it safe and I'll make it well worth your time, if you know what I mean."

I didn't know what he meant, but the meaning was so ominous that I decided not to decline. "OK," I said. "I'll do it. But if we win, you have to serve me breakfast in bed."

"You got yourself a deal!" the captain declared.

I knew that Smitty had to be on the team. He had a full-ride scholarship to play the sport of his choice at Iowa State and could run like a deer. Art "The Wop" Pollicelli would be the other end. Mike Huston was a wiry little guy who could also run like the wind. He and Pete would be good in the backfield.

I knew Chain pretty well and figured I could count on him to recruit for me. Chain was black and a real street fighter—he got his nickname because he always fought with a chain. We had a number of black guys in our company and they were all really, really big. Chain came through with an entire front line and they were all built like elephants. In fact, five of them went on to play pro football after the service.

I needed a center and gave that recruiting assignment to Smitty. He came into the barracks the next day with a stocky fellow from headquarters. "Meet Stan," Smitty said. "He played center for a football team in Ohio."

Stan stuck out his hand to shake and grinned with the ugliest set of teeth I've ever seen in my life.

"Looks like he's been chewing crushed rock, doesn't he?" Smitty said.

That didn't seem to bother Stan at all, who continued to grin as we shook hands.

The day of the game arrived. "All right, guys," I said. "You men up front, stop the defense for three counts. I'm going to either hand off the ball, or fake to Mike and Pete. If I hand off, they're on their own. If I fake, I'm going to throw the ball just as high and far as I can, and Smitty, you'd better be under it!"

That plan worked like a dream. I don't care where I threw it, Smitty was right there to catch it.

We were way ahead in the fourth quarter and decided to go for a shutout. Everyone played their hearts out as the opposing team tried to score. Their quarterback went back for a pass and I dove to get him.

BAM!

All I saw was stars! Mike Houston had dived for the quarterback at the same time I had, but the quarterback ducked and Mike and I had met head on. Mike started screaming and shaking, a sign of going into shock. I told him to lie down and put his hands on his stomach. That would keep him from feeling the gash on his head. Art gave me his T-shirt, which we applied to the cut to stop the bleeding. Smitty got a Jeep and took Mike to the dispensary.

I went to the shower to clean up and felt blood on my head. Lo and behold, I needed to go to the doctor for stitches, too! I got there just after

Mike had received his 32 stitches. The doc gave me three. My dad always did say I was hard-headed!

What's a few stitches? The important thing was that we won 35-0 and I got breakfast in bed.

Mike and I weren't the only casualties of that football game. Smitty came up to me and asked to go outside. He guided me to a space that was secluded and glanced around to make sure no one was within earshot. The he whispered "That big guy that tackled me hurt me. I think I have a prolapse like the pigs used to get back home on the farm. Dad used to shoot them because he said they'd never be the same again. What do I do?"

I assured him that he had a normal condition known as hemorrhoids. "The doctors can put a salve on them to make them go away," I explained.

I borrowed a jeep to drive Smitty to the dispensary. As we bounced down the roadway, Smitty groaned in pain. "I can't sit, Dad. It hurts." Smitty stood up behind the driver's seat and held on to my shoulders and said, "This should work!"

So I drove on with Smitty standing in the jeep behind me. Sure enough, an MP saw us driving along and turned on his siren. He pulled us over and looked up at Smitty. "You can't stand up in a Jeep, troop."

Smitty gave the MP a crisp salute even though the MP wasn't an officer. "I've got to stand up, sir! I've got hemorrhoids!"

This threw the MP for a loop but finally he said, "You could sit on a pillow."

Smitty shrugged his shoulder and nodded his head while the MP looked on in bewilderment. "It would take six Army pillows to make one good enough, sir!"

The MP waved us on with a laugh and Smitty got his Preparation H.

The word around the compound was that the NVA were building up around Pleiku and that they were recruiting Viet Cong in the area. They were firing rockets and mortars at headquarters and the infantry compound in the early morning and the early evening. Both targets were distant from the dog compound and the ammunition dump, so we dog handlers felt relatively safe. We knew that both the NVA and the Viet

Cong were deathly afraid of dogs. We were told that many of them were Buddhists and believed they had to have their entire body intact in order to go to heaven. But a dog would take a bite of flesh from their bodies and, therefore, prevent them from going to heaven.

Rumors abounded that our intelligence officers would take two prisoners up in a chopper and question them. Of course, the prisoners wouldn't talk. Then they would cut off a finger of one of the prisoners and throw it out the door of the Huey. That prisoner would dive out and try to catch his finger so his body would be complete when he died. The remaining prisoner would talk.

Even though they were afraid of dogs, they were crafty enough to investigate the perimeter to see if any of the dog handlers were lazy. If they found a guard shirking his duties, that's where they would infiltrate. Those of us who didn't use drugs were religious about walking our dogs throughout the night, but the dopers often held pot parties on post. Four or five of them would gather at one man's post for their party and leave their own posts unguarded.

And that's just what happened one particular night. The NVA found unguarded posts and tried to enter the ammo dump when one of the dogs got their scent, tore loose from the bush to which his handler had tied him to, and attacked the NVA soldier.

If there was a suspected penetration, standard operating procedure required us to shoot three quick shots into the air to signal the sergeant of the guard. Everybody in that group fired three shots and shortly thereafter a truckload of guards arrived. The guards fired off flares and M79 grenade launchers in the immediate area, while the truck picked up the dogs and their handlers to remove them from the dump. Dogs were supposed to alert and alert only. As soon as there was any firing, they were to be removed from the area. All dog handlers were removed from the dump as the guards continued to fire small arms and grenades in the immediate perimeter area to scare the enemy away.

When everything had calmed down, the guards found the body of an NVA infiltrator. They all praised the dog handlers for stopping an invasion of the ammo dump.

A few days later, I was walking my post with Shep when a mortar came in. I immediately headed for a reventment, which is a protective

264

structure made of two sheets of steel spaced about three feet apart. Soil is piled on the backs of each inch thick sheet of steel to a height of four feet. The end product is like a small hill with a three foot slit in it. We had just entered when a mortar hit near where we were. I remember Shep and I sailing through the air. As I flew, I thought "Am I dead?" I saw Shep land on the ground and then everything went blank. Then I heard music…wonderful music. It sounded so pretty. And then someone came to me. All I remember is that I was very happy to see him and that he was happy to see me judging by the smile on his face. He took my hand and we started to rise toward a bright light showing through the clouds. I remember looking back at my body lying on the ground. A huge piece of inch thick steel was lying flat on my back. But it was flat! It hadn't cut my body in half. It had hit me flat and I thought "I'm not dead…it just knocked me out!" I told the man holding my hand "I'm not dead! I have to go back." Our hands parted and he left me. I had taken philosophy of religion classes in college and that made me question everything about my religion. So as I headed back to my body I memorized the shape of the piece of steel. I wanted to make sure that I hadn't been dreaming. If I had been dreaming the shape of the steel would be unknown to me. Later I woke up as Shep was licking my face. I turned over and looked at the steel that had hit me in the back and the shape was exactly as I had remembered it. So there is no question in my mind that my spirit was met by someone and together we were headed to Heaven. I wish I knew who had come to meet me, but I have no idea. Maybe that's the way it's supposed to be. But this I know: I believe that you and I have a soul and that one day that soul will join the spirit worlds we call Heaven and Hell.

My entire back and my buttocks turned black and blue. I surmised that I was darn lucky to still be healthy and alive. I wondered about the other guys that may have been hit and were still alive but not healthy. Jesus said that we should visit the sick so I began to go to the hospital and read letters and the Bible to guys that were hurt. I saw a number of them die. And I saw that smile they had as someone came to escort them on their journey to the next world. That was always the moment the heart monitor sounded…just as their spirit left their bodies.

I read letters to a fellow who had been hit by a claymore mine. The Gooks had turned it around in the perimeter and set it off when he came to inspect it. The mine had blown his hands off, caused internal injuries and damaged his legs. He told me that he had been an all-state football player in Florida. Now he couldn't catch a ball and he probably would never be able to run again. "What am I going to do when I get back to the world? I'll never be able to get a job without hands. What girl in her right mind would want to marry me?" He knew that I was an M.P. and asked me to bring my .45 pistol and end his misery. I declined. Then he asked if I would just bring it and leave it by his bed. I didn't do that either.

War hurts people…soldiers and civilians…and they'll never be the same again.

One night a mortar round hit right beside the revetment we were in, and it sent me and Shep sailing through the air.

Shep detected an NVA inside the ammo dump. I called Pete for backup and we went into the ammo pad where I had seen the enemy, but couldn't find him anywhere. We roamed the entire area with no success. The dogs kept taking us to a garbage barrel and we kept pulling them away to pick up a human scent somewhere. We thought the dogs were alerting on the garbage. Gus pulled Pete back to the barrel again and in his frustration, Pete kicked the barrel over.

"Well, I'll be damned," Pete said. "Come take a look at this, Dad."

And there it was, an opening to a tunnel.

"Good gosh. They're coming up right inside the dump and stealing our own ammo to shoot back at us!" Pete said.

We reported what we had found and all sorts of activity began to take place. Two semi loads of CS gas were dumped into the hole. We had been exposed to CS when we were in training and let me tell you, it's horrible. It makes a person's eyes burn, irritates the skin, and makes it almost impossible to breathe. I expected lots of coughing and crying. I figured we would see NVA emerging from the hole with tears running down their cheeks and their hands high in the air. But there was nothing, not even a peep!

Tunnel rats were brought in, troops specially trained to combat the enemy in their own tunnels. Now those guys had my complete admiration. Usually, they were on the smaller side so they could navigate the tunnels. They were armed with a pistol, a bayonet, and a flash light. That's it! The Army issued them a.45 caliber pistol but most didn't use one. The .45 made a horrible racket when it was fired, especially in a tunnel. The sound would deafen the rat and of course, his hearing was important in his work. Most carried a Smith and Wesson Model 29 revolver loaded with .44 caliber shotgun shells. That made much less noise, was lighter to carry, and had a lot of knock down power.

The Viet Cong had gone underground years ago when they were fighting the French to avoid air power and bombing runs. They had food caches, ammunition caches, headquarters, R&R centers, hospitals, and a maze of tunnels connecting one to another. Spiders, snakes, scorpions, bats, booby traps, and VC awaited anyone who entered their confines.

I don't know how any one of our tunnel rats kept their sanity with all those threatening things lying in wait for them, but they did. The close confines alone would do me in with claustrophobia. Tunnel rats were usually quite small in stature and that made sense. The VC were small and their tunnels would correspond to their size. Our tunnel rat arrived and the little guy grinned and popped into the entrance as though it were just another day at the office. He spent three hours down there before he surfaced. When he did, he spoke with authority and no one questioned his information.

"You just threw away two truckloads of gas," he laughed. "The Gooks had a U-bend in their tunnel to channel the gas away from them. They've been down this road before with the French. Of course, the French used poison gas back in the day. They've got food, ammo, a bowling alley, an R&R center, a headquarters, a hospital, and it looks like they bring in girls to entertain the troops, all right under your US Army ammunition dump! Of course, they all di di maued the area, but they'll be back when the dust settles. You might as well let them steal some mortars and small arms ammo to shoot back at you from time to time, or if you stop them they'll just blow the whole damned works straight up into the troposphere!"

Smitty looked at Pete and I. "Well Dad, I think it's time to di di mau ourselves. I hear they need dog handlers in An Khe." We all decided to put in for a transfer to An Khe immediately.

After detecting the NVA internally and the finding the tunnel, I got directed to go to Cam Ranh Bay to meet with Intelligence officials. I flew down on a C-130 cargo plane and met with them, explaining what we'd found.

Afterwards, I went to the dog compound to visit with old friends. I walked into the barracks and saw familiar faces. We shook hands and renewed acquaintances. After a while, I noticed that everyone had a SP4 (Specialist 4th class) patch on their shoulders. How could this be? Smitty, Pete and I were selected to go north to Pleiku because we were the best in the unit. We didn't do drugs. We walked our dogs. We took care of our dogs and the kennels, but we were still E-3s, privates first class.

I had a wife at home I was trying to support. She couldn't get a teaching job because school boards were afraid she would leave as soon as I came home. So she was living with her sister in California and waiting tables, while I sent money home to her. And now I find out that a bunch of duds get rank and I didn't? I was fuming mad.

Payson had been reduced to E-2 for striking an officer way back when we first arrived in Cam Ranh Bay. But now he was a SP4. Johnson had been busted for possession of marijuana. He was a SP4, too. Mike had been arrested for bootlegging back in Georgia and given the choice of going to jail or the Army. Yup, he was a SP4. Jerry had beaten his dog to death. The Army wouldn't give him another dog, so they made him an administrative assistant and he was a SP4.

I was furious. What happened to rewarding a person for a job well done? I needed that extra income.

When I got back to Pleiku, I informed Pete and Smitty what I had found in Cam Ranh Bay. Pete was beside himself and what he said can't be printed in this document. He was ready to go to headquarters and duke it out with the CO. We decided that wouldn't do any good; we'd probably end up in the slammer.

"Let's write to our congressmen," Pete said. "They're supposed to represent us."

So we did. Smitty and I wrote to Iowa US Senator Harold Hughes, explaining our situation, while Pete wrote to Senator Albert Quie in Minnesota. We told them how we had been moved up north because we were good soldiers and that we had been screwed out of rank because of the move. We believed that rank had been given just because of tenure in one location rather than for job effectiveness. I personally thought that a quarter and that letter might get us a cup of coffee. A few weeks went by and Pete got a letter from Albert Quie. Smitty and I got letters from Harold Hughes.

"We have researched the facts and found that what you say is true. We have ordered the Army to award you SP4 status and grant you pay— retroactively!" So we got SP4 pay immediately and a nice check to make up the difference between our PFC checks and the SP4 amount clear back to the date we had been assigned to Pleiku.

Once upon a time, there were two good senators…

I received the Sunday edition of the Des Moines Register and was reading the headlines when Smitty grabbed the want ads. "Hey, Dad! Let's have an auction. Just like we have back in good ole Panora." He stood up on a foot locker and announced that he was holding an auction. I doubt that any of the guys had any idea what an auction was with the exception of a few of us who had come from the farm. But everyone knew that wherever Smitty was; a show was about to begin. They gathered around Smitty with questioning looks on their faces. "All right, let's start off with this beautiful John Deere B! Just look at the paint on that sucker…what a cherry! Who'll start the bidding with $500?"

Everyone looked at him like he was a Martian that had just landed in their back yard. "Oh, what the heck," I thought. I raised my hand and bid on the B.

"YES!" Smitty announced. "I have a bidder at $500! Five, humde, humde, humde, five…do I hear $600? 6, 6 humde, humde, humde…do I hear 6?" No one bid and I couldn't because I had the bid at $500.

"Just look at the rubber on that little jewel," Smitty said with a grin. "That'll plow a thousand acres before it even shows any wear! Heck, the tires are probably worth $600 by themselves! 6, 6 hundred, humde, humde, humde…do I hear $600?"

Chain had never witnessed an auction before. If he wanted tires; he jacked the car up and stole them! But he was getting into the fun and shyly raised his hand.

"YES!" Smitty screamed. "I've got 6! And now 7! 7, 7 hundred, humde, humde, humde…do I hear $700?"

More guys gathered in our little throng and Smitty gained momentum with their appearance. They all stood there with dumb grins on their faces as Smitty welcomed them by saying, "You're in luck boys! This dandy little John Deere B hasn't been sold yet and it's going at the basement price of $600! You can get in at $700…it's a steal at that price!" They all stood there like tobacco store Indian statues.

"Start 'er up," Smitty commanded to the imaginary owner. He stood there squinting as if he were watching the owner starting up the tractor. Just then, he broke into a wide grin and said, "Just listen to that engine, boys. Runs like a Singer sewing machine!" Everyone automatically tipped their heads as if they could hear the engine and the way Smitty was leading the group; they probably could! $700 and you can own that little baby! 7, 7 hundred, humde, humde, hum de…do I hear $700?"

Walt grinned as he raised his hand just like he had seen Chain do.

"YES! I have $700. Do I hear 8? 8, 8 hundred, humde, humde, humde…$800?"

More guys grinned and bid. Smitty chatted with the imaginary owner as everyone paid close attention to their conversation and learned that the engine had just been overhauled, it had new rings, pistons and valves, didn't use any oil and was a miser on gasoline.

The John Deere B sold for an astounding $7000 and Smitty had found a new niche in the Army. He sold cows with calves, horses, combines, pick-ups and baled hay to an adoring crowd of men who had absolutely no idea what they were bidding on…but they loved every minute of it. And a new tradition began…

I gave a sigh of relief as the date of my R&R finally arrived. All branches of the military gave a week of "Rest and Relaxation" during our tour in Viet Nam. Those of us that were married could meet our wives in Hawaii. Single soldiers got the choice of Bangkok, Thailand or Sidney, Australia.

I took a C-130 ride from Pleiku to Saigon where an airliner would take me to Hawaii. I was floored by the sights I saw in Saigon prior to my flight to Hawaii. People were busy shopping, sightseeing and going to and from business appointments. Traffic was heavy and there were even traffic jams! I saw retail stores, bowling alleys, bars, restaurants and churches. No one was wearing olive drab except those in the military. Otherwise, men and women alike wore brightly colored clothing. And no one carried a gun! I hadn't seen a peaceful surrounding like this in seven months. It was like Saturday night in Spencer, Iowa.

Our plane was filled with military personnel anxious to see their wives for the first time in months. We landed in Honolulu and were immediately placed on the army blue transportation busses. I had sat in the back of the plane so I was the last one onto the last bus. Four busloads of us headed to the reception area where we would join our wives. Each bus had an official greeter that welcomed us to Hawaii and explained what was about to happen: "Your wives will be waiting in two lines for you. Now understand that your wives may have changed from when you last saw them. Some will have lost weight and some will have gained. They may have a different hair style than when you saw them last. Since this is sunny Hawaii, they may be wearing sunglasses. Nothing makes a woman cry more than her husband not recognizing her and walking right on by. So please, take your time when you get off the bus. Walk slowly and check every one of them out so you don't make that mistake. Now, have a wonderful time in Hawaii with your wife."

While we were getting this bit of advice, Ginny was listening to a chaplain in the reception area. The women were lined up in two lines facing each other as the chaplain walked between them and told them what to expect. "These boys have been out in the jungle for months. They haven't seen you since they left. They are probably thinner than they were when they left. You have changed too. I'll bet he never saw the clothes you are wearing. Is your hair the same? So it might be easy for them to walk on by you. Don't you **dare** get angry if that happens. But be sure to give him a piece of your mind because he could have been like all those other guys and recognized you." The first bus unloaded and sure enough, after a time there was a name called over the loudspeaker for a wife to come join her husband. Neither one of them had recognized each other through the line up!

As the next two buses unloaded the banter from the chaplain continued, now relating the fact that those who were still waiting needed to talk to their husbands about being on time, how rude they were to make them wait etc. Ginny jokingly told the greeter that there wouldn't be any problem in her case. "Lee will be the last one off the bus. He's always late!"

Of course, I had sat in the back of the bus too! As I followed the other guys to get off the bus, I joked with the driver and said "I sure hope I find her!" I stepped past him and got onto the first step to exit the bus. WHAM! Ginny tackled me right on the step of the bus and we both fell into the driver's lap.

He looked at me with a grin on his face. "Looks like you did just fine!"

We kissed and kissed and kissed…right on the driver's lap! It was so good to see her and hold her that I felt like I had died and gone to heaven.

We immediately went to our hotel room to do what lovers do when they have been apart from one another. Unlike our little cabin in Augusta, this place was luxurious! It had a full kitchen, a dining area, a sofa, chairs, a TV and a sliding glass door that opened to a patio overlooking the ocean. But like our little cabin in Augusta, it had twin beds! I busied myself moving the beds together.

"You have to put these on first," Ginny said as she handed me a present wrapped in ribbon. "Go into the bath room and put them on." I went into the bath room and opened the present. A nice new pair of black, gold and white boxer shorts looked up at me. I put them on and joined her in bed. As I looked at her, I noticed that she had made panties and a bra from the same material! She smiled and said "Four more pair and you'll be coming home!"

I drew a tub of hot water and crawled in. I hadn't been able to soak in a tub in a long time since we only had showers in Viet Nam. And hot water! What a joy! I sat in the tub and reached over to flush the toilet. What a wonderful sound! I soaked and flushed for the better part of an hour.

Ginny had brought homemade bread in her suit case along with other fixings she knew I would enjoy. Our first meal was spaghetti, which is my favorite meal. And the homemade bread slathered with butter was a treat I hadn't had it quite a while. She introduced me to beef stroganoff which is another of my favorites to this day. I really didn't want to go out to a restaurant. I just wanted the joy of watching my wife cook a meal and I wanted to see the satisfied look on her face as I ate it.

We went to Sea World to see the show there. We rode an escalator down to the arena and it was fun! I felt like a little boy again; enjoying a simple thing like an escalator. I told Ginny, "I'm going to ride it again!" So I rode up, came back down, rode up and came back down while Ginny hid in the corner like she didn't even know me. Onlookers were enjoying watching my show but Ginny didn't. It felt good to embarrass here again. I told her I really didn't enjoy crowds and commercialism. I just wanted to be with her and no one else. So we rented a dune buggy and drove around the island to see the sights. We stopped at a high cliff where the trade winds blow up from the ocean with such force that I could lean over the edge of the cliff, be perfectly horizontal and the wind would hold me up. We drove by pineapple fields and jungle and happened upon a WWII concrete bunker on the top of a hill we had chosen to hike. I pointed out how the bunker was made and how it compared to the bunkers we had in Viet Nam. We continued on and the road which overlooked a beautiful bay a few hundred feet below us…Hanama Bay. It looked like a black honeycomb with aqua colored cells instead of yellow honey. "Let's go swimming," I said. So we drove the dune buggy right down onto the beach and dove in. We swam a hundred yards or so out into the water and just relaxed for a few hours there. While we were enjoying ourselves in the water, the tide went out. Suddenly, water than had been four feet deep was only a foot deep and we couldn't swim…we had to walk. It was then that we found out what had caused the beautiful honeycomb effect we had seen. Lava had flowed into this bay and giant bubbles of gas had burst leaving a hollow center where the gas had been. Hard, sharp lava surrounded each cell. The cells were four feet deep and the lava walls around each cell were three feet high. So we had no choice but to balance on the lava walls to walk back to the dune buggy. By the time we got back our feet were sore from the rough lava and we were both burned to a crisp. Ginny looked like a lobster!

The next day was Sunday and we were both looking forward to going to church together. We got up and started walking in search of a church. We walked a few blocks and found one. It was small as churches go and it was made entirely of lava rock. We walked in and sat down. Everyone

273

was dressed in beautiful Hawaiian clothing. The entire service was done in their native tongue so we didn't understand a word that was said. But when they got to the Lord's Prayer, we looked at each other and we knew. The rhythm of the prayer was unmistakable. We joined hands during the Lord's Prayer for the first time in eight months.

The minister came to see us after the service in his flowing, flowery robe and a crown made of flowers upon his head. "I'm sorry the service wasn't in English for you," he said. "But you just happened to come on the 100th anniversary of King Kamayamaya. We wanted to celebrate his birthday in our true Hawaiian tongue and in clothing reminiscent of his time. I hope you enjoyed it." We assured him that we had.

It ended all too soon and Ginny escorted me to the airport to see me off. We walked down the runway together and the sound system played another verse of Peter, Paul and Mary's "Leavin' on a jet plane:

Now the time has come to leave you
One more time let me kiss you.
Then close your eyes and I'll be on my way.
Dream about the days to come
When I won't have to leave alone
About the times, I won't have to say

So kiss me and smile for me
Tell me that you'll wait for me
Hold me like you'll never let me go.
I'm leavin' on a jet plane
I don't know when I'll be back again
Oh babe, I hate to go.

We kissed and Ginny said through her tears, "When I see you again, we'll never have to be apart again."

I flew back to Saigon and climbed aboard another C-130 for my trip back to Pleiku. I slept for most of the flight. That is, until we came close to Pleiku and the plane made a violent dip. The plane made violent dips and turns for a while and finally smoothed out. The pilot announced over the intercom "Sorry, boys. We were taking sniper fire and I was taking evasive actions. We should be on the ground in a few minutes." We flew along for a while and then the captain came on again. "The sniper must have hit a hydraulic line and our landing gear won't go down. But we have a manual back up system and we should be able to get it down with that. Bear with us."

His co-pilot came back and began to pump what looked like a hydraulic jack. He pumped for a while and then went back to the pilot who announced "There wasn't enough fluid in the system to get the landing gear all the way down. So we're going to have to go in as it is and we may do a belly flop; so cinch those safety belts up tight."

Growing up on the farm has its advantages. I had worked with hydraulics all my life. "Just a minute," I said. "Any fluid will work in a hydraulic system. Let's empty anything we've got into the hydraulic reservoir! Pop, water, coffee…whatever you've got." The co-pilot unscrewed the cap from the hydraulic reservoir and pumped as we all dumped canteens, cans of pop and thermoses of coffee. The pilot announced that the landing gear was almost down but his light hadn't come on yet. "OK boys," I said. "Line up and pee in the reservoir! We need every last drop!" We stood in line and took our turns while the co-pilot diligently pumped away. Then we heard a small "click" as the locking pins fell into place.

"I've got a light!" the pilot yelled. We all gave a sigh of relief and strapped ourselves in for a delightfully perfect landing. I've always wondered what kind of look went across that mechanic's face when he drained the system!

I told everyone in the barracks what a wonderful time I had experienced in Hawaii. Smitty was forlorn because he missed his girl, Nan, so much. They weren't married so going to Hawaii was out for them. But once Smitty got an idea in his head, he was pretty hard to stop.

"Hey, Dad! Guess what! I'm going to Hawaii! Johnson got a "Dear John" letter from his wife and he gave me his ticket to Hawaii! Now I can see Nan!"

"Darn," I thought. "How does that kid do it?"

Smitty went to the MARS station and called Nan to tell her. Their connection was very poor and they couldn't understand each other with the exception of the date and the destination of Hawaii.

Smitty's plane to Hawaai had mechanical problems and got delayed by an entire day. Meanwhile, Nan had arrived in Hawaii and waited in line with the other ladies as husbands got off the bus. One by one, couples were reunited as poor Nan watched, waiting for Smitty to disembark from the bus. But alas, everyone was finally gone and Nan stood all alone. She wandered the airport in Hawaii checking every gate and eventually laid down on a bench to cry. It was at that exact moment that Smitty walked into the exact spot where Nan was crying. The airport in Hawaai is a big one and how Smitty just happened to walk into the right gate can only be explained by his guardian angel.

We continued to get internal alerts at the ammo dump in Pleiku. Charlie kept coming out of his tunnel, taking mortars and other ammo, and disappearing. While the Army tried to figure out how to fix this problem with gas and tunnel rats, I got more and more nervous. The NVA had an enormous tunnel complex beneath our ammo dump. They were stealing our ammo and shooting it right back at us! You see, Communist mortars were 82 millimeters in diameter. Ours were 81 millimeters. Thus, our 81 m.m. mortars would fit in an 82 m.m. mortar tube. But theirs were one m.m. too large to fit in our tubes. Imagine how much easier it was to steal mortars from us than it was to bring them down the Ho Chi Minh Trail on a bicycle? That's also true for other ammunition. Communist ammo is one caliber larger than ours. NVA were sighted in the mountains surrounding Pleiku and scouts found a hidden road, camouflaged with undergrowth, and there were tank tracks on that road. Though no tanks were found, we couldn't deny that they were in the area. We found out later that the tanks were in tunnels that went all the way from Hue to Cambodia! Since they were hidden in the tunnels during the day, our observation planes wouldn't see them.

President Nixon had begun pulling troops out of Vietnam to satisfy the citizenry back home, and we realized that there wouldn't be enough of us left to defend ourselves if the NVA decided to attack. On top of that, Ho Chi Minh announced that one day he would like to retake Pleiku and build a memorial on Artillery Hill. Our prospects didn't look good.

An Khe had a reputation as a dumping ground for poor dog handlers. But An Khe was also home for the 101st Airborne Division and you don't mess with the 101st! An Khe had requested more dog handlers, and usually the brass in Pleiku picked their poorest handlers and sent them. But Smitty, Pete and I had already decided: We were going to volunteer for An Khe.

Sergeant Clifford was flabbergasted when he saw our names on the volunteer list. "What the h*ell* are you doing? I won't let you go!"

"I've already volunteered," I said.

"Look. I'll make you sergeant of the guard. You'll have an office, a Jeep, and you'll never have to walk a post again, just draw up the guard schedule and check on alerts. That's it!"

"No thanks. Smitty and Pete are going to An Khe, too, and we all stick together."

Sergeant Clifford finally gave in.

"You and Pete are the best handlers I've got," he said, "and I sure hate to lose you, but I won't stand in your way. Can't say the same for Smitty. That guy's the biggest screw-up I've ever been associated with. I don't know how you put up with him but I sure admire the way you two stick together." Smitty was a screw-up and a darn good one at that. But I had promised his parents at the airport in Des Moines that I would look out for him, and that's exactly what I intended to do.

I assumed that we would be moving to An Khe shortly, so I described everything that had been happening to Ginny in my next letter. I hadn't informed her of the internal alerts or the tunnels because I didn't want her to worry. But since we were going to be leaving Pleiku shortly and the mail would take a week or so; I thought I would be safe in describing the situation to her and I figured she would be relieved that I was making the move.

Little did I know how much paper work would be involved in changing our orders. It took three weeks for all the paper work for our orders to complete and by that time, Ginny was beside herself that I was still in Pleiku. I was just as worried as she was! Every night was a trial wondering if the Gooks would attack or not.

The tension broke when I heard Smitty's familiar voice. "Hey Dad, the transportation company is here and they want to stand us in football. You ready?"

We had beaten the transportation company badly at our last game and Mickey, our good friend in transportation, wanted a rematch. He had found five of the biggest guys I had ever seen for his front line. Any pro coach would have salivated just looking at them.

Game on! Nothing like a good football game to forget our worries!

We huddled and I gave my usual directions to Smitty: "Go down the right sideline just as hard as you can, count to five, look up and catch the ball because I'm unloading before those big gorillas tackle me!"

That was one of the reasons I loved Smitty. No matter where I threw the ball, he would be right there under it, catch it, and run in for a touchdown. It was like throwing to a cross between a deer and an octopus. He could run and he could catch.

After the game, which we again won handily, we announced to Mickey that Smitty, Pete, and I were going to An Khe.

"No!" Mickey yelled. "You guys are the best friends we've got. Who we gonna play football with? How 'bout volleyball? Horse shoes? You guys are the only outlet we have."

"Well," Smitty said. "We're gonna di di mau to An Khe and, like the Egyptian undertaker said, 'I guess that about wraps it up!'"

CHAPTER 7
AN KHE

We said our goodbyes to our friends in Pleiku, and then loaded our dogs and luggage into a deuce and a half for the trip to An Khe. We rode through the familiar rolling hills of that area, and the topography began to change the farther east we went. The hills became steeper and there were more trees. We were going from the central highlands with its agriculture, rice, bananas, and rubber trees into mountainous territory.

Far ahead we could see the outline of Hong Cong Mountain and it reminded me of the loess hills in western Iowa, more of a big hill that a mountain. It also reminded me of the trip a group of us college kids made to go skiing in Colorado. We saw the Rockies when we came close to Denver and they looked like they were just a few minutes away. But we drove and drove and drove until we finally got to the mountains. The same was true here. Hong Cong Mountain seemed to be just around the bend, but we drove and drove and drove before we finally got there.

The truck delivered us to a dilapidated barracks with a set of kennels and a deteriorating bunker next to it. I found out later that our barracks had been an old French motor pool. Apparently, the French had built the bunker, too, and no one had taken the effort to maintain it since then.

The word was that the rest of the military was as afraid of dogs as the Gooks were. That's the reason we were stuck a couple miles out in the middle of nowhere; they felt safer with the dogs far away. We were in a kind of a no-man's land.

We were told that our Mess Hall was with the 101st Airborne, two miles away,. The only transportation we had to the Mess Hall was a Jeep belonging to the sergeant of the guard. We could eat if he was in the mood, but since he liked to go to the club at night and sleep in the morning, breakfast was out. And if he was gone, we had no ride to the Mess Hall for any other meals.

Our facilities were primitive to say the least. We had a two-hole out house. A 55-gallon barrel had been cut in half and a half set below each hole. A trap door on the back side of the outhouse could be opened so that the barrel halves could be pulled out and dumped or burned.

Our showers and sinks adjoined the outhouse. A large tank sat on the roof of the shower, our water source for showering and shaving. If the sun shined and heated up the water in the tank, the shower was somewhat comfortable. However, we were up in the mountains and it was cold, even when the sun shone, so our showers were often cold and very invigorating. A tank truck with "Potable Water" printed on the side delivered water for the tank, but we ran out frequently.

None of us trusted the sign on the truck because we saw how the operator handled his operation. We didn't mind showering and shaving in that water but we sure weren't going to drink it. So we bought cases of soda pop and kept them on hand. We all drank pop. I don't think anyone of us drank any water the whole time we were in An Khe.

The ammunition dump at An Khe was quite a bit smaller than the one at Pleiku, the latter a mile long and a half-mile wide. The one at An Khe was just a few hundred yards long and a 100 yards wide. Two men were assigned to walk the dump at An Khe. In comparison, 24 men walked the dump in Pleiku.

Pete and I trusted each other and decided that we would work together. He took the west half of the dump and I worked the east half. I could easily see reasons for the dump having been blown up six times in the past, especially during TET. The concertina wire had not been maintained. There were a number of holes in it and, in fact, there were well-worn paths through it into the dump. Viet Cong and regular villagers had been entering the dump and stealing ammunition. The Viet Cong used it to supply the North Vietnamese and villagers sold it on the black market. Once they had all they needed, the Viet Cong threw backpacks full of plastic explosives into the small arms pit. The plastic set off the small arms ammo and that would often set off the rest of the dump. By the time we arrived they weren't interested in blowing up the dump. They just wanted to steal ammunition.

The ammo dump at An Khe didn't have a lighting system like the one in Pleiku. We could easily see if someone approached the perimeter at Pleiku, but not at An Khe. One night when Shep alerted on a scent, I couldn't see what we were following. I only knew that he had detected a South Vietnamese by the way Shep alerted. We followed the scent to the concertina wire and stopped. We were not supposed to go past the concertina wire. Once there, we were to call the infantry who would come to the area and recon it. So I called the infantry sergeant of the guard about the alert and the location. Then I continued checking out my area. Soon I had another alert, followed it to the perimeter wire, and called in that one. By the end of my shift, I had called in 13 alerts! I couldn't believe there had been that many infiltrators.

As the sun began to make its entrance for the day, I went to the center part of the ammo dump where Pete and I had parted company the night before. We had agreed to meet there the next morning prior to being picked up.

Pete was wild-eyed! "Man, I had 14 alerts last night! I think this place is crawling with V.C. How did it go for you?"

"I had 13 alerts myself," I replied.

"I called them all in but didn't see any infantry show up at all."

"Same here," I said.

The sergeant came in his Jeep to pick us up and we explained everything to him.

"They're testing you," he said. "The Gooks know that a new group of guys just came in and they wanted to see how good you are at your job. They're cagey little devils. They know just how far to come to test you but still get safely away if they have to. It was probably just a couple of them trying different locations to see if you were walking your post or not. If they had detected you in one location but not another, they would have spread the word that you were hunkered down in one spot and not patrolling. Then they would have known that the other locations were still safe to enter.

"You guys did a good job," he said." If you had that many alerts it shows me that you're doing your job. But don't worry about the infantry not responding. They're not going to show unless there's rifle fire or mortars. Just keep on doing your job."

Pete and I looked at each other in amazement. It looked to us like we were on our own.

The way the other dog handlers there handled themselves reflected a total lack of leadership. They had a "why try" attitude and seemed to accept the fact that, since the dump had been blown before, it would be blown again and there wasn't much they could do about it. Tower guards were smoking pot, reading books, and sleeping while on duty.

Smitty said, "Hey, Dad! I think it's time we did a little advertising!"

Since we had learned that the NVA were afraid of dogs because they might lose a part of their body and not go to heaven, we advertised by taking our dogs into a village to let the locals see that we were around. They, in turn, spread the word and sooner or later the NVA got very nervous about being around us.

We surprised the sergeant of the guard when we asked to use the Jeep for an hour to make a run into town, but he relinquished to Smitty's incessant arguments. I drove and Smitty sat in the passenger's seat with Brutus. I'm not sure who had more fun, Brutus barking at people with no muzzle on his snout or Smitty baring his teeth and growling like a dog at everyone we passed. Smitty leaned out the side of the Jeep toward some poor unsuspecting soul riding a bicycle on the side of the street and growled like a dog. The poor guy never took his eyes off Smitty as he slowly lost the balance of his bike and landed on the road with a thud. Turning around, he was face to face with a snarling and barking Brutus.

When we got back to the barracks, Smitty grinned. "The word is out. I'll bet it gets back to Pleiku by tonight!"

Now, our latrines were not the flush type. We had a "Papa San" who emptied the barrels and burned their contents on a daily basis. Pop was about five feet tall, weighed maybe ninety pounds and looked a hundred years old. His hair was gray and on the top of his head he wore a long pony tail, a symbol of age and wisdom with the Vietnamese. The longer the "top knot" as we called it; the more respect the owner would be shown. He had five or six chin whiskers which also earn respect in their culture but his chin whiskers looked like a bad field of corn that didn't get enough fertilizer! He wore the typical rice straw conical hat on his head. The hat showed its age just like his pants and shirt. He would open a trap door in the back of the latrine, pull the barrels to a burning hole and dump them, pour in a gallon of diesel fuel and a juice can full of gasoline, and then light a match. When the burning had been completed, he would shove the barrels back into position in the latrine and close the door.

One evening, I got a bright idea. I told the guys "Let's soak the burning pit with aviation fuel and see what happens when Papa San burns tomorrow."

Everyone jumped on the idea and soon we were hauling av gas in anything that would hold it: waste baskets, steel pots, cans, etc. The gas soaked into the ground but we kept at the project and eventually had the hole brimming with gas. Overnight, it soaked into the ground so there was no evidence when "Pop" showed up the next morning.

He opened the door, pulled out the barrels, dumped their contents, poured in his diesel fuel along with the juice can of gas and then pulled out his matches. We were hiding behind bushes, buildings, and elephant grass to witness the event.

Pop's match never even got a flame. With a tremendous roar flames shot up, the contents of the pit flew everywhere, and Pop's straw hat circled 40 feet straight up in the air!

Have you ever laughed so hard you couldn't stand up? There wasn't a soldier standing!

When the smoke cleared and the hat had landed back on the ground, we could see Pop. He was covered head to toe with the contents of the barrels. His "top knot" was gone along with his chin whiskers, his eye brows and his eye lashes. He looked at us and said "Beau Que work, TT money," which meant "Lots of work for little money." He was okay, except that he needed to take a shower. We were all happy to lend him clothes and a towel. I wanted to do something special for him since he had been the victim of my idea. So I took him to my cot where I had a cache of food that Ginny had sent in care packages. One of my favorite snacks is dried apricots and Ginny had packed them in a number of baggies tied with twist ties. I gave Pop one of the baggies and said, "Eat it Pop! Number 1 Chop Chop!" Before I could stop him, Pop threw the whole works into his mouth, baggie and twist tie included! He chewed and then smiled; rubbing his belly to communicate that he liked the flavor. Every guy gave Pop some Pee for the entertainment. And Pop was happy, too, because he went home a rich man by Vietnamese standards.

Pete and I were pitching horseshoes one day when a Jeep pulled up.

"Where's the guy with the birthmark on his face? I'd like to speak to him," said the major.

"I'll go find him," I volunteered.

Oh brother, I thought. *What has that scatterbrain done now?*

Pete joined me as we went to the barracks to find Smitty. Pete and I reviewed in our minds the escapades Smitty had been involved in over the past few days. We knew he had been to the village a couple times. Did he sell something on the black market? Had he messed with drugs? He was always saying something out of line—had he offended an officer?

As usual, he was sound asleep in his bunk.

"Smitty! Get up! There's a major looking for you and he looks really important!"

Smitty jumped up from his bunk and marched down the aisle, out the door, and straight up to the major—in his Army-green boxer shorts and nothing else. I had all I could do to hold my laughter as Smitty stood there facing this immaculately dressed officer.

"Yes sir," said Smitty. "How's it hangin'?"

I almost swallowed my tongue when he said that, but the officer just laughed and stuck out his hand.

"I just wanted to shake the hand of the man that put fear into the minds of all the Vietnamese in the area. We heard about you driving around the village with your dog snarling and growling at every person you saw. Let me tell you, the word spread that guard dogs are in the area, so the Viet Cong and NVA soon got the message."

As he talked, Smitty did that nervous twitch of his where he simultaneously squinted the right side of his face and brought his right shoulder up to his face. It wasn't long before the major was twitching in unison.

"Anyway, pilferage in the food yard has dropped dramatically since that day," the major said. "I'm in charge of the food yard and I wanted to thank you, first of all. And, secondly, I wonder if you'd consider walking your dogs in the food yard. We store food for all the officers' clubs there. You could help yourself to anything you want as payment."

"Sure," said Smitty. "Anything for the good old US of A!"

The major smiled and saluted Smitty.

Smitty gave him an Iowa farmer wave and said, "Don't worry sir. We'll keep it under control."

Smitty's agreement with the major proved to be a very good deal for us. We were welcome to anything in the food yard as long as we walked it. Previously, GIs and locals had stolen food for themselves and to sell on the black market.

"You've cut our losses immensely," the major said. "You dog handlers can't eat enough to come close to what used to walk out of there. If you're happy with food as your payment, I'm pleased as peaches!"

Smitty was a great shopper and always came back from walking the food yard with a gunnysack full of goodies: steaks, lobster, potatoes, lettuce, salad dressing, bread, butter, ketchup, mustard, and so on. We salvaged an old barrel and built a barbecue grill. Metal grating from who-knows-where became the grill top. Most of us had long ago purchased small refrigerators from the PX and they kept our food from spoiling.

Charcoal could be purchased locally, it being a major source of energy in Vietnam; at least it was back then. The Vietnamese would cut down trees and pile them. The piles were set afire and, once they were burning good, they would cover them with dirt. That prevented oxygen from getting to the fire and resulted in lump charcoal. Water and other waste got burned away, leaving carbon. The carbon oxidized when we burned it and created the heat to cook on our charcoal grill.

We weren't the best housekeepers. Oh sure, we washed our clothes, brushed our teeth, took showers and made our beds. So our barracks looked pretty darn good, in fact, better than our dorm rooms looked in college. But our kitchen was a mess! Everyone brought something they liked back from the food yard, so we had fish, chicken, lobster, pork, beef, etc. for meats. Bacon and eggs were popular for breakfast for most of us, although some preferred cereal with milk. All foods were packed for commercial use, which meant that one didn't just bring a leg and a thigh back. Rather he brought a whole case of chicken! The same goes for eggs, bacon, fish, and so on. That presented a problem in that we didn't always consume the perishable food before it started to perish! And thus, we often ate spoiled meats.

We all gambled when the foods, especially meats, began to smell a little bit and perhaps even have a little mold around the edges. After all, if you scrape the mold off and cook it on a good hot fire, it should be all right we figured. Sadly, that's not the way it always worked out.

Many of us experienced the "Backdoor Trots" and this presented some problems aside from the fact that we were sick. Our toilet facilities left a lot to be desired. That, in and of itself, was okay. The problem is that Vietnam had lots of poisonous things like scorpions, snakes, plants, and spiders.

Spiders like dark, moist areas that attract a lot of bugs. Now can you think of a more perfect environment for a spider than the area right below the hole in an outhouse? It's dark, it's moist, and it certainly has a lot of bugs! Soldiers have those "ugly, hangy-down things," as Meta Joss used to describe them. Because we knew about the spiders, we always took a stick and swept the area around the hole before sitting down. That way we took care of any spider that might be lurking below. Now picture a guy with the backdoor trots deciding whether he has the time to check the hole before he explodes. Generally, the decision was to SIT! Consequently, we had a number of guys who got spider bites in some very tender spots on their bodies. I'm not sure which was worse, the trots or the bite.

One night while walking my post Shep alerted, and it was a very strong alert. I thought the sapper must be inside the wire because his alert was so strong. The scent came from the other side of a small hill down close to the concertina wire. Thank goodness I kept my hand on the leash and didn't let him go. I followed along as Shep pulled on the leash. The closer we got to the top of the hill, the harder Shep pulled on the leash. Finally, he was up on his hind legs pulling on the leash and frothing at the mouth.

Wow, I thought. *This is the real McCoy! How did a Gook get this close without Shep picking up his scent sooner?*

We crossed the top of the hill and I had all I could do to hold Shep back because he had a lot more leverage going downhill. As we reached the bottom of the hill, I could see a man's form crouching near the concertina wire.

I was about to let go of the leash and tell Shep to attack when a familiar voice rang out, "Hey Dad, you got any nickels?"

It was Walt Hensley experiencing food poisoning and he had come to this out-of-the-way spot to relieve himself. The reason he had asked for a nickel might be of interest to you. We weren't allowed to have the American dollar in Vietnam. We had to use Vietnamese currency. All Vietnam's currency was paper—even the change was paper! The currency was called PEE and it was one place where you could hold a hand full of pee and not get your hand wet!

Poor Walt had used the toilet paper from a C-Ration container, which doesn't amount to much more than a Kleenex. When that wasn't enough to get the job done, he had resorted to using PEE. The nickel was the smallest denomination. I gave Walt a handful of change so he could finish his job.

When I got back to the barracks, I dubbed him Nickel Man and it stuck. That's what everyone called him for the rest of his tour. I wrote Ginny about Nickel Man and, aside from the laughter it brought to her friends, she felt sorry enough for him that she sent a box of toilet paper for me to hand out. I gave Walt a roll for future use and he wrote Gin the nicest thank you note!

So we went from having to hitch a ride to the Mess Hall to cooking our own steaks, burgers, baked potatoes, and salads. We had any kind of pop we wanted; we'd just take a case from the food yard and bring it back to the barracks.

We were eating like kings. But the charcoal grill was messy and it took time for the charcoal to heat. Plus, our little refrigerators couldn't handle the amount of food we were collecting.

After supper we would add more charcoal to the fire and sit around the heat, talking and brainstorming:

"Wouldn't it be great to have a big refrigerator so we could keep everything in one place?"

"Why don't we bring a pallet of pop and beer back to the barracks? Those cases are hard to carry."

"We could use a nice stove and oven."

"I'd like to have a sink and silverware and dishes—I'm tired of paper plates."

"Coffee! I'd give my left arm for a hot cup of coffee in the morning."

I guess we humans are never happy. My great grandparents were probably happy to live close to a stream so they had access to water. Great grandma had to start a fire to make hot water and great grandpa had to haul water to the house from the stream. They probably bathed in the stream. Grandpa and Grandma dug a well and used a hand pump to bring in the water. Grandpa pumped in the morning so there would always a bucket of water on the kitchen counter for drinking and cooking. They heated water on the first warm day of spring and took a bath in a wash tub. Some of their neighbors that were well-to-do had a hand pump in the kitchen!

Mom and Dad had a well with a pump that supplied water through pipes to the house. They had a water heater that supplied hot water, and we had a bath tub so we could take a bath every Saturday night before going to town to do shopping, and of course we had to smell good for church on Sunday.

These days we are on city water that has been tested and treated for bacteria, organisms, and other nasty things that were in the water that my great grandparents seemed to survive on. We even have a water conditioner to soften the water, clean it with a carbon filter, and purify it. We have an additional filter in our refrigerator to further cleanse the water and cool it for drinking! We have the choice of using a tub or a shower.

Who knows what our kids will have that will be an improvement over our present water system and accompaniments?

Anyway, all of us troops were complaining about how tough we had it to use charcoal for cooking, paper plates and plastic ware, little refrigerators throughout the barracks, "Who's got the ketchup?", and so on.

Someone said, "Hey! There's a supply yard in the base camp! I'll bet they have all those things! Do you suppose the supply yard is having the same trouble with stealing that the food yard had? Maybe we could make a deal with them too."

Everyone looked at Smitty.

He shrugged his shoulders and squinted his eyes at the same time. "I'm on it," he declared.

The next morning Smitty got me out of bed with one of his typical invitations. "Hey Dad, let's go down to the supply yard and see if we can make a deal!"

Normally, Smitty would sleep all day long and I'd have to shake *him* awake for his walk at night. But when he got an idea in his head he was always full of energy and ready to go.

"Knock it off Smitty. I need my beauty sleep!"

"Aw, come on Dad. Walking the food yard has paid off big time. Who knows what we can get if we walk the supply yard, too. Besides, we need a fork lift to bring up a pallet of beer and pop, and the supply yard has one. Come on, it's only a short walk."

We ambled down to the supply yard. Any normal person would have asked for whomever was in command of the supply yard, gone to his office and asked in a normal and dignified way about making a deal. But Smitty had a talent that I'd never been exposed to before. He knew that he needed inside information in order to make a deal. And he knew that inside information was best gotten from whoever was lowest on the totem pole. So he always met with janitors, gardeners, trash handlers, guards, laborers, and the like.

Smitty zeroed in on a soldier who was raking leaves in the corner of the supply yard. He had his hat on backward, his shirt was unbuttoned, and his shoes were not tied.

"What's happnin' man?" Smitty asked with a smile as he strode up to him.

"Jus' cleanin' the place up a bit," he replied.

"You the man!" Smitty said, and the guy lit up like a Christmas tree. Finally, someone appreciated him for all his hard work. He immediately broke into a grin and I knew that he was putty in Smitty's hands.

Smitty now moved into attack mode. He tilted his head and winked while at the same time he twitched his shoulder. He usually did this three times in a row for effect. The guy seemed a little shocked at first but stood there watching Smitty do his shoulder-eye twitch. People never knew whether to focus on Smitty's birthmark on the right side of his face or the twitching.

"Got any trouble with people stealing things in this here supply yard?" Smitty asked as he did his shoulder-eye twitch a couple more times.

I had watched Smitty do this a hundred times. At first I thought it was magic, but I learned that it wasn't. Smitty had invented his twitch to confuse people. They wondered, *Do I look at his birthmark or his twitch?* The result was predictable: He always got people to cooperate with him.

And then the next magical thing happened. The guy did the very same shoulder-eye twitch in unison with Smitty.

"Are you kidding, man? The brass steal from the yard and sell whatever they steal on the black market. And what the brass don't steal, the Gooks steal for their own use or for the black market. I get it on the shelf today and tomorrow it's gone!"

They discussed the stealing for a while longer and Smitty gathered a few more gems that he could deal with, all the while twitching with each other, patting each other on the back, and laughing.

Finally, Smitty knew he had the information he needed and asked where he could find the commanding officer.

"He's over there in that office." He said as he pointed to the building. "But you'll never get in. They won't even let me go in there!"

Smitty did a half salute to the guy, which he always did to regular GIs. It was a combination of mockery of the military and respect to whomever he was talking to. The guy responded with a big grin of gratitude to the man with the birthmark who had shown him some respect.

Smitty headed directly to the office.

"Smitty," I said. "The guy just said you can't go in there. What are you going to do?"

"Just walk in like I own the place," Smitty calmly replied with a grin on his face.

A first lieutenant met us at the door. He looked like an ROTC college type who wouldn't mind turning people away if they didn't have the rank or orders to get in, probably used to saying, *What's your business here? You don't have an appointment? I'm sorry, sir, but you'll have to leave.* Then with a smug smile he would turn around and leave.

But he hadn't met anyone like Smitty before and he probably never would again.

Smitty was always on the offensive. Before the lieutenant could ask his formal questions, Smitty said, "I feel sorry for you, sir." He did his shoulder-eye twitch a couple times. "I don't know how you keep your sanity trying to supply all the units up north when people are sneaking in here at night stealing all your supplies."

The guy visibly melted right before my eyes as he responded with a shoulder-eye twitch and a blank look on his face, staring at Smitty's birthmark.

A few days later Smitty and I were told to report to the supply yard. Apparently Smitty's groundwork was beginning to pay off.

"You can't believe the amount of stealing that goes on here!" the lieutenant there lamented. "We have armed guards but that doesn't seem to work at all. I think they may be part of the problem. They're probably getting paid to look the other way or getting rich themselves by selling stuff on the black market. We hire locals to dump the outhouses and clean up—no telling how much they're walking away with. But the Inspector General is my biggest headache. We've got to have so many of every item on inventory here in order to pass inspection. Units up north may need a new radio for one that got blown up. I've got one on inventory that they could have but I have to keep it on inventory in order to pass an inspection. So they've got a broken radio that they can't use and I've got a perfectly good radio that I can't give them. I'm telling you, this is not the way to fight a war!"

Smitty smiled and twitched. The lieutenant smiled and twitched. They had become blood brothers.

"I don't know how you keep your sanity," Smitty said. "That's a lot of responsibility for one guy to handle, and I'll bet if the IG finds a problem, you're the one they point to."

The look on the lieutenant's face told me that Smitty had just hit the mother lode. I believe the lieutenant would have jumped off a cliff for him.

"You ever seen what a guy looks like after he's been killed by a dog," Smitty asked with a twitch. "They either rip out his groin or they tear off his face. Ain't pretty, but it sure stops the next guy from messing with my dog!"

The lieutenant's mouth was wide open with surprise and his face had gone white.

"Yes, sir," Smitty continued. "We stopped people from stealing from the food yard and we can stop people from stealing your supplies. Once they know there are attack dogs roaming the area, they just clear out. And the Gooks? Did you know they believe they have to have their entire body in order to go to heaven? One good chunk of flesh gone from a dog bite and they're doomed forever!"

Smitty did his shoulder-eye twitch a few more times and the lieutenant matched him move for move.

"I think I need to introduce you to the colonel," the lieutenant said.

I could hardly believe what I was hearing. We'd been told by the first guy we met in the supply yard that we would never get into the office and now the lieutenant was going to introduce us to the head man!

"Colonel Perkins, this is Specialist Smith and Specialist Halverson with the 981st MP unit," the lieutenant said. "They are attack dog handlers and I believe after extensive discussions with them that they can stop the stealing of material from the supply yard. Did you know that a dog can rip out a man's groin area or rip a man's face off with just one bite? And did you know that the Vietnamese believe they have to have their entire body in order to go to heaven? Just one bite and they're doomed for eternity!"

The lieutenant must have had straight A's in college because he had just given Smitty's entire sales pitch almost word for word.

"Is that right?" asked the colonel. "Do you think you can stop the pilferage? And how do you propose to accomplish that feat?"

The colonel was obviously a hard sell.

Smitty did his shoulder-eye twitch a few times and the lieutenant smiled as he did the twitch in unison with Smitty. The colonel looked from Smitty's birthmark to the lieutenant's movements with wonder on his face.

"I think one night a week should work," Smitty said. "We won't walk the same night every week, we'll do it randomly so no one ever knows which night we're walking the dogs. But once we start walking, I'll guarantee you three things: The Gooks will never come to the supply yard, the GIs will be scared to death, and you'll pass your next IG inspection."

That last comment clearly got the Colonel's attention by the look on his face. "What do you expect for pay out of this?" the colonel asked.

I knew then that the deal was closed.

"How about the use of a fork lift?" Smitty said with a twitch.

Both the colonel and the lieutenant said, "Deal!" as they twitched together.

Most of us were sound asleep after walking the last shift the night before. Vaguely, I heard the sound of a motor and a voice yelling "Last trolley to Frisco! Last trolley to Frisco!" I was shaking the sleep from my head when Pete, who had a fiery temper said, "What the Hell is going on?" I could tell that he was ready to do war with whoever had interfered with his sleep. Pete led the way to the door and threw it open. He burst outside with a determined look on his face and suddenly, a fork lift turned around the edge of the barracks. Pete changed like a summer thunder storm. He doubled over in laughter and pointed at Smitty who was driving the fork lift. A pallet of Black Label beer was on the forks of the lift and Smitty shouted triumphantly, "Last trolley to Frisco!" He drove around the barracks a few more times until everyone had seen his little show and parked by the barracks dropping the pallet of beer. "OK, boys. Belly up to the bar! I'm off to get pop for all the non-drinkers." A while later he showed up with a pallet of Dr. Pepper. He dropped it beside the beer and left to return the forklift to its proper place at the supply yard.

I had grown up in an entirely different environment than Smitty. I'd been taught to ask permission. I'd been taught to observe all the rules.

So I tended to assume that there must be a rule preventing me from doing something I would like to do and as a result; I never even tried.

But Smitty didn't operate that way. He always found a way to convince people that what he wanted was to their benefit as well. He used that birth mark, shoulder shrug and winking of the eye to throw people off and when they least expected it; he would close the deal. He always left a deal making session with the group of people he was working with standing there shrugging their shoulders, winking their eyes and wondering what the Hell had just happened!

"How did you get that fork lift?" I asked.

"Just got on it like I owned it!" Smitty replied.

"But you've never run a fork lift, have you?"

"Hey, Dad. Once you've run a John Deere A you can run anything!' he laughed.

"How did you get a full pallet of beer?"

"Just drove up to the pallet, raised it up and drove off! Ha. They even opened the gate for me! When I got back they opened the gate and waved to me."

That was the beginning of a series of episodes that made our little "Puppy Pusher" outfit very much like the show "MASH." Smitty had the supply yard and the food yard in his hip pocket and could literally get away with murder in either place. And it wasn't like he was sneaking around getting away with it. Without exception, the men at both the supply yard and the food yard were just delighted when Smitty showed up. They would wave and laugh as he went through his antics and drive off with anything he wanted.

The ammo pad had helicopter flares. They were about eight feet long and loaded with white phosphorus which would burn very hot and very bright. Smitty would throw one over his shoulder and march around the dump as if he were a revolutionary soldier carrying his musket. The guards at the ammo dump were in stitches as he tramped around with that flare on his shoulder. Rather than put it back where it belonged, Smitty would throw it into the truck, bring it back to the barracks and deposit it in a small storage shed. Over time that shed had flares, claymore mines, M-60 machine guns, grenades and belts of various ammunition.

It was a disaster waiting to happen.

Our relationship with the food yard and the supply yard continued to grow. Absolutely everyone at each site adored Smitty and his entertaining. A sergeant at the supply yard commented "He's nuts! There's never a dull moment when Smitty is around and when he starts to shrug that shoulder and wink his eye; look out because he's after something!" And the more he conned them into something, the better they seemed to like it. In fact they bragged about what Smitty had last picked up with the fork lift and deposited at the dog handler's compound.

"Hey, Dad! Guess what I found at the supply yard! A pool table!" Ever the fuddy duddy I said "You can't take that Smitty. It's probably destined for an officer's club somewhere. They'll raise holy hell if it doesn't show up."

"Nah. They'll just put in a requisition for another one…happens all the time! Officers can get anything they want." And so before long here came the fork lift with a pool table perched on its forks. Since we were stuck out in the boonies in an old French motor pool to keep us far away from the regular troops, we had anonymity and a number of buildings that had been used for storage, offices, repair facilities and parts. One of these buildings was perfect for the pool table. We set the table in the middle of the room, hung the racks and cues on a wall and commenced playing pool in all our off hours.

Soon we furnished the back area of that building with a gas fired stove, oven, refrigerator and freezer. We didn't have enough electricity to run the refrigerator and freezer but if we kept the doors shut, everything kept quite well. How nice it was to move all our condiments spread out in everyone's individual little refrigerators into one big one in our kitchen.

One day Smitty arrived with a load of walnut paneling on the fork lift. "Hey, Dad! I'll bet we'll be the only outfit in Viet Nam with walnut paneling in our bunker!" His enthusiasm spread through the other guys like the Black Plague and before long everyone was pitching in hanging the paneling in our bunker. One thing led to another and someone got the idea that we should build a stage in our bunker. "Why not? The Filipino dancing girls they bring in for the officer's club need a little practice. This would be perfect for them!" Before long we had built a reputation among the transportation company, the infantry, the supply yard and the food yard as a place they could all come for a show. Because of us, these guys got a treat that previously only officers got. They loved the "Puppy Pushers" and that only opened the flood gates for Smitty's imagination.

Roeder got into the program. "How about a sauna? After a long night's walking the ammo dump, wouldn't it be nice to relax in a sauna?" That's all Smitty needed…a challenge! He worked the guys at the supply yard and he worked and he worked, but there was no such thing as a sauna in Viet Nam. Someone is the supply yard asked "Why not use a conex shipping container? You could place a water heater near it, set it on high and pipe the steam into the conex." Before long we had Roeder's sauna and we had hot water in our showers. Not even the officers had that luxury!

While searching for a water heater, Smitty stumbled upon a generator that had been sitting in the supply yard for ages. It wasn't long before we had lighting 24/7 and could power all our appliances.

I wondered "What will he come up with next?"

We had arrived at An Khe just ahead of TET, the lunar New Year. During TET the Vietnamese fought without ceasing. When the week was over they took a rest. The Army needed the ammunition at An Khe because it supplied our troops in the Central Highlands and along the DMZ.

The Army is always looking for the latest in technology and they decided to use the latest invention to prepare for TET in An Khe. If it was successful; it would be used at every ammunition dump in Viet Nam in the future. A professorial looking officer arrived with his crew at the ammo dump. He took a circular looking mechanism to the top of the bunker in the middle of the dump as his crew went about the business of burying what looked like rabbit ears from old T.V.s These were buried in a systematic fashion around the perimeter of the dump. We all wondered what the heck was going on but went on with our business. After a few days, the announcement was made that we had a new computerized defensive system in place and dogs would no longer be needed. We were shown how the system would work. The rabbit ears were sensors that could pick up vibrations in the ground. They sent their information to the circular "mother board," which was like a compass with degrees marked on it. The sensors would identify the degree at which the infiltrator stood and a rifle mounted on the circular device could be aimed at that specific degree. When discharged, the bullet would hit the infiltrator. They ran a trial run and had an imaginary infiltrator walk in the perimeter. The sensor beeped, the degrees were read, the rifle was pointed at that degree on the compass and lo and behold; if you looked down the sights you could see that you were aimed directly at the infiltrator! It was perfect and the eyes of the professor gleamed as we all looked at him in amazement.

The first night was a success. They were able to stop an infiltrator outside the perimeter wire. This would have been an outside alert for our dogs, the Gook would have seen us coming and disappeared. But they had stopped a Gook outside the perimeter wire! The professor was beside himself with delight.

The second night was much more fun. The "Mother Board" lit up like a Christmas tree. The professor announced that a "Human Wave Attack" was taking place and "Spooky" was called in. Spooky was also called "Puff the Magic Dragon" by many of us. Spooky was a modified DC-3 with three mini-guns aboard. Two mini-guns fired from two passenger windows on the pilots side of the plane and a third fired from a cargo door, also on the pilot's side. Mini-guns can fire up to 6000 rounds of 7.62 mm. rounds per minute. Imagine what three of them can do? The firing is so rapid that one can't hear each round…there's just a steady BRRRRRRRRRRRRRR. The next morning there were hundreds of monkeys lying dead on the ground! The Gooks had figured out that something was going on and had herded the monkeys into the area. It took two days to clean up the mess.

I can still see the commander of the ammunition dump looking at the poor professor and yelling, "Get that F-in contraption out of here and bring those dogs back!"

Imagine my amazement when the commander of the ammo dump called and said, "Get down here right away. One of your dogs has killed three sappers and has a fourth one by the seat of the pants. His leash is caught and he can't move, but neither can the sapper. You come get the dog so we can take the sapper to Intelligence for questioning. We can't find the handler and we imagine he's dead. I've got a medal ready for his family because the guy and his dog have saved the dump and a lot of lives."

I went to the ammo dump and found Smitty's dog Brutus in the perimeter wire. I wasn't afraid to handle Brutus since I fed him as often as Smitty did and we'd become close. His leash had caught on a root. He had the pants of the sapper in his mouth and wouldn't let go. The sapper's legs were caught in his pants and he couldn't go anywhere either.

I remember looking at the sapper's bare bottom and thinking, *If this wasn't war, this would be funny.*

I took Brutus and released the sapper.

After putting Brutus in a kennel, I started my hunt for Smitty, expecting to find his body somewhere in the perimeter wire. But he was nowhere to be found. Finally I thought of a small shed where lawn mowers and other tools were kept. I opened the door and there laid Smitty—sound asleep! He had taken a sleeping bag and a couple pillows to the dump, and had gone to sleep. He had picked up some bad habits in Pleiku and that concerned me greatly. At any rate, he had been sound asleep while his dog took care of four sappers!

I shook him awake. As we walked to meet with the commander I explained that he'd be getting an award. He got the Medal of Valor with oak leaf cluster—for sleeping!

Young lieutenants were drawn to the ammo dump like flies to a watermelon rind after hearing about all the sappers that had been stopped. They rode in their jeeps with their legs hanging out the side like they were riding a golf cart back home. Most of them carried special weapons as if they were John Wayne himself. Sawed off shotguns were popular with them...good for close range fighting in Viet Nam. They usually wore bush hats because that was fashionable. So they rode around the ammo dump in all their glory and I'm sure they had pictures taken of their bravado that they could send back home. The problem with their constant travel through the dump was this: The dogs rode back to the kennels in a vehicle and when the jeeps drove through; the dogs thought they were done for the night. So they quit working and waited for the ride home!

Pete was exasperated with the situation and met me where our posts joined. "We're stopping the next jeep that comes through," he said. "We're military policemen and have the right to check anyone for their military identification. Hopefully, if we stop them enough they'll get tired of it and leave us alone. You stop the next jeep that comes and order them out of the jeep and ask them to show their I.D. I'll hide behind a berm with Gus and sneak up from behind. If they give you any trouble; I'll put Gus right into the back seat with them."

We didn't have to wait long. Another jeep came down the path and I stood out and held up my palm showing the "Stop" signal. The jeep stopped and I ordered them to "Please get out and place your military identification on the hood so I can see it."

Someone inside the jeep said, "Step aside and let us through. We're on an important mission."

At that same time Pete said, "Watch him, boy!" as Gus jumped into the back seat right between the two men sitting there.

In the twinkling of an eye; four men stood at the hood of the jeep pulling their wallets from their hip pockets as Pete again said, "Watch 'em, boy." Gus strained at his leash and growled. No one took their eyes off Gus as they wrestled with their wallets.

I noticed then that we hadn't stopped some ROTC rocket jockey with his dandy little sawed off shot gun. Oh no, we had stopped a two star general, two sergeants and a sergeant major! "Oh brother," I thought. "We're in trouble now! We just stopped and carded a general!" I felt the sweat trickling down my back as I checked the I.D. cards. There were only three. The sergeant major did not have one. I told the general and the two sergeants to get back in the jeep.

Pete looked menacingly at the Sergeant Major and ordered, "FRONT LEANING REST...NOW!" The sergeant major looked at him in disbelief and started to laugh.

Pete said, "GET 'IM, BOY!" and Gus went absolutely wild as he lunged at the sergeant major, barking and growling with slobber foaming in his mouth. The man went from a standing position to front leaning rest without moving a muscle and without taking his eyes off Gus. "You stay there until our commanding officer clears you," Pete said. I radioed for our C.O. to come and clear the man.

The C.O. arrived and the sergeant major's eyes were about to pop out of his head, but they never left Gus. The C.O. gasped when he saw the general and again when he saw a sergeant major in front leaning rest. He immediately cleared the sergeant major and then went to the general and apologized as if he had burned the guy's house down.

The next morning Pete and I were called to the C.O.'s office. "What the Hell were you two yahoos thinking?" he asked. "You stop a general and card him for God's sake? And a sergeant major? The Army calls that insubordination punishable with an Article 15. I've written up two article 15s here and I want you both to sign them."

"We have a perfect right to stop and ask for military identification," Pete said. "I'm not signing any Article 15…I'll take a court martial."

"Same for me," I said.

Just then the phone rang. The C.O. answered it and immediately turned red. Then he said a bunch of uh huhs and finally he broke out into a big grin and said "Thank you, sir! I'll tell them sir!"

He looked at us and said "Well, I'll be damned. That was the general you stopped last night. He says to take good care of you boys…you're the best soldiers he's seen over here!"

Pete was the only guy I trusted at this point. We both wanted to get home safely and decided that we would walk the dump together until TET was over. We took other guys shifts and walked the dump 24 hours a day for a week. I remember falling asleep while walking my dog and waking up when I hit the ground. Toward the end I didn't even wake up when I hit the ground. We walked in shifts, but we walked the entire dump every minute of every day. It was the only ammo dump that didn't get blown up that year, and Pete and I were awarded medals for it. The commander laid the medals on our chests as we slept—he didn't want to wake us up for the presentation.

We would be on easy street the next week as the North Vietnamese rested from their Lunar New Year activities.

The officers decided that they wanted someone from our unit to enter the "Soldier of the Month" competition. The competition covered the topics of the code of justice, military etiquette, military history, knowledge of rank, and an understanding of our mission. Having a Soldier of the Month was a real feather in the cap for any company.

Everyone in the company took an initial exam and I came out with the highest score! Immediately, I got easier duty so I could focus on studying for the battalion-wide contest. Soldiers from every company would be studying just like me and we would all meet in Quin Nhon for the honor of being battalion Soldier of the Month. All of this was well worth the effort because the winner would get a two-week furlough to escort a body to the States, attend the funeral, and then spend a week back home.

The day finally came for the competition. I had studied hard and had been quizzed by officers for weeks. I crawled into the backseat of a Jeep, along with my commanding officer. The battalion commander and his driver were in front. We left our compound, which was located in the foothills at the base of Hong Cong Mountain. The road meanders through mountain passes with hairpin curves, lots of vegetation and wild life on both sides, and descends from the central highlands to the South China Sea.

A particularly dangerous portion of that road is called An Khe Pass. This pass has 200-foot high cliffs on either side carved out by centuries of Mother Nature's erosion. It has a hairpin curve at one end so narrow that it's one-way traffic only. That curve is the most dangerous part of the journey because the vehicle has to slow down. The enemy could position themselves at the top of the cliff at this curve and roll grenades down the cliff. A well-placed grenade could do a lot of damage and, if it hit the driver, the vehicle could go over the edge. There were plenty of vehicles at the bottom of the ravine to bear witness to the effectiveness of that technique. With the vegetation so dense, the enemy was fairly safe from gunfire because they were hidden.

As we neared this curve, we drew small arms fire and grenades. We didn't dare venture farther into the curve and we couldn't turn around because the road was only wide enough for one-way traffic. Without any hesitation we all jumped out of the Jeep, positioned ourselves on each corner of the Jeep, grabbed the bumper at our corner and lifted the Jeep up, turned it around, got back inside, and left as fast as we could.

When we got back to the compound, we all jabbered excitedly to everyone else about what had happened. One fellow obviously was a "doubting Thomas" and said, "Yah, right. Let's see you all get a corner of that Jeep and prove to us that you can lift it."

With absolute confidence, we each grabbed a corner and lifted…and lifted…*and lifted*…until our faces were beet red. We couldn't even get one tire off the ground! I realized that it's true what one can do with the adrenaline rush that an emergency brings.

All I could think was, *All that studying for nothing!*

"Hey Dad!" Smitty shouted in my ear one morning. "Get up and take a look at this! There's so much frost on the ground that it looks like it snowed last night. Winter has set in and we won't be able to plow 'til spring. I sure wish I was back in Iowa milking a good ole Guernsey cow right now. Nothing like putting your hand on a warm tit when it's cold outside!"

Everyone roared with laughter at Smitty's remark. Most of them had grown up in the city and had no idea where their milk came from, let alone how to milk a cow, but Smitty's picturesque language always got their attention.

I unzipped my sleeping bag and crawled out to take a look. There was an impressive layer of frost on the ground and on the landscape. The concertina wire looked like a giant white sea serpent all coiled up and ready to strike. Telephone poles and lines sparkled in the morning sun. That winter wonderland existed in the middle of a war zone.

I thought of Pastor Hatlen, a retired minister at First Lutheran Church. Whenever it snowed and the parishioners complained, he would say, "Look at the beautiful snow! It's God's way of covering up all the sins of the world."

How right he was.

The Army in all its wisdom had declared Vietnam a tropical war zone. Of course, it was tropical in Saigon where the war had started. But we were hundreds of miles north of Saigon, up in the mountains, and the weather there was *not* tropical.

Because the Army had supplied us soldiers with tropical gear, we were freezing to death! We were issued tropical fatigues. You could almost read a newspaper through the fabric. Our boots were the tropical kind with fabric sides that allowed the skin to breath.

Our bedding consisted of sheets and mosquito netting. We were issued large brown bottles of quinine pills. We were to take two quinine tablets a day to fight the malaria we could get from a mosquito bite, but there wasn't a mosquito within 100 miles!

This situation created a wonderful opportunity for an industrious person. The black market thrived on the dilemma the Army had created. Wool blankets, sleeping bags, winter clothing, hats, gloves, regular fatigues, and so on were all available there. Seamstresses did a thriving business sewing parachute fabric into blankets and coats. Those people were amazing. There were both male and female tailors, and, if you could dream it, they could make it.

The jackets were extremely popular because they could be personalized with a saying sewn onto the back of the jacket. Mine said, "For those who have fought for it, freedom has a flavor the protected will never taste." Smitty had a vicious dog snarling with blood dripping from its teeth: "Hell dogs." Pete had a man and his dog in silhouette: "Puppy Pusher." P.J. had a large hand giving the finger. "F**k the Army."

I listened to everyone chattering about the frost and how stupid the Army was, which made me think about the farmers at the coffee shop back in Sioux Rapids. I could almost hear them talking about the last snow and how the county supervisors had screwed up by not keeping the roads clear. And in six months they would all be complaining about the heat and the complications that it presented.

I almost felt at home.

MACV had gotten shelled the night before with rocket fire. MACV was just up the hill from us, close enough that we could feel the shock waves when the rockets hit, but far enough away that we didn't have to worry about shrapnel.

The Gooks were sending an "in your face" message by rocketing them instead of targets that had infantry or material. MACV stood for Military Assistance Command, Vietnam. It had been created in 1962 to provide assistance and advice to South Vietnam. MACV assisted the MAAG, short for Military Assistance Advisory Group, in controlling every advisory and assistance effort in Vietnam. In 1964, MACV absorbed MAAG when the number of combat units deployed became too large for an advisory group to control. LBJ didn't want to be the first president to lose a war. Since the advisory groups weren't working and the South Vietnamese were not responding, LBJ and his advisors decided to take over the war. Robert McNamara, ex-Ford executive, ran the war from his banker's chair in Washington, D.C.

Washington created MACV/SOG the same year, SOG standing for Studies and Operations Group. We all came to know them as Special Ops. The US government denied its existence and it wasn't until years later that the SOG story became public.

Special Ops were responsible for clandestine operations, such as crossing the border into Cambodia, Laos, and North Vietnam to carry out intelligence gathering or raiding missions on the enemy's home turf; gathering intelligence about POWs and rescuing them when possible; rescuing downed pilots; training agents in North Vietnam to gather intelligence or form resistance groups; spreading "black propaganda" on fake broadcasting systems in enemy territory; kidnapping or assassinating key military personnel; and inserting rigged mortar rounds or other booby traps in enemy arms caches. SOG was a joint services unit composed of members from all four branches of the armed forces: Navy SEALS, Marine Recons, Air Force Special Operations, and Army Special Forces.

By 1966, MACV had outgrown its offices in Saigon and new ones had to be built. A giant set of offices went up at Tan Son Nhut Air Force Base, near Saigon in southern Vietnam, and became known as Pentagon East.

General William Westmoreland commanded MACV from 1964-1968, followed by General Creighton Abrams. While the main headquarters of MACV remained at Tan Son Nhut, MACV compounds were all over Vietnam. MACV personnel wore a shoulder patch on their uniforms, a red and gold shield with the upright sword. That same insignia appeared on large signs at each of their compounds, and they had one just up the road from our dog handlers' area. MACV got rocketed because they were in charge of intelligence and the battle plan for the American forces.

I could almost hear the rockets sneering, *There, see how smart you are!*

I made friends with a number of guys in the infantry. We dog handlers lived in relatively safe conditions since we were always inside the compound, guarded by fortified perimeters with infantry units searching the immediate area outside the compound, and were close to firepower. But the infantry had to patrol the jungle on their own with nothing but intelligence to protect them. And guess where they got their intelligence: black marketers and whores. They will show up wherever the action is and they always know what's going on!

The Army had beefed us up with more people as they were afraid of what TET 1969 would look like and they were afraid of a surprise attack after TET, which had never happened before. Besides, we now had a food yard and the supply yard to guard as well as the ammunition dump. The commanders of the food yard and the supply yard gave us glowing recommendations because stealing had gone way down since the dogs began patrolling their areas. It seemed like Smitty walked away with half their products and materials but apparently it had been a lot worse before we came along. While we had walked the food yard and the supply yard only once per week, the army decided that we should walk them every night just like the ammo dump. So four new men appeared to join our ranks. A new problem arose immediately. We only had one vehicle and that just couldn't deliver all the guys and dogs to all the places we had to be. But the army hadn't considered the fact we had to use the company vehicle much more that we had in the past. The commander didn't like that because it infringed on his use of it. He complained and we complained. When we both needed the jeep, the commander always won out because he had rank.

"Let's find us a vehicle of our own!" Smitty announced. "There's plenty of junkers sitting around that got hit with an RPG or a land mine.

"I'm a good mechanic," Leonard said. "I helped my uncle in his shop before the army got me."

Smitty's ideas were always like a fever. Everyone caught the fever and began looking for a vehicle that we could salvage. There were plenty of jeeps that had been damaged but they couldn't carry very many men with their dogs. Deuce and a halves were plentiful too but were too big and bulky for our needs. Be that as it may, we all dutifully looked for something we could use.

Smitty had a network that was matchless. He had the infantry boys and the transportation guy all looking for us. And one day Mickey showed up. Mickey was from Bull Shoals, Arkansas. He never tied his shoes, never buttoned his shirt all the way and never wore his army issue hat. He was about six foot three and weighed at least 230 pounds. The big guy shuffled along with his boots flapping on either side of his unbloused pant legs. "Hey boys! How y'all a doin'?" Mickey grinned with his big Ozark smile. "I think I found you boys just the truck you want. It's a dandy little three quarter ton pick-up truck that took a hit at An Khe Pass. She's got a little front end damage, but with a little work I think you can get 'er runnin'."

"You the man!" Chain shouted. Chain and Charley Butler were our two black dog handlers. Chain's street language was contagious and everyone else yelled "You the man, Mickey!"

Mickey grinned that "Aw, Shucks, it wasn't nothin'" smile of his and enjoyed our adoration as if he were standing in the first day of warm sunlight after a long, cold winter. "I got to pull a flatbed over to Quin Nhon next week and I'll pick it up on the way back."

There was another chorus of "You the man, Mickey!" as he continued to stand there enjoying the moment. And with that he turned those untied boots around and shuffled to his deuce and a half to go back to his compound.

A week later the flatbed arrived at our compound with Mickey driving and blowing the air horns on the diesel truck he was driving. Mickey's head was hanging out the driver's window with that big Ozark grin of his. Perched on the flatbed truck was our three quarter ton pick-up. It was in nearly perfect condition except for the right front. It had hit a land mine and the fender, the right wheel and the undercarriage were damaged. Mickey unloaded the truck and we all stood back and admired our new find as if it were a new born colt. We all had visions of sugar plums dancing in our heads.

Smitty got into the driver's seat and made engine noises as he turned the wheel left and right. He beamed like a little boy with his brand new *Daisy official Red Ryder BB gun!* "Won't be long now, boys! We'll have this thing running in no time and then we will take her on a Sunday drive just like the banker back in Panora!"

Everyone was looking for parts for us…the infantry, the supply yard people, the transportation guys and the MPs. It was like a giant scavenger hunt. We got leads on three quarter tons that were out of commission from all over the place. Leonard proved to be a man of his word. He tore into the engine and removed damaged parts from it and the front end so we would be able to assemble when the proper parts were found. The city guys stood in awe of Leonard and his wrenches. "Man, the only thing we ever learned to do was put the car up on blocks and take off the tires and pull the radio," Chain said. "That's how we got our spending money back home."

Leonard placed his orders for parts with Smitty who would diligently go to the motor pool to get them. We needed a new fan, water pump, hoses, v-belts, spark plugs, wiring and so on for the engine. The supply room at the motor pool had most of these parts and Smitty would haul them back for Leonard who finally stood back to admire his handiwork. "I think she's ready to start, guys." he said. "Who wants to do the honor of cranking her up?" Chain immediately volunteered. "Man, I've never started or driven a vehicle," he remarked. "All we ever did was strip them down!" Chain had been a gang banger in the streets and had never experienced what a bunch of farm boys could do once they put their minds to it. And he liked what he saw! Chain turned the key and the engine turned over but it didn't start. He tried again with no success. He was so dejected that I thought he might cry.

Leonard ducked under the hood and yelled "Turn 'er over. Again. OK. Again. OK, once more." Chain responded in kind and finally Leonard announced "We've got spark and we've got air but we don't have any gas!" He crawled beneath the engine and soon popped back out. "We need a fuel pump. A small piece of shrapnel blew a hole in the bottom of it…can't see it from above or I'd have caught it sooner."

Smitty and I made the trip to the motor pool and requested the fuel pump from the sergeant in charge who had an unlit cigar in his mouth. "I've only got two of them in stock," he said around his stogie. I've got to have one on display in case the inspector general decides to honor me with his presence. The other one is the only one I can let go and I'm not sure the "Puppy Pushers" are the right candidate. What if the infantry needs it?"

Smitty started his shoulder shrugging and eye twitching routine and the sergeant unconsciously joined him; his cigar bobbing and weaving in time with his shoulder. "C'mon man," Smitty said. "We've got a war to fight out there and we can't do it with a fuel pump on the shelf! It's got to be in our vehicle." It wasn't long before the sergeant gave in. He escorted us outside to our jeep. He stood there with his unlit cigar and a scowl on his face as we backed out and headed back to our compound with our precious cargo.

Leonard had already removed the old pump and promptly installed the new one. "OK, Chain. Give it a crank!" Leonard used the familiar terminology of a true Southerner. Chain turned the key and the engine came to life. We all stood in quiet reverence as the motor hummed it's little song to us. Chain broke out in a grin as if he had discovered gold and finally, all at once; we began to cheer! We had done it!

With renewed vigor we began to tackle the next project. "Hey, Dad!" Smitty yelled over the engine noise. "If we can get the engine going, the rest is a piece of cake!" And that pretty much summed up the attitude that all of us had.

The front axle, the spindle, the brakes and lining were not to be found at the motor pool. But one of the infantry guys had spotted a three quarter ton in the jungle not too far from us. He said that it had been hit by an RPG in the engine compartment and thought the front end was OK. "I think she's even got a good set of tires."

Leonard and a group went to the site loaded with wrenches and jacks. Sure enough, the front end was just fine. Chain was beside himself with excitement because the vehicle needed to be jacked up and parts had to be removed. And that was something he had experience with! Before long they had removed the entire front axle, brakes, hoses, fender and bumper. We now had all the parts we needed to have our own vehicle. Everyone had that smile…the smile of a father with a new born baby.

We were all obsessed with the three quarter ton pick-up. Some of the guys that had no mechanical experience worked double shifts so the rest of us could work on it. Chain had no mechanical experience but he was bound and determined to take part and be the first to drive it. Leonard led the restoration like a general and it seemed as though he had done this a hundred times before. The front end was pulled and replaced with the salvaged one. Brake lines were replaced along with the fender. Leonard looked at Chain and said "She's ready for a practice run," as he winked at the rest of us. We all knew that this project was like getting a new Bicycle for Christmas to Chain.

Chain got behind the wheel and cranked the engine which jumped into life without hesitation. "Now what do I do?" Chain asked.

"Put 'er in gear and drive around like you're checking the cattle," Smitty exclaimed. There was a period of grinding gears, which put a frown on Leonard's face but finally the grinding stopped, the motor raced and Chain dropped the clutch like many first time drivers do. The truck jumped and lurched as it tried to keep running with the sudden load Chain had given it. Chain's head bounced back and forth like a pinball but finally it all smoothed out. He gave that Cheshire cat grin and drove the pick-up around the barracks a couple times.

"Give 'er some gas," Smitty yelled. "let's see what she'll do!" As Chain increased the speed, it was evident that something was wrong. The truck vibrated rhythmically and a pronounced wobbling sound came from beneath the frame. Chain stopped and looked at Leonard with a pleading look on his face. "Did I do something wrong?"

Leonard didn't respond as he crawled beneath the truck and began to investigate. "Put the gear shift in neutral," he yelled. Chain did so. Leonard continued his research under the pick-up and finally we heard a string of curse words emanating from below the truck. He got out from under the truck and dusted himself off. "The damn mine sent some shrapnel into the drive shaft," he said. "It looks OK until you spin it and then you can see it's out of balance. I don't have the equipment here to rebalance it so I guess we're going to have to find another one."

"I'll take care of it," Smitty volunteered. Smitty and I got in the jeep and headed to the motor pool once again. The sergeant glared at us chewing on his ever present unlit cigar and I could tell that we had worn out our welcome with this man.

He rolled his eyes and said "What'll it be now, boys? I suppose you're looking for an Abrams Tank today? Well sorry, I just gave the last one away about an hour ago.

Smitty didn't notice the sarcasm. "Hey Sarge! We need a drive shaft for the three quarter ton."

The sarge scowled. "I've got one. That's it hanging on the wall over there. It's the only one I've got and I'm keeping it. Number 1: I've got infantry units and transportation units that might need that shaft to fight Uncle Sam's war...not going out on a pleasure ride like you boys are going to do. Number 2: If I have an inspector general come through, he's going to want every piece of equipment I'm supposed to have on inventory. And when he asks for a drive shaft, it's going to be right there on the wall...front and center!"

Smitty began his shoulder twitch and head nodding as he tried to argue his case but the sergeant just put his hand up as if he were stopping traffic and said "Nuff said, troop!" He escorted us out to the jeep and stood there frowning with his unlit cigar as we drove off.

Smitty had to go back to the dispensary so the doctor could check his "Zipper Injury." It was a short walk through some hilly elephant grass. The doctor said his injury was healing just fine and that he should shower regularly and keep the wound clean so no infection would occur. We were just leaving when a three quarter ton pick-up drove into the parking lot. And this wasn't any ordinary pick-up. Oh no, this one shined like it had just come off the show room floor. The tires had even been shined with what looked like boot polish. An extremely fat little fellow jumped from the driver's seat, raced to the other side of the pick-up and opened the door for an inspector general. I wondered who the fat little guy's father must have been to land him such a cushy little job as driver for a general. He had beads of sweat on his forehead and neck and his uniform was soaked in the arm pits. His hat balanced on his head rather than covering it because it and his uniform appeared to be two sizes too small. "Little Lord Fauntleroy" came to my mind. The general marched into the dispensary with the little lord bouncing along behind.

"Dad! There's our drive shaft!" Smitty announced.

"Are you kidding?" I replied. "That's a general. He'll have us in Long Binh Jail!"

"Nah. He'll just go to the motor pool and get the drive shaft they won't give to us. Let's run back to the kennels. You get Shep and act like you're guarding the dispensary while I pull the drive shaft. If that fat guy sees Shep he won't come out the door." I got Shep and Smitty got the tools he needed. Back at the field hospital I walked back and forth in the area of the entrance door. "Little Lord Fauntlaroy" came to the door to check on his vehicle, but when he saw Shep he immediately turned around and disappeared from view. Smitty crawled beneath the truck and went to work removing the U bolts that held the drive shaft in place.

"Hey Dad! I got 'er. Let's di di mau!" Smitty announced as he rolled out from beneath the truck. He threw the drive shaft over his shoulder and we moved out smartly toward the kennel area. We got about a hundred yards from the dispensary when Smitty said "Hunker down into the elephant grass, Dad. We gotta see this!"

From our lofty perch on the hill we watched as the general and his fat little driver exited. The little lord escorted the general to the passenger side of the vehicle and opened the door for him. Then he quickly walked as best he could to his side of the truck and settled down behind the steering wheel. He turned the key and the engine of the beautiful machine came to life. He shifted into reverse, turned to look out the back window and let out the clutch. The engine raced but they didn't move. The little lord looked at the general who looked back at him and pointed towards the road as if to say "That way. Let's get going." The little lord grabbed the gear shift and went through the motions of putting it into reverse obviously thinking he hadn't put it in gear. He again looked out the back window and let out the clutch. Once again the engine roared but the truck didn't move. We observed quite an exchange of words between the general and his driver at this point and it was all we could do not to break out in uncontrolled laughter. We lowered ourselves further into the elephant grass as both of them got out of the truck and began to look around. The general barked at the driver to try it once again. He did and got the same results. The general threw his brief case on the ground and the little lord looked like he was going to cry.

"Time for us to get outta here." I said.

"Hey, Leonard," Smitty yelled through the barracks door. "Git yer tools and get out here on the double! We've got a driveshaft to put in the ¾ ton!"

Leonard came out of the barracks in his boxer shorts and tried to wipe the sleep from his eyes. He looked at the driveshaft on Smitty's shoulder in amazement. "Where did you find that?"

"Found 'er in a ditch down by the dispensary," Smitty replied with that typical grin on his face. He twitched his shoulder as he looked at Leonard. "Times awastin' and that three quarter ton ain't gonna run with this thing on my shoulder! Now let's get crackin'."

Leonard let out a war whoop as he went back into the barracks. "We've got a driveshaft , Chain! Get your clothes on cause we're gonna need someone to give it a test drive."

Leonard got under the pickup in a flash and Chain stooped to watch him work. He looked like a little boy waiting to open Christmas presents. It didn't take long before Leonard came out from beneath the truck and said, "Start 'er up. Let's see what she'll do."

It started right away and everyone grinned in anticipation. Chain ground gears as he tried to put it into gear.

"Grind me a pound!" someone in the background yelled and everyone else laughed with glee.

The grinding stopped and Chain let out the clutch. The motor immediately died. He restarted it and ground a few more gears.

"Let the clutch out slowly," Pete shouted.

The engine raced as Chain looked straight ahead with nervous tension all over his face and slowly let out the clutch. The truck lurched forward, halted, lurched again, halted again, and then died. Chain's face turned down with a look that said, "I dropped the ball before I crossed the goal line."

"What gear do you have it in?" Leonard asked.

"I don't know. I've stolen parts from a truck like this but I've never *driven* one!"

"Put 'er into gear again," Leonard demanded as he watched. "Well, there's your problem. You put it into high gear! You've got to pull the gear shift clear over to your left and then pull it down."

Chain started the vehicle again and put it into gear under Leonard's watchful eye. Chain looked at Leonard with a questioning eye and Leonard winked back at him. "That's right. Now let the clutch out slowly and let's go!"

Chain drove the pickup around the barracks a few times in low gear. The corners of his smile met in the back of his head! He wasn't going to chance shifting gears and embarrassing himself again, so he just left it in low gear and wound the engine like a rubber band. He finally stopped and got out with the look of someone who had just ridden a bronco for the full eight seconds.

Everyone took their turn and most of the guys could run it through the gears.

"Won't it be nice to go anywhere we want without asking the CO for his vehicle?" Smitty said. "Come on, Dad! Let's take 'er for a spin,"

He went directly down the drive and turned to the left.

"Where you going?" I asked.

"Down to the motor pool," Smitty laughed.

He parked and we went inside where the motor pool sergeant stood behind his desk with his ever present unlit cigar in his mouth and a scowl on his face.

"Hey Sarge," Smitty grinned. "You ready to give us that driveshaft yet?"

"No," he said emphatically as he pointed to the bare spot on the wall where the driveshaft had previously hung, "and it's a damn good thing I never gave it to you too! An Inspector General came in here earlier today and he needed one. If I hadn't held on to that driveshaft; my butt would have been in a sling! He was madder than hops and his fat, little driver was in tears, claimed his driveshaft just disappeared out of nowhere! You boys wouldn't have any idea how that could have happened, would you?"

"Nope," Smitty responded. "Like you said, it's a darn good thing you held on to it. Well, see ya at the fair!"

The Sarge followed us out as we got into the three quarter ton. I watched his face as Smitty put it in gear and backed up. The Sarge calmly reached into his pocket, pulled out a lighter, lit his cigar, and grinned.

Kentuck worked at the ammo dump. He had not learned to tie his shoes and accentuated the problem by not buttoning his shirt! Inspections were not a daily routine in Vietnam like they were in Boot Camp. The only time we had inspections in Vietnam was when we had an Inspector

General stop by to check our post, ammo dump, or barracks. The commander at the ammunition dump had the problem of what to do with Kentuck in the event an Inspector General stopped by for a surprise inspection. He chose to put Kentuck in the most inconspicuous spot in the ammo dump: the bone yard.

The bone yard was where spent shell casings were delivered and stored for eventual re-loading. It was grueling work because most of the shell casings were from howitzers and were heavy. But Kentuck was a big boy, and happily carried and neatly piled the casings with his shirt flying in the wind and his shoe laces dragging along in the dirt. The bill of his hat was always turned to the right about 45 degrees, which drove the officers mad; the bill was supposed to be aimed straight ahead. Every time I saw Kentuck I thought of Gomer Pyle.

The day came when the Inspector General stopped at the ammo dump. The first place he went was to the bone yard where a grinning Kentuck said, "Hey, how y'all a doin'?" and kept right on with his work without even saluting.

Our commander was sick until the inspector completed his inspection and announced that the best man in the unit was back there in the bone yard.

One day Kentuck came to me with a letter in his hand. "Hey, Dad, my wife had twin boys! Shucks, ain't that sumthin'?"

When I ran for Soldier of the Month, I had learned that the Army would grant a leave to soldiers who escorted a body back home. Of course everyone wanted to escort a body home and get out of a war zone, so the Army had limited this job to Soldiers of the Month and soldiers whose wives had given birth to twins. I submitted an application for Kentuck and a few weeks later I received his orders; Kentuck would escort a body home, and then spend a week's leave with his wife and two sons.

It came as a complete surprise to him. He took his orders and hitched a ride on a V-100 to go to Pleiku where he would ride a C-130 to Saigon, pick up the body and escort it home. As they drove through An Khe pass, there was a soft WHOOMP. The whoomp was soft because the rocket propelled grenade the Gooks had fired had entered Kentuck's body before it went off. His body absorbed all the shock of the RPG. That saved the lives of the rest of the G.I.s riding the V-100 with him. They picked up what was left of his body and placed it in a body bag.

I wondered, *Could all of this possibly be worth two little boys growing up without their father?*

Every community has that one person that seems to do everything wrong no matter what comes along and thus, provides entertainment for everyone else. Ours was Roeder. I remember standing for inspection in Cam Ranh Bay. MPs are supposed to be experts in military etiquette, dress and demeanor. Our shaves had to be close, hair had to be the proper length and combed, buttons had to be buttoned, shoes spit shined, uniforms starched and pressed and so on. In short; we had to be the model example of what a military man should look like.

The inspector general moved from man to man on this cold, crisp morning at 6 a.m. He looked each of us up and down from head to toe nodding as he went. Generals never smile with approval. They just look at you like you're garbage and frown. If the frown remains and he moves on; take that as a compliment.

The general continued along the ranks of men until he got to Roeder. His gasp was audible. He just couldn't believe what he was seeing. "What did you shine your shoes with? A Hershey bar?" he yelled.

"Yep," replied Roeder. "One with almonds in it."

I tried to hold my laughter back as the general's face turned red with anger and his eyes bulged.

"And how about your shaver? Did you put a blade in it? You have stubble, you know," the general ranted.

"I didn't get a chance to shave," Roeder replied. We all held back our laughter once again as we thought of Roeder getting out of bed in the morning. The guy could sleep right through bugle call…I think he could sleep through a bombing raid. At any rate, the rest of us would be showered and shaved; ready to go and Roeder would still be sleeping contentedly. Someone would jar his bunk and tell him we were going to mess for breakfast. Now Roeder loved to eat and this would always bring him around. He would hurriedly pull clothing from the pile in his foot locker, pull on his boots without tying them (That could be done in breakfast line.) and race to the mess hall. He never folded his clothes so he resembled a green colored map with lines all over for roads and rivers.

"Bring me a shaver," barked the general. And with that, he dry shaved Roeder. No shaving cream. No water. Just a shaver being pulled over his stubble. To his credit; Roeder never made a peep as the shaver scraped away at his beard leaving trails of blood in its wake. "Now. Do you think you can remember to shave in the morning," the general asked.

"Yes, sir, general sir," Roeder replied.

"And where did you get that uniform?" the general quizzed.

"From Uncle Sam's supply," Roeder said. I was beginning to choke on the laughter that was boiling inside me as the general looked into Roeder's eyes and for the first time; I think the general understood that he wasn't dealing with the average soldier here. In fact he kind of melted and even smiled a little bit.

"Just have them starched next time you send them to the laundry and remember to button all your buttons," he said sympathetically.

Roeder provided us with that kind of entertainment through our whole tour. One day the veterinarian asked us all to bring in stool samples from our dogs. We all went to the supply room and got paper sample cups and wooden tongue depressors to collect our samples. As we were standing in line to give our sample cups, names of the dogs and our names to the vet, Roeder walked in with a gigantic dog turd in his hand! He was so proud that he had searched the pen and found the best specimen for the vet. His proud face turned red as he looked around and noticed the rest of us holding our paper cups.

What would life be like without a Roeder around?

Our sergeant of the guard reached the end of his tour. He would be reassigned back in the states and a replacement would arrive the next day. We were all surprised when sergeant Yates, one of our trainers in Okinawa, showed up as his replacement. Everyone welcomed him to our unit and it was a happy reunion.

Pete and I had to leave the reunion early since we had first shift at the ammo dump. By this time, Gus and Shep knew each other as well as Pete and I. Normally, dogs should stay on their leashes so they don't get into a dog fight and so they don't attack a man. But Pete and I had worked with our dogs enough that they followed our commands and we could trust them. So we often worked our dogs off leash. Unbeknownst to us, Yates had come to the ammo dump to observe us. The next morning he told us that he had observed us the night before and had seen us working the dogs off leash. "They ran around like someone's pet!" he yelled. "They won't attack because I saw them walk right by personnel at the ammo dump. I'm writing both of you up for an Article 15! You've ruined those dogs!"

"Just a darned minute," Pete responded. "Follow me." Pete took Yates to Gus' kennel, took out his billfold and pulled a crisp $100 bill. He placed the bill in Gus' kennel and said "Watch, 'im, Gus. Watch 'im." Gus returned a low, guttural growl. "OK sergeant Yates. That bill is yours. All you have to do is go in there and get it."

Yates stood there for a while, his attention torn between the $100 bill and Gus, who continued to growl. Finally, he turned to Pete and said "Well, I guess I was wrong. Looks like you boys are doing a pretty good job."

The Army required every soldier to attend a reenlistment session near the end of his tour. The re-up officer welcomed me into his office and began his conversation about my signing up for more time in the Army.

"You have tremendous potential to become an officer," he told me. He laid out what kind of money I could make as an officer, explained that I would gain a lot more status as an officer, and that Ginny would have many benefits as an officer's wife that she presently didn't have.

My first question was, "How do you rationalize being separated from your wife and how is she taking being separated from you?"

I could tell that he hadn't expected that question by the way his jaw nearly dropped to the floor. He explained that it was hard at first, but that the Army had all sorts of women's groups where they could sit around and cry on each other's shoulders.

I told him that if my wife had any crying to do, I'd rather be there by her side so she could cry on *my* shoulder.

"Well, consider all the leadership training the Army can give you," he mentioned. "You'll be a lot better individual with officer training."

I asked him if he thought he was better than me because he was an officer.

His jaw hit the floor again and he was at a loss for words. His decision to become an officer apparently came from his need for money, status, and security.

I didn't have those goals so I didn't reenlist.

The chop, chop sound of a Huey hung directly over our barracks. We didn't think anything about it because choppers flew over all the time. But this one hung above us for quite some time before it finally dropped down and landed in our yard. Pete and I had run the midnight shift the night before so we were still in our bunks. The screen door opened and someone yelled "Ten Hut!" We hadn't heard someone bark at us to come to attention since we had been in training back in the states.

Pete had been woken from a good night's sleep and since he had a hot temper to begin with, he hopped out of bed flaming mad! "Who the f__ do you think you are yelling attention when we're trying to get a good night's sleep? Now shut up and get out of here!"

I peeked through my mosquito netting and saw a pair of spit shined boots. They were magnificent. I peeked a little higher and saw a pair of fatigue pants that had a pressed crease in them. Not just a crease! No, this crease was like a knife blade on the front of the pants. I climbed out of bed and came face to face with a sergeant major! And was he mad! Apparently, he didn't like Pete's welcome and at the top of his voice he yelled "On your feet, front and center!" Pete and I stood beside our beds in our boxer shorts while this non-com eyed us from head to toe with a gruesome look on his face. I was afraid he was going to order us to drop to the floor and do push-ups!

I was wearing a pair of the boxer shorts Ginny sent me every month. This pair happened to be from the month of April and had the fly sewn shut. He eyed the shorts and said with a menacing voice "Those aren't Army issue, troop!"

Pete jumped on that like a frog on a mayfly. "We're not required to wear army issue underwear," he said. "We can wear civvies if we want to." The sergeant major and Pete eyed each other like a couple boxers being introduced in the ring just before the championship fight.

He smoldered at Pete's statement and while he was considering what to do next; another man walked through the door. This man had stars on his baseball cap. He exuded authority. "I'm General Caskey," the man said.

"Oh great!" I thought. "Here I am in front of a general in a pair of funny looking boxer shorts and nothing else. And Pete just used the F word with his personal aid, who by the way was still smoldering over the comment and our obvious lack of respect for authority and the Army.

"We hovered over this place looking at the map trying to figure out what it is. It doesn't show on the map at all. So what are you and what are you doing here?" the general asked.

"We're military police sentry dog handlers, sir," I replied. "We guard the food yard, the supply yard and the ammunition dump here."

"Is that so," the general responded with a pleased smile on his face. "I've heard about attack dogs but I don't know much about them. Could you give me a demonstration?"

We took Caskey and his not too happy sidekick back to the kennels to see the dogs. As soon as the dogs smelled the scent of strangers they went absolutely berserk. They were barking wildly, clawing at the fencing of their kennels and some were trying to bite them through the wires of the fence. Caskey and the sergeant were obviously impressed and scared to death with this demonstration of canine ferocity.

"Would you like to see one go through the obstacle course?" I asked.

"Absolutely!" Caskey replied.

I took Shep out of his kennel and took him to the course. "He's been taught to run off leash," I explained. "He won't attack you unless I give the command, but I will leave his muzzle on just to be on the safe side." I'd spent many painstaking hours training Shep; so it was very satisfying to see him jump through the window, hop over the hurdle, climb the ladder and jump from the platform all on his own.

I had added one more touch to this exercise. I had taught Shep to stop in front of whoever was on my left, sit and then raise his paw to that person as if he was saluting them. Shep completed his run, sat down in front of Caskey and raised his paw in salute. I doubt Caskey had ever smiled as widely as he did at that moment. I gave a sigh of relief because I knew that demonstration would stop any retaliation the sergeant major might have dreamed up.

"That was amazing!" Caskey said with a beaming smile on his face. "What else can they do?"

"Well, sir, they can detect a sapper from quite a ways away. On a night when the humidity and wind direction are just right, a good dog can tell if someone's trying to sneak in from as far as half a mile away! At a quarter mile we can tell if the man is black, white, North Vietnames or South Vietnamese just by the way he's reacting to the scent."

Caskey looked at me like I was a used car salesman. "You're kidding. How can a dog know the difference between a North Vietnamese and a South Vietnamese?"

"They have different diets…they eat different foods. So their bodies exude different odors and the dog can tell the different scents. The dog doesn't know they are different people but he reacts differently to each scent and we can read that by the way the dog reacts."

"Wow!" Caskey exclaimed. "So what do you do if your dog picks up the scent of a North Vietnames?"

"We call the C.O. of the ammunition dump and tell him that we have detected someone out there. He calls the infantry unit and they send a squad out to investigate. We tell the squad leader where the sapper is and they take it from there. If the infantry unit arrives quickly the sapper will still be out a few hundred yards. They'll fire a couple M-79 grenade launchers and that'll take care of it. If they are slow in coming; the sapper may be within a hundred yards. At a hundred yards we can read the dog's alert and pretty much tell the infantry where to aim their M-16 and get them. And if the infantry doesn't show and the sapper gets inside the wire; we will order the dog to kill. And I can guarantee you this: The sapper won't get in because the dog won't miss!"

"Amazing," he said. "Can you show us how that works?"

"Yes," I replied. "But we'd have to have a decoy."

"He'll do," Pete blurted out pointing at the sergeant major. Pete looked at me with a devilish grin on his face and stated, "Unless he's scared!"

I wasn't sure what the look on the sergeant major's face was. Part of him wanted to take Pete out behind the barracks and give him a lesson in hand to hand combat and part of him was scared to death that he might have to face off with an attack dog. His eyes were wide open in fear and his mouth was gaping at the outrageous suggestion made about a man of his stature.

"Ha, ha." Caskey boomed. "Sergeant Jones has faced the enemy in Korea and Viet Nam. I'm sure the threat of a single dog doesn't scare him in the least. Right, Sergeant Jones?"

Jones face almost twisted off his shoulders as his look went from Pete to General Caskey, And what could the poor guy say? A simple specialist had questioned his manhood just as if he had slapped him in the face with his glove and challenged him to a dual. Caskey had just announced that Jones had no fear. His integrity was in question here and he had nowhere to turn.

Jones finally regained his composure and worked up the courage to give a weak smile. "I'd be glad to act as a decoy," he said.

"Good man," Caskey replied with a beaming smile on his face.

We walked with the two men back to the kennels to get Gus, Pete's dog. Gus was an old dog and we knew it by his teeth. They were so worn down that he would have to "gum" a guy to death rather than bite him. But his ferocious attitude more than made up for his teeth.

All the dogs were barking wildly and jumping up and down at the fence trying to get at the two strangers. Caskey boldly tried to pet a few of them as we walked along the fence line but kept a safe distance just the same. Jones maintained a distance as far away from the kennels as he could without appearing petrified. He walked along behind us with that discouraged look on his face that said he was going to have to do something that he absolutely didn't want to do.

Pete finally got to Gus' kennel. Gus was in such a state of fury that his mouth was full of foam. He looked like he had rabies. I saw Jones reaction when he saw this brute of a dog with the foaming mouth. He was ready to run but duty had called in the form of his general's request. Gus had seen four tours in Viet Nam and was a seasoned veteran. He had killed sappers at the perimeter wire of the ammo dump and therefore had tasted blood. And once a dog tastes blood, he wants more. Pete slipped the muzzle over Gus' snout and this only made Gus madder. He clawed furiously at the muzzle to get it off while Pete slipped on the choke chain and leash. Pete yanked the choke chain and Gus calmed down and for some reason he looked directly at Jones as if to say, "Once this is off, you're mine!"

Pete, Gus and the general led the way to the pasture behind the kennels. I walked behind them and Sergeant Jones lagged well behind hoping for the Gooks to pull a surprise attack, I'm sure. But no miracle happened that would save him from this experience.

Pete stopped and pointed at the elephant grass covering the pasture. "You can go out as far as you want and hide," Pete said. "We'll keep Gus facing the opposite direction so he can't see where you go. We'll give you five minutes."

Poor Sergeant Major Jones looked at General Caskey with a pleading look on his face and I'm sure he was thinking of Christ's words at the crucifixion: "Oh, general, let this cup pass from me."

But Caskey just smiled and said, "Better get moving…the clock's ticking!"

The entire pasture had grass three or four feet tall and interspersed throughout were tufts of giant elephant grass which grew up to ten feet in height. Jones left us and began jogging in a zigzag pattern, which was smart because the scent he would leave would change direction and make it more difficult for Gus to follow. At least that is what Jones was thinking and I'm sure he was hoping it would work. He jogged about a hundred yards to the tallest growth of elephant grass he could find and dove into the center of a ten foot wide plant that looked like a miniature jungle. There he knelt confident that he had outsmarted Gus.

Pete removed the choke chain from Gus and replaced it with a leather collar. This change sends an immediate message to an attack dog: "You are no longer under my command and you are free to do whatsoever you want." Caskey noticed the change right away. Gus no longer sat on his haunches waiting for Pete to give him a command. He stood on his hind legs and began sniffing the air. His ears moved like the dish on a radar truck as he continued to sniff the wind. His concentration was intense and not a sound came from him. All of the sudden his demeanor changed. His ears bent to a specific direction…and that direction was exactly where Jones was hidden. A low growl came from deep in Gus' throat. This growl was so blood curdling that the smile left Caskey's face as he realized this was not a game. This dog meant business. Gus strained at his leash as he pulled Pete along and followed the scent of Jones, zigzagging exactly as Jones had done on his way to his hiding spot. Gus dragged Pete along as he bulldozed his way through the elephant grass and leapt onto Jones with such ferocity that all of us, including Pete, were taken by surprise. Before Pete had realized that Gus was already attacking Jones, the dog had knocked Jones to the ground and was intently trying to bite him through the muzzle still on his snout. Jones was screaming bloody murder and Pete was trying to regain control of Gus. But Gus still had the leather collar on and in his mind, anything he wanted to do was fair game. Jones tried to rise and Gus knocked him to the ground. Gus stood over him with his fore legs on either side of Jones neck and growled a warning: "Stay still." Then Gus would again try to remove his muzzle at which time, Jones would attempt to regain his feet. Gus knocked him back down, growled his warning and returned to trying to remove his muzzle. Jones moved again and Gus gave up on his muzzle and began clawing at Jones body. The more Jones moved the more Gus clawed. The two of them rolled around on the ground together and I was reminded of Verne Gagne and Hans Schmidt in one of their wrestling matches. Pete was frantically trying to get his hands on the choke chain so he could once again control Gus. He finally got the chain around Gus' neck and commanded "Out!" Gus immediately sat on his haunches and the party was over.

Poor sergeant major Jones! I looked at him and remembered the creased pants I had noticed when he first came into the barracks and hollered "Ten Hut!" The pants were now in shreds. I looked down at his combat boots that previously had a mirror like shine. Gus' claws had dug ugly scratch marks into the finish and they looked to be at least an eighth of an inch deep. "How many years has he spit shined those boots?" I wondered. "Well, he's going to have to start all over again now!" His face and hands had scratch marks all over them. None would require stitches but they were impressive cuts just the same.

"That was outstanding!" Caskey said as we gathered ourselves together and began our trek back to the kennels. Jones gave him a look and that look said more than any words he could have uttered.

"I can't believe he found Jones that fast! It was like he was waving a flag!" Caskey said with a grin of elation on his face. "That was simply amazing, wasn't it sergeant major Jones?"

Jones glowered at Caskey. Then he glowered at Pete. And finally, he glowered at Gus. He ran his finger over the tattered uniform that had once been immaculate. Then he studied his combat boots. He looked like he was viewing the body of a dear friend at a funeral. He focused on the deep scratch marks that Gus had left in his once mirror like shine and sighed. He knew that he was beaten. Caskey loved the demonstration that Gus had given him and Jones would never be able to punish Pete for insubordination without Caskey's support. So it was over and he knew it.

"How about a tour of your facilities?" Caskey asked.

He had already seen the kennel area so we showed him the storage room where we kept the dog's food and supplies. He was surprised to find that we fed the dogs a can of meat at every meal. Apparently he had thought we fed them dried dog food. "What kind of meat is it?" he asked as he studied a label. He got a look of disgust on his face when he read that the contents were horse meat. "Damn shame," he commented. "Horses are such a beautiful animal and have such a rich history with the army."

Next was the toilet. He was familiar with the outhouse style of facility we had with the half barrels beneath the seats. "Who burns the contents of the barrels?" he asked. "Do you take turns?"

"No. We have a papa-san that takes care of that. We pay him well and I think he would work for free just for some of Ginny's cookies," I replied. "She also sends me dried fruits and pop is really fond of the dried apricots. In fact I gave him a baggie of them once and he shoved the whole bag, twist tie and all into his mouth and swallowed it before I could warn him." Caskey laughed. Jones glowered.

Jones turned the faucet for the hot water expecting it not to run since no one had hot water other than officers. He gasped when it not only ran but was hot! "How did you get hot water?" he demanded.

"Well, sergeant major," Pete replied with a twinkle in his eye. "It's tied into our steam bath."

"Steam bath!" Jones retorted with fire shooting from his eyes. "Officer's clubs don't even have steam baths!" It was clear that Jones believed officers should have a more luxurious life style than regular G.I.s. He thought nice things were a right of rank; not creativity. By this time Smitty had joined us and led the tour through the steam room, pointing out the burner and the piping. Caskey grinned with pleasure and nodded his head in admiration. Jones glowered.

Smitty led us to the building that had our pool table and cooking facilities. "That pool table was supposed to go to the officer's club!" Jones bellered. "They've been wondering where it went." He stood triumphantly in the door way because he knew he finally had us. And then Smitty began his shoulder twitch and head nodding. Jones looked at the birth mark on Smitty's face and then at the shoulder twitch and head nodding. Just like everyone else I had seen react to Smitty's act...Jones' brain froze! He just stood there like a dummy, transfixed with the sight before him.

Satisfied that Jones was in the typical hypnotic paralysis, Smitty said "Hey, sarge! They can come and play pool any time they want. Why don't you set up a contest? Officers against dog handlers? How about you? Do you shoot pool? Smitty placed $5 on the pool table and looked directly into Jones eyes. Jones stood there like he had just realized he had purchased the Brooklyn Bridge. He didn't know what to do. He was obviously irate that we had a pool table but this weird G.I. with the birth mark and the strange twitching of his shoulder and head had just challenged him to another duel. And if there's anything a career army man can't pass up, it's a challenge to his manhood or his abilities!

I stood there in awe of Smitty. How did he know that a challenge would hit Jones' buttons? Jones hesitated for just a moment and then reached into his hip pocket and pulled out his billfold. He placed $5 on the table and gave Smitty a look of defiance.

Smitty simply shrugged his shoulder and dipped his head. "You wanna break or should I?" Jones shrugged his shoulder and dipped his head. He waved his hand at Smitty to go ahead and break. Smitty broke sinking two balls. He ran the table. Jones glowered.

Caskey laughed as Smitty picked up his two $5 bills. "I should do something official while I'm here," he said. "Let's have an inspection of your bunker." We all looked at each other as Caskey headed out the door with Jones at his side.

"Hey Dad!" Smitty grinned. "This ought to get Jones going!"

Bunkers are notorious for going out of condition. Most units built them when they first set up a compound and then forgot about maintaining them. Usually, 55 gallon drums are filled with sand and make the foundation of the bunker. Regular sand bags are then piled on top of these barrels to a height of 7 or 8 feet. Wooden or metal beams form the ceiling and are placed on top of the sand bags. Then more sand bags are placed on the beams, usually two deep. Over time the fabric in the sand bags begins to deteriorate in the sunlight and the elements of weather. These need to be replaced as they break down. But like a house that needs painting, replacing rotted sand bags is something that can be put off until later. Inspectors General loved the bunkers because if they couldn't find anything else to GIG (Penalize.) a company on; they could always find fault in the bunker. Bunkers are dark and dank. Soldiers rarely go in them unless there's an attack. They are usually full of spiders, bugs of all sorts, scorpions and so on.

Caskey and Jones entered into the familiar darkness of the bunker and waited for their eyes to adjust to the darkness. They both jumped in alarm when Pete turned the lights on. "Lights!" Caskey said with delight. "Why doesn't that surprise me? I've never been in a bunker that had lights!" Jones scowled.

"What the heck?" Jones said in surprise. "Walnut paneling?"

"Well, I'll be damned," Caskey said in reply. "And a stage!"

"That paneling was supposed to go to the officer's club," Jones frowned. "I should write you up right here and now!"

"What's the deal with a stage?" Caskey wondered.

"Well, sir," Smitty said with a twitch, "The officer's clubs get dancing girls from the Philippines. The girls usually arrive a day or two earlier than their show and they need a place to practice. So we made a place for them to practice. We invite the ground pounders and the transportation company up and everyone gets to enjoy the show. The girls like the practice and the guys love the show. They need a little entertainment just as much as the officers."

"Can't argue with that," Caskey stated nodding his head in agreement.

"But sir," Jones interjected. "That paneling was meant for the officer's club!"

The general grinned with satisfaction. "Boys, this isn't my first rodeo. I've got a pretty good idea how you operate and I'll tell you what…if you have any lobster in the freezer, I make a pretty mean butter sauce!" Jones looked like he's swallowed a piece of broken glass.

"No problem-o," Smitty said. "I'll be right back." Smitty returned from the food yard with a case of lobster and handed them over to Caskey, who was busy in the kitchen. Jones was busy taking inventory of all the kitchen appliances we had and no doubt was preparing for a savage court martial.

We all ate lobster and listened to the war stories Caskey had to tell. He really seemed to be enjoying himself. It was as if he had arrived on vacation and was just letting down from the rigors of managing the war in Viet Nam. Finally, he stood up. "Well, boys, this has been a real joy but I'm afraid it's come to an end and we'll have to be going…got a war to fight, you know. I told you that we stopped because this place wasn't on the map and we wanted to investigate and see what it was. I promise you that it will continue to remain anonymous and will never be on the map. This outfit is refreshing and if we let others know about it, we would ruin a beautiful thing…isn't that so, sergeant major Jones?" Jones scowled.

Smitty escorted the general to his helicopter with his hat at the usual thirty degrees off center. The general saluted and Smitty gave him his typical farmer wave as the chopper took off.

Pete and I walked the ammo dump together on our last night of duty. We walked together this night since it would be our last. Shep and Gus were good friends and they needed a last walk together too. Suddenly, Gus alerted. "Oh great!" I thought. "Our last night and we've got an infiltrator." Gus pulled Pete off the path we normally walked and dragged him through the brush. I followed along. Gus followed the concertina wire and then veered towards one of the towers. And there he was! The figure of a man was huddled directly beneath one of the towers. "How did he get that far without a tower guard seeing him?" I wondered.

Pete followed Gus towards the man saying "Watch him, Gus. Watch him." Gus was ready for action and he looked more like a Belgian horse than a dog the way he was pulling Pete along. Gus was foaming at the mouth by now and began barking vigorously. The victim stood up at about the same time Pete was ready to say "Kill 'im, Gus." The man was wearing an army uniform!

"What the Hell are you doing?" Pete yelled. "I almost turned my dog loose on you. He'd have killed you so fast you would have stunk before you hit the ground!"

"Reading my book," the guy said. "The light's better down here." It was obvious the guy was on drugs.

"You've got till I count five before I turn Gus loose on you," Pete said. "If you aren't in that tower by five; you're a dead man!" The man hardly touched the ladder on his way back up to the confines of the tower where he and his buddy peeped over the edge in mortal fear.

"Damn," Pete said. "I darn near turned Gus loose on him! Do you realize that if I had; we'd probably both be in Long Binh Jail for manslaughter!"

We both had our "Short Timer" sticks back at the barracks and after tonight; we would have no more dangerous duty. Short timer sticks were about a foot and a half long and were carved out of "monkey pod," a tree indigenous to Viet Nam. The Vietnamese were good carvers and could reproduce just about anything with a simple knife and some wood. The short timer stick had a dragon's head at the top and was segmented to look like a shaft of bamboo. The end of the stick had a shell casing…partly for decoration and partly to keep the wood from splitting. We would carry them for the duration of our time in Viet Nam so officers would notice them and not give us any orders that would put us in harm's way.

I put Shep away in his kennel for the last time. I wondered if he would fly back to Okinawa to pick up a new handler when Pinky sidled over to me. "Hey, Dad. Would you mind if I took Shep and sent my dog back to Okinawa? Shep's a good dog…a lot better than mine." Pinky was a decent guy and I knew that he would take good care of Shep, so I agreed. We shook hands and Shep had a new handler.

When the war ended, Shep and all the other dogs were put to sleep. There was a heart disease specific to dogs that existed in Viet Nam. The Army didn't want to bring the disease back to the states.

CHAPTER 8
GOING HOME

The day I had been waiting for had finally arrived! I flew to Cam Ranh Bay on a C-130 and waited in line to get on my "Freedom Bird," the name all of us G.I.s had given to the 727 that would fly us back home. We all happily boarded the plane and waited with much anticipation to take off. The engines were started and we were beginning to taxi to the runway when we all heard a "Whooooooooomp!' It was the unmistakable sound of a rocket exploding. Immediately the siren started to blare its warning. Bases have a fire siren that goes off whenever there is an attack. Soldiers are conditioned by that siren to grab their steel pots, flak jackets and rifles and then head for the safety of the bunker.

I thought to myself, "This can't be happening! Here we are in Cam Ranh Bay, one of the safest places in Viet Nam and we're being attacked. Our officers had continued to talk about winning the war, but I had read in the Des Moines Register that public pressure was forcing Nixon to consider withdrawing. He said something about "Peace with honor," whatever that meant. Evidently, the Gooks knew they had the upper hand and they were making their move.

I looked out my window just in time to see another rocket explode right off the wing tip. The captain came over the intercom and announced that we should all leave the plane immediately and get into a bunker. Without even thinking, I stood up and yelled, "I've waited a year to get out of this Hell Hole and I'm not getting off this plane for anybody!" The other G.I.s on the plane caught on and spontaneously started chanting "Hell No....We won't go!" Ironically, we were using the exact same chant the draft dodgers back home had used when they burned their draft cards to avoid the military!

I was in the front row and could hear the pilot telling the tower that we wouldn't get off the plane. The tower responded by screaming back at him, "Get that bird in the air and get it the Hell out of here!" The pilot threw the throttles ahead and soon we were roaring down the runway. The plane lifted off, banked and made its turn as is the usual pattern. We could see the explosions hundreds of feet below us, but we were in the air and on our way home. We had all been holding our breath up to his point and a few of us gave a sigh of relief. Soon everyone was cheering the fact that we had successfully taken off and were safely in the air.

We stopped in Guam for fuel. Rum is made in Guam and the airport had duty free boxes of rum for sale. The most popular was the box with three different types of rum. Soon we were back in the air and G.I.s were sampling rum on the way to Anchorage, Alaska. There was singing and laughing and then…snoring! Our plane load of drunks landed and apparently, the pilot had bought rum as well because he ran into a truck on the runway and broke the nose wheel on the plane. The airport claimed it was because of the fog, but I still think our pilot was hitting the bottle!

I called Ginny and told her "I've got good news and I've got bad news. The good news is that I'm out of Viet Nam and in Alaska. The bad news is that our plane hit a truck and broke the nose wheel. We're stuck here until they get it repaired so I won't be landing in Des Moines at the time I told you. They say it will be about 6 hours. All I can do is wait until they get it repaired. When that happens, I'll call you and tell you when you can meet me in Des Moines."

So Ginny began her wait. As was the practice in her farm neighborhood, the neighbors all gathered each morning in her family's kitchen for coffee and the local gossip. That morning she told them that I was on my way home and should be in Des Moines sometime later that day. They were all thrilled for her as they knew how anxious she was. As she went about her daily chores, helping with the cooking and cleaning, she never went far from the telephone. As day turned into night, the wait became excruciating and there was nothing she could do. She slept that night on the floor by the telephone in case I would call during the night. She didn't want to take the chance that she wouldn't make it downstairs in time to answer it.

The next morning, as usual, the neighbors came for coffee. When he saw her Andy said "Gin, what are you doing here? Hasn't he called?"

That was the straw that broke the camel's back and the tears she had so bravely been holding back for the past 24 hours began to flow. And, guess what! The phone rang! I was finally in Seattle and ready to board my last plane home.

It took 24 hours for the airplane to be repaired. Parts had to be flown in from the "Lower 48" and then they had to be installed. The army fed us well and entertained us with the latest movies but despite their best efforts to appease us, we were antsy to get home and mad about the delay. I decided that my time was better spent writing another poem:

A Patriot's Message

I've just graduated and I've got me a girl.
I'd like to start working and give marriage a whirl,
But I got my draft notice in the mail today
And I might have to fight in a land far away.

The "Hawks" say it's a war that we really must fight
'Cause the Commies are moving with all their might.
The "Doves" say it's crazy, the dominoes won't fall;
Vietnam doesn't affect us at all.

I just want my job and my girl—that's all I know.
Canada's no choice or I surely would go.
You see, crossing the border is a serious move;
I'd give up my rights and the family I love.

I could never come back to work or to live.
That seems like a lot for a young man to give,
So I'll just let myself get drafted and hope for the best,
Come back in one piece and forget the whole mess,

John Wayne was my idol, I saw every show.
Did he feel like this when he had to go?
I'm scared and I'm worried, I just hope I live,
But I'll put in my time and give all I can give.

But there's something wrong here, it's terribly wrong.
The Viets should welcome us with cheer and with song
But they look at us quietly with hate in each eye.
They're our friends in the day and they fight us at night.

We're fighting for their freedom, they can't act like that.
But then I looked closer and I felt like a rat.
Their rice is their life, they can't live without food.
We blew up their fields, we bombed them out good.

They're dead, grandma and grandpa in their twilight years;
Babies and parents are left in a trail of tears.
The land is dead, too, bombs and defoliant spray.
Its people won't eat well for many a day.

When I saw what was happening, I didn't want to kill,
But when they shot at me I shot back, I would still.
And I sleep with those corpses, those men I did fight.
I kill them again almost every night.

How can you fight with such stupid rules?
The Gooks cross the line and we can't, the damn fools.
We go by a village and hear a rifle crack,
And must ask permission so we can fire back!

We sleep and eat in the muck and the mire,
And buddies are killed by what's called "friendly fire."
My enemy is not the Gook in my sight;
It's the people that sent me and won't let me fight!

We had tanks on the ground, B-52s in the air,
But what good is machinery when the soldiers don't care?
The Gooks are amazing; they fought with our junk;
Dud bombs and wire, and they fought with such spunk.

I remembered John Wayne and his welcome home,
The parades and the cheering, the beer and the foam.
Except for my family, none seemed to care,
They didn't say anything, like they just didn't dare.

Jobs were impossible; there were none to be had
Vets were seen as drug addicts and mental cases; it was so sad.
That's how they greeted us, outcasts in our own land.
And the draft dodgers got amnesty; now ain't that just grand!

There's a feeling of guilt that most people feel
About our return and it hurts a great deal.
They'd like to thank us for doing our best
In a war they detested, a dilemma at best.

Please don't regret the feelings you have.
They're normal, they're healthy, and our nations salve.
It was wrong; you know it and I know it too.
Let's not repeat it, for me, and for you.

I went 'cause I got drafted; I was forced to go
By the country I love and I do love it so.
I love it enough to here state my mind
So that internal strength we one day may find.

The wrong was in drafting my buddy and me,
When our Congress and Senate couldn't even agree.
My buddy is dead now; he was one of a kind.
And when we came home, the Hawk changed his mind.

Now you Hawks listen and you listen well.
Don't draft my child or you'll go through Hell !
Don't push us to war when we people don't care.
When the war is worth fighting, we'll all be there.

We were finally told that we would be boarding soon and would be on our way. I called Ginny and informed her of my new schedule. I had checked flights out of Seattle and knew when I would be arriving in Des Moines. "Reserve a motel room close to the airport because I won't get in until eight in the evening," I told her.

We got back on our "Freedom Bird" and left the barren fields of Alaska behind us. We landed in Seattle, Washington and I quickly left the plane and headed into the airport. We all had to fly by what they called "military stand-by." That meant that ticketed passengers got on the plane first. Empty seats were counted and a military person could have one of those seats. Our military ticket was good as long as there were empty seats available, but if there weren't any, we would have to wait for the next flight that went to our destination and hope there was an empty seat for us. Thus, I wanted to be first in line.

As I walked into the airport, a hippie type spit on me and called me a "baby killer." I looked at his ponytail, his tie-dyed shirt, his granny glasses and the hate in his eyes. Then I thought about working with the orphanage in Okinawa and the orphanage in Pleiku. I thought of all the babies and youngsters that had a home because we had repaired the orphanage for them. I thought about the young boy in Pleiku that I had fed and received warnings of attacks in return. And for the first time in my military career; I felt like killing! I went into the bathroom to splash water on my face and calm myself. The hippie followed me in and called me a baby killer again. And that's when I'd had enough. I tackled him driving him into a stall and onto the toilet. Then I stuck his head into the toilet and flushed. His ponytail disappeared into the bowels of the toilet as he sputtered and gasped. I gave it one more flush and left with a feeling of great satisfaction.

I was able to be the first in line for the flight to Des Moines and there were empty seats for military stand by. I got on the plane just as darn quick as I could because I didn't know if the cops would be after me because of my encounter with the hippie or not. When they backed the plane away from the loading area and the jet engines began to whine, I gave a big sigh of relief. I was on my way home to Ginny.

As my plane landed in Des Moines, Ginny was sitting in the waiting area. A nice man asked her if she was waiting for a G.I. She replied that she was and he said, "What are you sitting here for? Get out there and meet him at the plane!" So, she headed for the runway and he followed. As the people began to come down the stairs, with each uniform, he would ask if that was me. When she finally saw me and said "That's him", he gave her a shove right to the base of the steps!

We left for the Sleepy Bear Motel just outside the airport. We had barely been married for a year and most of the year I had spent in Viet Nam so you can imagine the joy of being together once again. I opened the door to our room and you'll never guess what I saw. Twin beds! Once again, I busied myself shoving them together to make one good bed!

A siren blaring woke me up. As I had been conditioned to do because they always blew a siren when we were being attacked, I got up and started to search for my M-16 and my steel pot and flack vest. I couldn't find them anywhere so I decided I'd better head to the bunker without them. I threw the door of our motel room open and headed down the hallway naked as a jaybird. In my mind I was still in Vet Nam until the elevator bell rang and brought me back to reality. The doors of the elevator opened and a drunk who had just left the bar was gazing at me…standing stark naked in front of him! I stupidly smiled, waved at him and said "Good night." The elevator doors closed and the drunk disappeared. I went back to the room and found that I had locked myself out and Ginny was still sound asleep. I had to bang on the door for quite a while before she awoke and let me in. The next morning when we left, I discovered that a fire station was right across the street from our motel. That's where the sound of the siren had come from. It took twenty years before I could listen to a fire siren without absentmindedly reaching for my M-16. Sometimes, I still do.

CHAPTER 9
BACK IN THE WORLD

My tour in Vietnam lasted a year. Since I spent about six months going through Basic Training and Advanced Individual Training before going to 'Nam, I had about six months left on my enlistment. That meant that at the end of my tour I could go back stateside for six months of additional service.

The military offered an option called the "early out." If a GI agreed to serve another three months of duty in Vietnam, the Army would release them from duty three months early. Choosing between a three-month extension in a war zone and six months duty stateside was a tough decision for some. Many of the GIs in Vietnam extended for an early out, and I can tell you that it was a sad affair when one of those soldiers got killed in action.

"What a shame," people would say. "He could have been back in 'Freedom Land' and still be alive."

Nonetheless, many of those who had been drafted into Uncle Sam's military were so fed up with war and the Army that they were willing to take that risk just to get out of the service as quickly as possible. Not me. I had a wife at home and I wasn't taking any chances. I wanted to come home to her in one piece!

I arrived home from Vietnam in June, 1970, and went home on leave. It surprised me to find that my body had adjusted to the monsoon season and the heat in Vietnam to the point that I froze when I got back to the Iowa summer. Everyone else was in their shirt sleeves, but not me. I had to wear a jacket to be comfortable. We visited friends and relatives while I was on leave, and everyone remarked about me wearing a jacket in the heat.

My leave ended all too quickly and Ginny and I packed for our trip to Maryland. The Army assigned me to a Nike Missile site at Edgewood Arsenal, a part of Aberdeen Proving Grounds in Maryland. The Army paid for air travel to Maryland or any other destination we chose. But if we chose another destination, it was on our nickel to get from that point to our duty station. I had landed in Des Moines and now it was my responsibility to get from Des Moines to Maryland. We had only one problem: no money!

I lay in bed the night before we left, wondering how I would come up with the money to pay for gas and meals. Would I have to beg Emery, Ginny's father, for spending money? Could I call Dad? I don't think I would have slept at all that night because of my worry, except for the fact that we had a horrific thunderstorm and I've always slept well when I could hear the pitter-patter of rain on the roof.

Voices woke me the next morning and I came downstairs to find Emery surrounded by his neighbors and having coffee. They were discussing the terrific hail storm they'd had during the night. Crops had been damaged severely, windows got broken, shingles were ruined, and in the early morning hours the lawn had looked like it had snowed.

One of the neighbors said, "You ought to see your car! It looks like someone took a ball peen hammer to it!"

Another neighbor said, "You should go see your insurance agent. I bet they'll pay for the repair."

I went out and our '64 Chevy looked like it had a bad case of acne. I went to Humboldt, where Ginny had taken out insurance on the car and inquired about what could be done.

The agent looked the car over and said, "It will cost more to fix it than the car is worth. We'll just total it out and give you a check!"

A few minutes later, I left his office with a check for $750 and our worries were over! We may have had a dimpled car, but we had travel money!

Ginny and I arrived in Maryland and I reported for duty. We were assigned an apartment in Married Housing, but we had an option. We could live off base and receive a housing allowance. The housing allowance wouldn't cover even the cheapest apartment, but I didn't care. I hated the Army and didn't want to live in its midst if I could help it.

So we found an upstairs apartment in a farm house located in Edgewood, Maryland. How wonderful that felt! We were in the country, had pastures to look at and walk in, cows were mooing right outside our window, gineau hens woke us every morning, we could hear the familiar sound of a Model M Farmall tractor working in the fields, and best of all we had privacy and no military personnel in our surroundings.

We had to pay for a month's rent in advance. We paid that sum and moved into the apartment, but we didn't have anything left to live on. Ginny and I had our privacy but like Grandpa Brown used to say, "You can live on love for a little while, but sooner or later you're going to need a little grub!"

I had a few days leave time left so Ginny and I enjoyed our new digs together. I read in the paper that the people were demonstrating at Edgewood Arsenal. "What the heck?" I thought. "I think I'll go down and see what it's all about." I went to the gate where they were demonstrating and mixed with the demonstrators. They were the typical demonstrators. The guys had pony tails and tie dyed shirts. The women had long hair, dresses and were braless. At first, they thought I was a plant because of my dress and my hair cut. But I explained that I had just come back from Viet Nam and was interested in their point of view. They fell all over themselves telling me why we shouldn't be in Viet Nam, about the atrocities that were happening there, the number of young men that were dying for nothing, the Vietnamese people that were suffering because of the war, corporations that were getting rich from the war and most of all, crooked politicians that were supporting the war but making sure their son didn't have to go. I couldn't argue with any of their points. I told them that I had been there because I had been drafted. I didn't really believe in the war but I did believe in doing my duty. They seemed to appreciate that. So we enjoyed each other's company. I gave them the peace sign and left.

I took our car and reported for my first day on the job. I spent the day walking the perimeter of a Nike Missile site. And guess who was at my gate on the perimeter...the demonstrators. "Hey Lee!" they yelled. "How ya doin'?" They gave me the peace sign and I gave it back to them. There were no problems with the demonstrators on my watch.

My first day of duty finally ended and I got back in the '64 Chevy and headed for home. As I turned on the road to our apartment, I heard screeching brakes and felt a bump on the driver's side of the car. An older fellow had gone through a stop sign, slammed on his brakes, and almost stopped before he hit me. However, "almost stopped" wasn't quite good enough. His bumper had peeled the chrome strip from the side of my car. Amazingly, there wasn't a dent on the body. He had come just close enough that his fender grabbed the chrome strip and peeled it from the side of the car. The chrome lay in a coiled strip on the ground.

I picked it up and the man said, "Follow me, QUICK!"

He led me to the driveway of his home and, after looking both ways, he said, "Are you OK?"

I assured him that I was.

With a sigh of relief, he went on to say, "If I report another accident, they'll take away my driver's license. I'll pay you for the damages if you don't report this to the authorities. How's $600 sound?" He gladly wrote me a check for the $600 and I left him in a very happy state myself! "God does provide," I thought to myself.

I went home and unpeeled the chrome strip and hammered it into shape. I refastened it to the car and one could hardly tell there had been any damage unless they looked closely.

Our apartment came furnished with appliances, furniture, beds, a dinette set, dishes, and silverware. Ginny made cinnamon rolls and wonderful meals, things I hadn't smelled or eaten in almost two years. When I came home, I weighed 165 pounds. Not much fat on my 6'3" frame. It took about three months for me to gain 50 pounds. When I pulled guard duty, she would bring me meals at the base. It wasn't long before she was making enough for all the other GIs on duty with me and Ginny became everyone's favorite person!

One night we took a couple bottles of wine and went on a walk in the cow pasture. We wandered through the pasture until we found an isolated patch of grass surrounded by a ring of trees. It was as if God had guided us to a perfect little romantic spot! We drank wine and made love in our little paradise. When we were done, I felt something wet on my neck. I brushed it with my hand, thinking it was an insect of some kind. To my surprise it was a cow! I looked up and eight cows were standing in a circle around us. Apparently, they had enjoyed the show!

My military pay check wasn't enough to cover the rent and living expenses, so Ginny began bagging groceries at the PX for tips. The base had plenty of retired generals who shopped there. The PX allowed military wives to carry groceries for the generals because they knew our wives couldn't get jobs in the private sector. That was their way of helping out, and it was wonderful. Ginny soon had a number of old men who requested her to carry their groceries for them. They tipped handsomely and often she would come home with $30, $40, or $50. We had a real celebration when, at end of one pay period, we had $25 left over. We went to a pawn shop and bought a TV for $20.

My supervisor, Sergeant Phillips, asked me one day if I could drive a tractor.

"Are you kidding," I said. "I grew up on a farm in Iowa and started driving a tractor when I was five years old!"

Phillips said, "Well, I cut grass in my off time and we need another person who can handle a tractor."

He introduced me to Gene, the owner of the grass cutting operation. Gene pointed to a Fordson tractor with a gang of reel lawn mowers mounted on it and said, "Show me what you can do."

I got on the Fordson, made a circle around the area, and got hired on the spot. So, in my time off, I mowed the military compound and the golf course. Sergeant Phillips and I handled the tractor mowers and Gene always had a raggedy group of men who handled the push mowers. Those guys ranged in ages and color, but shared one thing in common: they didn't just push the mowers, they ran with them. And I mean RAN! It was like they were in a track meet with lawn mowers. Since they did the trim work, they were still working when I left for the day.

One day I asked Gene "Why do those guys run with the lawn mowers? Do you threaten them?"

Gene laughed and said, "You be here early tomorrow and you'll see."

We got into Gene's old "Wonder Bread" van and headed into town. He pulled up at the liquor store and bought ten cases of Mogan David 20-20 and two cases of Jack Daniels.

We then went down to skid row where Gene opened the doors and said, "Hop in. When you're done mowing, you can drink till it's gone!"

Soon the van was shoulder to shoulder with men.

When they were done mowing, they all came to the van and began drinking and laughing and telling stories. I conversed with the men expecting to find illiterate, unemployable men, but I met a doctor, a lawyer, and men that had been business professionals.

They didn't stand shoulder to shoulder when we took them back. Somehow, they randomly positioned themselves back in the van. They didn't look comfortable, but they sure were happy!

We had eked out a living on my military pay check, my grass cutting and Ginny's bagging of groceries. But I had finally reached the end of my obligation in the United States Army and Ginny and I packed all our worldly possessions into the '64 Chevy and a small U-Haul trailer and headed back to Iowa and family.

We pulled into an Iowa gas station to fill up. I noticed a pick-up truck in the next bay. It had a kennel with a German Shephard in it. I went over to admire the dog and struck up a conversation with the owner. "I breed dogs and donate them to the Army," he said.

"No kidding," I said. "I just got back from Viet Nam and I was a military police attack dog handler."

"No kidding," he said as he pulled out his billfold and showed me a picture of the last one he had sent to the Army. It was Shep.

EPILOGUE

Lee "Dad" Halverson landed on U.S. soil, got off the plane and was immediately spat upon and called a "baby killer" by a demonstrator. He's had difficulty adjusting to noises like cars backfiring, sirens blowing and fireworks. Ginny advised him to talk about his experiences in Viet Nam and let it out instead of holding it in. It has been good therapy. Together they have raised two daughters: Missy and Ginger. Lee has rheumatoid arthritis. His family has no record of that disease. The military does not recognize it as one caused by Agent Orange.

William "Smitty" Smith arrived home at the Des Moines Airport and was greeted by anti-war protestors. He found that it was hard to adjust to civilian life and was haunted by sudden noises. Like many others, he didn't want to talk about his experiences in Viet Nam.

He moved to Oskaloosa, Iowa where he purchased an auction house. Smitty entertained his audiences just like he had when he sold the John Deere B back in Pleiku. Iowa holds an annual auctioneering contest and Smitty won auctioneer of the year.

He married his wife, Joy and together they raised two daughters. Both daughters enjoyed riding with Smitty as he made his rounds picking up and delivering livestock and sale items. Together they raised orphaned fawns and even had a pet bear.

In 2005; Smitty died from Multiple Myeloma which was caused by Agent Orange. I spoke at his funeral. Smitty was larger than life and I thought he would live forever; but I guess his "Guardian Angel" just ran out of gas.

Dale "Lil Brother" Bladorn went back to Jaynesville, Wisconsin and worked his entire career at the General Motors Plant there. He married his wife, Rhonda, and together they raised a son and a daughter.

Dale has diabetes which was brought on by contact with Agent Orange.

Charley "Pete" Peterson landed in Minneapolis, MN. He went down to the baggage area to pick up his bags and a war protestor spit on him from the balcony up above. True to his nature, Pete was on his way to have a "conversation" with the man when two of his friends grabbed him and told him to let it be. He married his wife, Sue, and together they raised two sons. Pete worked at the Hormel plant in Austin, MN. His union went on strike and Hormel brought in scab laborers to keep the plant running during the strike. Those scabs were Vietnamese. He felt that his country had taken two years of his life away from him and now they were giving his job to the very people he had laid his life on the line to protect. He eventually went to work for the U.S. Postal Service and is now retired.

John "Hawk" Hawkins died of cancer in 2008. Hawk was an all-state football player from Ohio.

Michael Dunaway died of cancer in 1999. Mike was a clean cut All-American boy and a close friend of mine. He had been nominated for soldier of the month while we were in 'Nam because of his knowledge, manners, dress, and demeanor. Such a nice young man he was.

Charles "Charlie" Butler died of cancer in 2002, the first black man I had ever known.

Richard Laberdee died of cancer in 1993. Richie was always a ball of fun. Nothing depressed him. I never had trouble finding Richie, I just followed the laughter.

Art "The Big Wop" Pollicelli came from Boston and died from exposure to Agent Orange. His father and grandfather were cops, and Art followed the family tradition when he got back to The World.

Bill Nunn has colon cancer attributed to Agent Orange.

Willie "Chain" Bolton has prostate cancer brought on by exposure to Agent Orange.

Stanley Everson has prostate cancer brought on by exposure to Agent Orange.

Bernard "Bernie" Siwek, has diabetes as a result of Agent Orange.

David "Mikey" Huston has diabetes from Agent Orange.

Ralph "Skip" Shaefer has kidney cancer from Agent Orange.

Steve Heiberger has kidney cancer from Agent Orange.
.

All these men were in my unit. Ten out of 54 men have died of cancer and eight have some sort of malady, whether it's cancer or diabetes.

Roughly a third of the guys I served with have died or became sick from exposure to Agent Orange. Our government told us it was safe, and they wonder why we don't trust them.

Glossary

1LT, first lieutenant, an O-2

2LT, second lieutenant, an O-1, the lowest officer rank in the Army

4-H, standing for "head, heart, health, hands," is an organization for farm children that teaches them skills they'll need if they become farmers

AH-1, or Cobra, a heavily-armed attack helicopter, also called a gunship

AIT, advanced individual training for a military specialty, in this case Military Police

Article 15, non-judicial punishment awarded by a commanding officer for minor offenses

Arty, short for artillery

Basic, boot camp, where recruits learned how to dress, address superiors, and perform physical training

C-130, four-engine turboprop military transport plane

C-4, plastic explosive

Cadre, leadership of a unit, composed of officers and NCOs

Cam Ranh Bay, key transportation hub during the Vietnam War, located on the South China Sea in far south South Vietnam

Charlie, an abbreviation of "Victor Charlie," the phonetic term for Viet Cong or VC

Class A Uniform, semi-formal military dress that can include a coat and tie

Claymore mine, a directional bomb that can be stood up on the ground and set off by a remote signal or a tripwire

Cobra, or AH-1, a heavily-armed attack helicopter, also called a gunship

Concertina wire, coiled razor-sharp wire used to inhibit entry or exit from a facility

CS Gas, chlorobenzalmalononitrile, a riot control agent, often called tear gas

Details, menial jobs, such as digging latrines and disposing of refuse

Deuce-and-a-half, a 10-wheel cargo truck

Doper, someone who uses non-prescription drugs, such as marijuana or heroin

Firefight, fierce gunfight with the enemy

Fragging—killing or maiming a hated superior by a subordinate

Gook, derogatory term for an enemy Vietnamese soldier

Hamburger Hill, Hill 937 in the A Shau Valley of South Vietnam near the Laotian border, so-named because participants in a battle that occurred there were chewed up like hamburger

Ho Chi Minh Trail, a primitive road from North Vietnam through Laos and Cambodia, used to as a path for supplying materiel to North Vietnamese soldiers

Hooch, living quarters in a military compound

Huey, a UH-1 helicopter normally used to haul troops or cargo, but sometimes modified as a gunship or for medical evacuation. Unarmed versions were called "slicks"

Jeep, also ¼ Ton or M-151, generic term for a four-seat, four-wheel-drive military vehicle with a removable canvas top

Kit Carson Scout, a North Vietnamese or VC who had come over to our side

LOACH, an OH-6, a small two-person helicopter used for observation and reconnaissance

Long Binh, a massive US military complex near Saigon, the then-South Vietnamese capitol

LSD, Lysergic acid diethylamide, colloquially acid, hallucinogenic drug popular during the 1960s

LT, short for either a first or second lieutenant

M14, a 7.62 mm (.30 caliber) center-fire rifle that can be fired in semi- or fully-automatic mode

M16, a 5.56mm (.22 caliber) center-fire, selectable semi- or full-automatic, standard-issue infantry rifle

M60, a fully automatic 7.62mm (.30 caliber) machinegun

M79 , a single-shot, break-action, shoulder-fired weapon used to launch 40mm grenades

Mama-san, any Vietnamese mother

MARS, Military-Affiliated Radio Station, often used by troops in Vietnam to connect with ham radio operators in the States who would patch their calls to friends and family

MedEvac, a helicopter, usually a UH-1, that has been modified to evacuate wounded troops from a combat zone

Minigun, Gatling gun, a six-barrel 7.62 mm (.30 caliber) machinegun

MM, millimeter or mike-mike, a small metric measure; about 25mm to the inch

Monsoon, heavy rain or the season when heavy rains occur

MP, Military Police

NCO, also **non-com**, non-commissioned officer, anyone above the rank of private first class

NVA, North Vietnamese Army

Peter Principle, a theory that a worker will continue to get promotions until reaching a level at which he is no longer competent

Pleiku, key city in the northern part of South Vietnam

Pop, a Midwestern term for a soft drink, such as cola

Post, a fixed military installation (fort) or, in the case of MPs, an area to be walked during guard duty

Revetment, a reinforced wall or enclosure designed to protect personnel and/or equipment from enemy fire

RPG, rocket propelled grenade, supplied by the Russians and Chinese to enemy forces

Saigon, capital city of South Vietnam

Sapper, also zapper, an enemy combatant adept at getting through wire barriers and into areas where Americans lived and worked when not out on patrol. Sappers would then plant bombs and traps to injure Americans in their supposedly safe environment

Satchel charge, a suitcase-like explosive container often carried by enemy soldiers, often sneaked into American compounds and later detonated

Slick, a UH-1 helicopter with no armament, configured strictly for cargo and troop transport or MedEvac

South China Sea, body of water separating Vietnam and the Philippines

Steel Pot, slang for helmet

The World, euphemism for the United States

UCMJ, Uniform Code of Military Justice

UH-1, also called a **Huey**, a helicopter normally used to haul troops or cargo, but sometimes modified as a gunship or medical evacuation helicopter

V-100, a four-wheel armored personnel carrier

VEISHA, a celebration of Iowa State University, its students, faculty members, and surrounding community. The name VEISHEA is composed of the first letters of the five colleges: V standing for Veterinary medicine, E for Engineering, IS for Industrial Science, HE for Home Economics, and A for Agriculture.

Vietcong, also **VC**, citizen-soldiers opposed to American forces, often citizens during the day and soldiers at night

West Okoboji, a 4000-acre lake just below the Minnesota border in western Iowa

Wop, a racial slur usually associated with a person of Italian descent, meaning "without papers"

www.ingramcontent.com/pod-product-compliance
Lightning Source LLC
Chambersburg PA
CBHW021608120626
46545CB00001B/125